Raising the Race

Families in Focus

Series Editors

Anita Ilta Garey, University of Connecticut
Naomi R. Gerstel, University of Massachusetts, Amherst
Karen V. Hansen, Brandeis University
Rosanna Hertz, Wellesley College
Margaret K. Nelson, Middlebury College

Raising the Race

Black Career Women Redefine Marriage, Motherhood, and Community

RICHÉ J. DANIEL BARNES

RUTGERS UNIVERSITY PRESS

NEW BRUNSWICK, NEW JERSEY AND LONDON

LIBRARY OF CONGRESS CATALOGING-IN-PUBLICATION DATA

Barnes, Riché J. Daniel, 1973–

Raising the race : Black career women redefine marriage, motherhood, and community / Riché J. Daniel Barnes.

pages cm. — (Families in focus)

Includes bibliographical references and index.

ISBN 978–0–8135–6199–8 (hardcover : alk. paper) — ISBN 978–0–8135–6198–1 (pbk. : alk. paper) — ISBN 978–0–8135–6200–1 (e-book (web pdf)) — ISBN 978–0–8135–7538–4 (e-book (epub))

1. African American women in the professions. 2. African American women in the professions—Family relationships. 3. Work and family—United States. I. Title.

HD6054.2.U6B37 2016

305.48'896073—dc23   2015004943

A British Cataloging-in-Publication record for
this book is available from the British Library.

Visit our website: http://rutgerspress.rutgers.edu

Manufactured in the United States of America

For my Nana, Myrtle L. Bishop
for my Mom and Dad, Gwen and Leon Daniel
and for the othermothers and just-like fathers, here and passed on,
who have contributed to raising me . . .

For Darnel, my love, for taking this journey with me,
and for Nailah, Nikhil, and Nasir,
the reasons for the journey . . .

CONTENTS

PREFACE

This book is an intervention. It adds Black career women to the research on professional women who "opt-out" of the professional labor force (Belkin 2003) and engages a conversation that to date has omitted Black women. By investigating the ways in which Black career women conceptualize their decision to be stay-at-home moms or change their relationships with work, I draw scholarly attention to the contemporary Black elite: their marriages, their child-rearing strategies, and their residential and school choices. And by centering the conversation on Black elite women, I challenge stereotypical myths and images of Black women as welfare queens and strong black women.

I have sought to complete the research and the analysis while keeping Black career women's everyday lived experiences at the fore (Collins [1990] 2000) and situating the inquiry in the literatures, theories, and methodologies that reside in several disciplines (anthropology, sociology, history, urban studies, women's studies, Africana studies, and family studies). I have explored a variety of topical areas (work and family conflict, child care, residential patterns, migration patterns, inequalities, gender strategies, race, and class), and this work has taken me to the southern United States, where my study is situated in Atlanta, Georgia, as well as our collective memory of Africa.

Part of this is the normal work that goes into completion of an ethnographic project, but I have also grounded the work in the Black feminist ethic of "talking back" to each potential stakeholder or gatekeeper, as bell hooks suggests (1988). This is a difficult process because it requires approaches that are often at odds: the scholarly and the communal. My objective then is not just to add to the scholarly canon but also to provide a platform from which to change and, in some instances, to save Black women's lives (Hull and Christian 1986, xxv). This is not to say that some magical answer, hidden within the pages of this book, will transform all the structures that have negatively affected Black women's lives; rather, I attempt to make one more aspect of Black women's lives visible, thereby rendering Black women visible. Making Black women's lives visible is a type of self-preservation, and that, according to Audre Lorde, is an act of political warfare (Lorde 1988).

I am humbled by the number of people who have asked about the results of this study. In its early stages of analysis, I presented it at various academic and corporate events and people repeatedly asked me about my findings, relayed their own experiences, or inquired when my analysis would be available. One group even asked if I might be available to offer workshops. I was repeatedly and pleasantly surprised when scholars mentioned they had read my work or were using it in their classrooms. Although widespread dissemination and discussion were definitely my goals, the continued interest solidified the study's importance. I knew it was important to me, but I often wondered if it was important to others. In addition, some Black women, after having heard about the study through various social networks, admonished me to hurry up and get it done because they "needed" it.

Of course, I am indebted to the women who graciously allowed me to poke and prod them and their families for the benefit of my research. They reminded me each day that this project was not about me. I hope that I have done their voices a service in my retelling. Fiction writers often say that their characters write their books and they are simply the conduits. While the analysis is mine and could therefore be severely flawed, the experiences belong to these women, and they make this study so important. I am grateful to each and every one of them and to their families. We continue to exchange cards, occasional phone calls, and social media posts; we have created an odd kind of friendship. I wish I could call their names and pay homage to their stories and the selflessness they exuded when I asked them if they would participate in the study. To each of them, I want you to know, *I am* because *you are*.

There are many people who have been on this journey with me at various stages of its development. Bradd Shore, Karyn Lacy, Peggy Barlett, and Carla Freeman were all a part of the early formation of the project. I received a generous fellowship from the Emory University Center for Myth and Ritual in American Life (MARIAL), directed by Bradd Shore, to investigate Black middle-class families. The Emory Center was a part of the Alfred P. Sloan Center on Working Families, directed by Kathleen Christensen. The multiyear fellowship provided me with the opportunity to fund the research, part of the writing, and to present the research at other Sloan Centers, including the University of Chicago, MIT, and UCLA. In addition to the Sloan Centers, the Ford Foundation Fellows program offered assistance at a critical moment in the analysis and writing.

I was also fortunate to be able to work with Myra Burnett at Spelman College and Cora Marrett, formerly NSF deputy director, as the project director for the NSF-sponsored Science and Social Transformation Collaboration Grant at Spelman College. This allowed me an opportunity to utilize Spelman's many resources and to exchange ideas with scholars in the United States, Ghana, Uganda, and South Africa. While working at Spelman, I benefitted from the great mentorship of Cynthia Spence, Harry Lefever, and Darryl White, faculty in the department of sociology and anthropology.

Since moving to the Pioneer Valley, my department colleagues—Kevin Quashie, Daphne Lamothe, Louis Wilson, Paula Giddings, Shani Roper, and Andrea Hairston—and outside advisers—Ginetta Candelario, Jennifer Guglielmo, Danielle Ramdath, Lisa Armstrong, Susan Van Dyne, and Marilyn Schuster—have made my time at Smith College immeasurably productive and enjoyable. Advice from Spelman College President Beverly Daniel Tatum, who left Mount Holyoke for Spelman just a few years before I came to Smith, was indispensable as I made the transition in culture and weather. Faculty Development Funds, particularly the Jill Ker Conway Fund, and research funds have helped me to finish the writing process and provided multiple venues for discussion and analytical inquiry. Correspondingly, presentations at Mount Holyoke College, the University of North Carolina Chapel Hill, Spelman College, and Wesleyan University gave me important audiences with whom to consider new ideas.

I am especially thankful to several faculty fellowship groups of which I have been a part; they allowed me to coalesce many of my ideas. With many brilliant minds from the Five College Consortium, I, as a faculty fellow in the Smith College Kahn Liberal Arts Institute, tackled the theme "Mothers & Others" Reproduction, Representation, and the Body Politic. This group, led by Naomi Miller and Ginetta Candelario, was particularly instrumental in helping me develop "strategic mothering" as a conceptual tool and, equally important, setting aside time in my busy teaching and writing schedule to simply think. Thank you to the UMASS Care/Work Policy group, headed by Joya Misra, and to some of my coparticipants, Miliann Kang, Naomi Gerstel, and Eiko Strader, primarily sociologists, for reading drafts of chapters and giving extremely valuable feedback. Our exchanges are wonderful examples of interdisciplinary networks of support and friendship.

I am also thankful to Joan Williams, director of the Center for WorkLife Law at UC Hastings College of Law, for her interest and support of my research. She and Shelley Correll at the Stanford University Clayman Institute for Gender Research provided a necessary lens and space through which to see my research as important to scholarly, public policy, and media initiatives through the multiyear Redesigning, Redefining Work Research group and summit at Stanford University.

Spelman College as both an institution and a group of people has played a tremendous role in my life. I realize this more and more each day as I try to share the profound teaching and unbelievable mentorship I received with my own students. Most notable, are Beverly Guy-Sheftall and "Sister Prez" Johnnetta Betsch Cole, after whom I daily try to model my academic achievement and commitment to communities of women and "black folk." Dr. Cole introduced me to anthropology, saw me through the application process, mentored, and advised me at various stages of my development as an anthropologist, wife, and mother. Thank you will never be enough.

There are people in the world of anthropology, particularly the Association of Black Anthropologists who have been mentors to me and helped me at various points with advice, close reads, or simply conversations. I have received tremendous mentorship from Faye Harrison, John L. Jackson, Marla Frederick, Deborah Thomas, Whitney Battle-Baptiste, Kimberly Simmons, David Simmons, Leith Mullings, Irma McClaurin, Pem Buck, Sabiyah Prince, and Dana-Ain Davis. I reserve a special thank you to A. Lynne Bolles who has been a great ally since Dr. Cole first introduced us. I am also blessed to have made extraordinary life- and research-affirming friendships with Bianca Williams and Corliss Heath. I'm pretty sure this project would not have been completed without each one of you advising and often cheering me on.

To my editor Marlie Wasserman at Rutgers University Press, thank you so much for your patience, reminders, prodding, and reality checks. We both have been through many personal ups and downs during this process, and I think the book is better for it. I also thank the editors of the Families in Focus series, most notably Peggy Nelson and Karen Hansen, for not only their careful attention to this manuscript but also to the ways my work builds on that of the late Anita Ilta Garey. I hope I have done her legacy some justice.

Special "shout-outs" to Pastor Aaron L. Parker and the "village" at Zion Hill Baptist Church in Atlanta (you are too many to name, but you know who you are). Also, thank you to the Neville family, the Earles-Ross family, the Bennafield family, the Rice family, the Newman family, the Peyton family, the Soudan family of Baltimore, the Cecil family of Richmond, the Burnett family and the Baldwin families of Springfield, the Wilson family of Northampton, the Williams family of Amherst, and the Battle-Baptiste family of Pelham. Thank you to our friends and neighbors at Deerfield Academy, the Thiels, the Cullinanes, the Lowes, the Otts, the Youngs, the Loftuses, and the Rajballie-Bognolos. You helped make my ability to combine career and family much more negotiable, despite the fact that I was more than one thousand miles from my family.

I thank my sorority sisters, so many to count who truly are my sisters (most notably Tiffanye Porter Sledge, Celeste Watkins-Hayes, Johnita Walker Mizell, and Rimani Kelsey-Rogers). I am so thankful for my sister-cousins Andrea "Nickey" Hardon and Elisa Tory Dixon, who were the wind beneath my wings long before my wings had fully formed.

I thank my family. I have truly been raised by a village, and part of that upbringing made this project so important to me. I thank my parents, Leon and Gwen Daniel, my godparents, Shireen and Ronnie Patterson, my Nana, Myrtle L. Bishop, Aunt Spring and Uncle Buster, cousin Butch and Gail, Aunt Rosetta,

Uncle Vanderbilt, Aunt Jackie, Aunt Pat, Uncle Leroy, and a host of cousins who have been with me and believing in me from the beginning. I thank the entire Bishop-Gadson family, the Daniel-Fears-Gideon family, and the Molock-Barnes family for all of your love and support.

And I offer inadequate but special thanks to those friends who blur the line between family and friends and offer an ever-present sense of calm to quiet the storms: Neuman "Larry" and Avis Leverett, Kanika Raney, Andrea Abrams, Leandris Liburd, and Maurita Poole.

I thank God. Some people do not believe in God. Some days I question Her/His efficacy, but most days I know I would not make it through without believing "there is a God somewhere."

I thank my husband, Darnel Emir Barnes, whose support, encouragement, and partnership forged me into the wife, mother, and scholar that I am. None of this is possible without him. I have heard the stories of men and women who have left their marriages stating, "I did not sign up for this . . ." Honestly, there are too many things he "did not sign up for" to name. I am grateful for you and to you. Thank you for taking this journey with me. Thank you to our brilliant and beautiful children, Nailah, Nikhil, and Nasir, "my crew" who often traveled with me or sent me good wishes when I presented at various conferences and were mostly patient with me when I was less than available.

And if I have missed anyone, please know it is an inadvertent omission and charge it to my head and not my heart. Ashe.

Deerfield, Massachusetts
December 20, 2014

Raising the Race

Introduction

Black Career Women and Strategic Mothering

"Every time my Dad would call to say 'hi,' he would ask me when I was going back to work," said Denise, a thirty-year-old Black woman and married mother of two.[1] "It was like a running joke, but it wasn't funny. I knew what he was really saying was, 'why are you still sitting at home with a baby?'" While Denise felt she made the best decision for her family, the persistent comments from both her mother and father signaled the career and family conflict Denise and other professional Black women experience as they are caught between familial expectations and social class directives.

I met Denise during the story time for preschool children at the Southwest regional library in Atlanta, Georgia. The library was situated in one of Atlanta's oldest Black middle-class communities and prided itself on offering books, magazines, and programming specifically for African Americans. Several moms were present with their children at story time each week, but Denise and I discovered we were close in age with children close in age, and we immediately hit it off. At the time, Denise, having just finished law school, was preparing to take the bar exam for the State of Georgia. As I got to know Denise and the other women who frequented story time, I realized they were highly educated Black women who were "taking a break" from work. None saw herself as being on maternity leave, and the "break" from career was more permanent than not.

I was surprised by their decisions to be at-home moms. I was a mother myself and had no intentions of stopping my career trajectory to raise my child(ren). My mother always advised me, "Babies have basic needs that any trustworthy and loving person can provide." Not only did her statement fit my career goals, but it also represented the sentiments of most of the Black community (Landry 2000). Growing up, I did not know any highly educated African American professional women who were stay-at-home moms. Most educated African American women were raised with the cultural model that encouraged pursuit of

1

successful careers, achievement of economic self-reliance, and development as a role-model for the Black community (Higginbotham 2001; Shaw 1996). By leaving their careers and relying (financially) on their husbands, these women were seemingly going against many primary tenets that worked to ensure the success of the Black community.

As I continued to spend time with Denise and the other women in the story time playgroup, among them a Ph.D. journalism student, a marketing and advertising executive, a school administrator, and a French language translator who had begun her career at the UN, I embarked on this book project with interest in exploring why Black women, who have historically always had to combine work and family, would leave, modify, or change their careers. I was interested in whether they defined their decisions as a response to career and family conflict, similar to professional white women. I also wondered if, like me and the other professional women I knew, they had been raised with a gender strategy that focused on ambition, higher education, and careers with marriage and children to follow. If so, how did they reconcile their decision to abandon that strategy and adopt a strategy more in line with ideal traditional gender roles and family lives?

I found Black career women who sharply focused their attention on representing, maintaining, and raising the race while grounded in a strategy I call the neo-politics of respectability. The women in this study were purposefully turning away from the myth of the strong Black woman, rooted in the larger-than-life historical persona of Sojourner Truth, which forced often debilitating expectations on Black women by requiring them to have superhuman physical, emotional, and psychological strength (Beauboeuf-Lafontant 2009; Harris-Perry 2011; Morgan 2000; Mullings 2001; Painter 1996). Instead, they were focused on developing and prioritizing stable Black marriage and family lives and saw this new tactic as one their mothers and grandmothers had not prioritized. Yet this seemingly new tactic could be added to the long history of what I call *strategic mothering*, which Black women have employed for centuries.

Strategic mothering is a framework I develop to account for the myriad ways in which Black mothers continuously navigate and redefine their relationship with work to best fit the needs of their families and their communities.[2] In this case, Black women see being "available" to their families as a necessary strategy that requires a departure from a cultural model and gender strategy that privileges career success combined with motherhood. In other words, they want to be not only good mothers but also good wives. Although this signals a departure from previous strategies, many practices that have ensured Black familial success and advancement persist, albeit in different forms and with different priorities. As a result I define strategic mothering as a way to discuss African

American women's roles as mothers and workers as multifold and multipurpose, often changing over the life course.

At the root of strategic mothering is an understanding that Black mothers have historically faced insurmountable odds that forced them to make life-altering decisions. As early as the seventeenth century, Black women are recorded as having been tried for killing both their owners who raped them and their children who were conceived during the rape by their white male owners. As Harriett Jacobs taught us in her autobiographical book, *Incidents in the Life of a Slave Girl* (1861), a Black woman often had to decide between the well-being of self and that of her children. Additionally, many scholars have noted Black women's strategies for survival of both self and family. Historian Jacqueline Jones, writing on Black women's roles as laborers during U.S. slavery, stated, "In their devotion to family ties—a devotion that encompassed kin and ultimately the whole slave community—Black women and men affirmed the value of group survival over the slaveholders' base financial and political considerations. The work of Black women helped to preserve that community" (Jones 2010, 41).

Because Black women, in particular, have historically seen their roles as mothers as multifaceted and multipurposed, strategic mothering considers the context in which Black women, in addition to being responsible for their own biological children, have also been directly responsible for other children in the community and indirectly responsible for the community as a whole (Davis 1972; Stack 1974). That responsibility, particularly for middle-class Black women, has been historically centered as caregivers, culture bearers, and community builders, and since the turn of the twentieth century such responsibility has been rooted in racial uplift. Caregivers provide various forms of mothering. Culture bearers teach the ways of the community by instilling pride, culture, and values as means of individual survival. Community builders work, both productively and reproductively, in the interest of the race. Through Black women's strategic mothering practices, which change and adapt over time, Black families have been able to survive.

Sociologist Shirley A. Hill demonstrates in her careful articulation of the intersection of race, class, and gender oppression and its historical depiction in Black family life that strategic mothering practices, employed over time in response to various social structures, are subject to change:

> Slavery, racism, and economic exclusion curtailed the ability and willingness of many African Americans to conform to mainstream gender ideologies that call for economically dominant men, dependent/submissive women, and marriage centered families. African American families were stigmatized as deviant and unstable throughout the twentieth century, although history shows that many responded to racial oppression

by creating more equitable and innovative family relationships. For
example, middle-class Black women virtually pioneered the trend of
combining family and employment, and . . . lower-class women often
resisted patriarchal marriages altogether in favor of female-centered
family structures. . . . The benefits of marriage to economically marginal
men simply did not compensate for their loss of autonomy or the more
reliable extended family resources. (Hill 2004, 201)

Since slavery, Black women have had to work: first, labor was a condition of
their bondage; later, they helped support their families in an economic system
structured around racialized discrimination that made it nearly impossible for
Black men to support their families without assistance from their wives. Black
women have historically been doubly stigmatized by discrimination based on
race and gender, rendering them unable to make the decision to be "at home"
without some economic and social penalty, from either white employers or
state policies.[3] In response, the Black community has emphasized a strategy of
education and professional credentials for Black women; that is, if Black women
had to work, these credentials could allow them better control over where they
worked and over their work conditions (Higginbotham 2001; Shaw 1996). Correspondingly, Black families have historically been seen as more gender equitable
in terms of work and family responsibility when compared to white families
(Hill 2004; Hochschild 1989; Landry 2000).

At the turn of the twenty-first century, professional African American
women and their families are experiencing a shift from older cultural models of
marriage and parenting that privileged matrifocal conceptualizations of Black
family life to a more nuclear model that privileges companionate marriage and
biological children.[4] In the older model, Black mothers relied on their families of
origin, notably their mothers, grandmothers, and "othermothers,"[5] for emotional
and often financial support. This reliance on maternal kin, originating in communal structures of the West African precolonial past, was retained throughout
American slavery because mothers, fathers, and children were frequently sold
away from each other, leaving nonkin women to care for children whose parents
had been sold (Gutman 1976; Sudarkasa 1996). The reliance on kin and fictive
kin has been adapted since Reconstruction to respond to incessant and persistent race-based discriminatory practices that make it difficult for Black families
to maintain a two-parent household (Stack [1974] 1997; Sudarkasa 1996).[6] Scholars have traced this expectation to precolonial Africa where women worked collectively to plant and gather food and take care of children (Sudarkasa 1996).
During American slavery, enslaved women, often impregnated without being
in relationship with males (white and Black), were then responsible for raising
the children of those unions (Jones 1985). When biological mothers were sold

away from their children, a community of women took care of those children (Davis 1971). Post-abolition employment discrimination made it necessary for both men and women to work in either the fields in the South or the factories in the North. Mothers were then forced to rely on "othermothers" to take care of their children (Collins [1990] 2000; James 1993). Inequities in employment opportunities meant Black men, often unemployed for long periods of time, had to rely on the women to take care of the household (Landry 2000). Daughters were taught to expect that Black men may not be consistently strong marriage partners. These multigenerational experiences have been passed down through Black women's collective memory to create a matrifocal cultural model.

Although differing from the nuclear model, a cornerstone of the modern (white) American family ideal, the matrifocal model has allowed Black women a way to protect themselves and the entire African American community from the vulnerability of dependence upon men. Consequently, by following the nuclear/companionate model, Black career women—mothers and wives who are altering their relationship with work to focus on their nuclear families—require a rupture with practices that have historically protected Black mothers and their children and, by extension, secured Black family survival.

Despite departing from the teachings of their mothers and grandmothers (many women recounted painful exchanges), Black women who are modifying their relationship with their careers and depending on the nuclear/companionate model do not see retreating or modifying their careers as a potentially detrimental reliance on their husbands. These Black women also recognize neither the conflict between their ability to negotiate a career and children nor the frustration with workplace family policies. Instead, the professional and upper-middle class Black women presented here see their work and family conflict as the challenge of reconciling cultural expectations, which place a Black woman's career goals and mothering imperatives at odds with maintaining a marriage. Additionally, in their daily negotiations, these women articulate their desire to challenge stereotypical assumptions about Black families and Black communities and work to present a different portrait of Black families.

In the following chapters, I describe how Black professional women navigate marriage, motherhood, and community by substituting a cultural model that privileges marital stability over work stability. Because of their raced, gendered, and classed position, Black career woman are developing strategic mothering practices wherein, once they are married, their marriages move from being something they can take or leave to something valued and necessary for family and communal success. I suggest they choose to stay at home or modify their careers to ensure the stability of their families and privilege their marriages above previous, more established kinship ties. The Black career women are concerned that pursuing and maintaining two ambitious careers might doom the relationship to failure and the children to uncertain futures. Despite the changes in tactics, I find these women employing strategic mothering practices, which Black women have done throughout history to ensure familial and communal survival. Not only do the women in this study discuss the ways in which they attempt to navigate career, marriage, motherhood, and extended family responsibilities, but they are also concerned with their representation to and for the Black community.

Keayba, a married mom of two and a family physician, expressed this point well when she illuminated the ways in which Black women's work and family responsibilities affect their communities in ways they typically do not for white women:

> There is a need for Black female doctors to be visible. For young Black girls this is really important. But you reach a point where you decide what things need to be done. Yeah, you want to contribute, but that is what contributes to the imbalance. For particularly white or Caucasian women some of them are driven and want to excel in their careers. Those who choose careers like that don't have family as a priority. Those who do take family as a priority make decisions on the front end that take family into consideration. For Black women it is an attempt at doing it all that forms the imbalance. You want to be a model and break the stereotypes, but you also have your own children and your husband that need your time and commitment. I think this is one of the reasons for me to do something differently for my career [balancing career and family]; it's because I have been an overachiever and do things with excellence and some of that is based on feeling the need to contribute.

Keayba, like many of the women featured here, expressed a degree of ambivalence in discussing her desire to locate and implement strategies that would allow her to navigate family responsibilities and the pull of the community.

As I talked with Keayba and the other women in this study, I wondered what this shift meant for Black career women who were choosing to modify their relationship with work to establish more stable relationships at home. Their reliance on their husbands and their concerns with "representing the race" seemingly take us back to bygone sexist and racist epochs. At the same time, each woman articulated a desire to move outside the "strong Black woman" framework that required them to do it all. I wondered if this could be an attempt at resistance and resilience. They seemed to be developing a strategy in which they exercised more control over their lives because they had some degree of choice—the choice to be at home or not, to work part-time or not—that most Black women do not have. They often however, made these choices in response to either structural pressures (e.g., layoffs), familial pressures (e.g., husband's request), or communal responsibility (e.g., undoing stereotypes about Black families).

Black Women's Strategies for Resistance and Resilience

Noted anthropologist Leith Mullings developed the framework of the Sojourner Syndrome in her research with Black women of various class strata in Central Harlem, as a way to understand the resilience and resistance strategies of Black women as they navigate class, race, and gender inequality. Using Sojourner Truth's reported words in her 1851 "Ar'n't I a Woman" speech, where she is presented as a woman "who ploughed the fields as well as any man, birthed several children, and watched them be sold into slavery with a mother's grief only Jesus could hear" (Gage 1863), Mullings compares Truth's enumerated responsibilities to contemporary Black women's responsibilities in their own communities: "Her [Sojourner Truth's] account embodies the findings of the research: the assumption of economic, household, and community responsibilities, which are expressed in family headships, working outside the home (like a man), and the constant need to address community empowerment—often carried out in conditions made difficult by discrimination and scarce resources" (Mullings 2005, 86). Nevertheless, according to Mullings, Black women's responsiveness to these responsibilities also represents a "strategy for fostering the reproduction and continuity of the Black community . . . [and] throughout, African American women's individual and collective efforts on behalf of their community have facilitated group survival. In other words, the Sojourner Syndrome is a survival strategy, which may have both short-term and long-term benefits" (2005, 87). From Mullings's perspective, understanding the structural constraints that impede Black women as well as the ways Black women resist these constraints signifies the power in the Sojourner Syndrome framework.

Not everyone has seen the Sojourner model and the accompanying expectation for Black women to be strong and to be "everything to everybody" as demonstrating either resistance or resilience. Historian Nell Painter's biography of the nineteenth-century abolitionist and early women's rights activist found that many accounts of Sojourner Truth's speech, including those from Gage, have been proven false or exaggerated. But for Painter, the importance in telling Truth's story is as much about why Truth herself and others remade her image and created the symbol of Sojourner Truth as it is about the realities of her life (Painter 1996). According to Painter, recrafting Truth as a symbol happened, in part, when, at the turn of the twentieth century, the women's rights movement dropped Sojourner Truth from its pantheon of symbolic women as the movement's consciousness became whiter. The image of Truth was then adopted as a manifestation of a strong Black woman, separate in many ways from the image of white femininity (Painter 1996). Because Black women could not expect the patriarchal protections of either the institution of marriage or the state, they placed a greater emphasis on their ability to take care of themselves, their families, and their communities.

Again, these efforts have had many costs, and some costs manifest themselves in challenges to Black women's health. Mullings and others have used the discussion of the Sojourner Syndrome to shed light on the health consequences that accompany Black women's responsibility to and for the Black community. Research suggests that Black women are at greater risk of stress-related complications with pregnancy, labor, and some chronic illnesses, not because they are Black but because the stress of dealing with the effects of racism produces detrimental health consequences (Jackson et al. 2001; Mullings 2005; Mullings and Wali 2001).

Recent studies investigating the lives of African American middle-class and professional women have extended the Black feminist critique of creating and perpetuating the myth of the strong Black woman (Beauboeuf-Lafontant 2009; Harris-Perry 2011; Morgan 2000, Parks 2013). Black feminist scholars have identified the strong Black woman, hailed as a heroine to most in the Black community, as a way to control Black women, in both the Black community and U.S. society in general (Collins 2000).

While the image of the strong Black woman in opposition to the frail white lady helped early twentieth-century Black women discuss their roles as mothers, wives, and activists, later articulations used this image to explain the problems within the Black community, namely the prevalence of female-headed households. When Black communities began rioting in the 1960s to protest continued apartheid-like conditions and lack of advancement, the strong Black woman was reintroduced by Daniel Patrick Moynihan as the Black matriarch. Moynihan, a sociologist, and self-defined liberal Democrat, who was assistant secretary of labor under Presidents John F. Kennedy and Lyndon B. Johnson and later senator from New York, suggested in his now infamous report that Black families were not able to excel and succeed because Black women were the heads and did not allow Black men their rightful place, thus rendering black men less than useful. This, according to Moynihan, resulted in high rates of teen pregnancies, male unemployment, and poverty (1965).

Recognizing that Black women were being criticized for making the best of difficult structural realities of racism and discrimination, Michelle Wallace, author of *Black Macho and the Myth of the Super Woman*, and other Black feminists critiqued the matriarchy misnomer,[7] which blamed Black women for their second-class citizen position and then celebrated them for managing to "survive" all of its indignities (Wallace 1979; Collins 2000; Giddings 1984; hooks 1981).

Despite critiques by Black feminist scholars, the Black community continued to celebrate Black women whom they represented as managing it all—work, children, and economic, political, and social insecurity—alone. Indeed, when I have presented this research and referenced the problems with the myth of the strong Black woman, Black women scholars in attendance have cautioned me against calling it a myth; so many Black women rely on and use it as a strategy for resilience. "It is a badge of honor," I was told, and one of the few stereotypes of Black women that is actually positive. For Black professional women, however, this myth, encouraging them to be superwomen who are beholden to their careers, spouses, children, families of origin, and the larger Black community, increasingly comes at a cost the women are not willing to pay (Beaubouef-Lafontant 2009; Harris-Perry 2011; Parks 2013).

Nancy, a physician and married mom of three, was negotiating this very contradiction when I talked with her. She had two children but had already lost two; one was stillborn, and the other would have been her oldest child's twin. Nancy told me that during her first pregnancy she had been working twelve-hour shifts well into her third trimester. "I was so tired all of the time, but I did not want to leave my patients," she said, reflecting on that time in her life. "Aaron [her husband] was busy building the business, and we were using my income to pay the bills and keep everything afloat. And then I lost the baby. . . . I didn't even realize he had stopped moving." She noted, "It was devastating, and I blamed myself a lot. I thought if only I hadn't been so busy. I thought I needed to slow down. Maybe if I hadn't been so busy and so tired I would have noticed when he first stopped moving and they could have done something."

When Nancy got pregnant again, she decided to take it easy but she admitted that didn't mean much: "I said I was doing fewer shifts, but then I was working with the health center, and I would take emergency patients or not leave when I was supposed to." She said that only the grace of God got her through that pregnancy. But as she worked out childcare, helped her husband with his business, and saw her patients, it became clear something would have to give. "At the same time that we were having the kids, and I was working crazy hours, Aaron was trying to manage everything with the company by himself," Nancy said, clearly commenting on this very difficult time for their family. She continued, "It was taking its toll on him, and our schedules were taking a toll on our marriage."

When Nancy decided to leave her position at the health center and manage her children and her husband's construction company full-time, she articulated a purposeful mothering strategy that privileged her ability to build a "healthy marriage and family," in which the needs of her family, and particularly those of her husband, were foremost. Nancy and many of the other women saw themselves as living differently than their mothers, grandmothers, and even some women in their age cohort. Their families of origin, particularly their mothers and grandmothers, raised them to be independent, and they were, but they were also making a decision to shift their reliance from themselves and/or the women in their families to their husbands. In doing so, they articulated a desire to ensure their nuclear family's survival. This shift in reliance, while primarily financial, allowed them to focus more on maintaining their marriages and the nuclear family structure more commensurate with the expectations of their upper-middle-class standing. As the research shows, the women in this study saw their focus on their marriages as a survival strategy, for themselves, their children, and the Black community. Not unlike the Black, primarily elite, club women of the early twentieth century, who attempted to redefine Black womanhood as a counter to the harmful effects of racism and sexism on the Black community, the Black career women presented here saw their turn to a nuclear-focused family form away from the Black traditional matrifocal family form as another resistance and resilience strategy.

The women interviewed for this study articulated a desire to benefit or preserve the Black community. But creating a new strategy for career, family, and community that relies on the protections of private marriage is risky business and places these otherwise powerful, successful, and independent women in a predicament where they are seemingly deliberately embedding themselves more deeply into a sexist and patriarchal system. As I completed the research I needed tools to help me think through what appeared to be contradictions in the women's lived experiences and articulated goals. I developed two ways to help me consider the current contradictions in Black women's strategic mothering: *neo-politics of respectability* and *constrained choice*.

The Neo-Politics of Respectability

The *neo-politics of respectability* is what I see as contemporary Black career wives' enactment of strategic mothering. I draw the terminology from Evelyn Brooks Higginbotham's concept, the "politics of respectability," a term she used to define the reform efforts developed by Black women who were a part of the uplift movement at the turn of the twentieth century ([1993] 2006). For Higginbotham, the politics of respectability is separate from the uplift movement in that the Black women who developed and constructed the reform actively redefined Black womanhood in direct opposition to the racist, scientific classification systems that were impeding Black lives.

Similar to early twentieth-century elite women, today's Black mothers and wives, with careers, attempt to resist and counter racist images that continue to use negative stereotypes to impede Black lives. Women of the earlier era responded to prevalent conceptions that Black women were ladies unworthy of protection by developing a framework meant to convince Black and white society of Black women's respectability; likewise, contemporary women are responding to current portrayals of all Black women as unmarriageable and incapable of parenting (Clarke 2011). Married Black career women with children counter these images, according to the women in this study, through the ideal of a stable Black marriage and family. I call this reworking of the twentieth-century paradigm the neo-politics of respectability to account for the twenty-first-century modifications to an earlier strategy. As Mignon Moore asserts in her book *Invisible Families*,

> The emphasis on respectability for the Black middle class today goes beyond a general concern about images that are portrayed to Whites or the enhancement of employment opportunities (as in the earlier "respectability" era). It is equally important for Black women to be seen by other members of the racial community as "people of good character," meaning that they show respect toward others, commitment and responsibility to the group through the demonstration of loyalty and accountability to themselves and to others for their actions. (2011, 12)

While Moore focuses on Black lesbian women with families,[8] the expectations for Black heterosexual middle- and upper-middle-class women, because they are educated career women themselves and married to professionals, come with deeper pressures to uphold the image of respectability. Part of upholding the image, particularly as it pertains to the early twentieth-century articulation of the politics of respectability, is maintaining public and private commitments to racial uplift.

This century-old framework may seem outdated, but the racial climate in the United States makes it continually relevant and salient. According to Kevin Gaines, author of *Uplifting the Race: Black Leadership, Politics, and Culture during the Twentieth Century* (1996),

> Racial uplift ideology . . . remains an influential framework among African Americans for understanding the challenges they continue to face. The persistence of racial stereotypes and prejudice fuels the perception among many Blacks that racist attitudes must be countered by positive images and exemplary behavior by Blacks. Moreover, the fragility of

African American social progress and conservative attacks on civil rights reforms since the 1980s have contributed to a renewed popularity of self-help ideology and efforts . . . Despite the significant changes produced by the civil rights movement, U.S. society remains deeply segregated, at the level of its schools, residential neighborhoods, and church life. Among African Americans the divide in income, social class, and cultural values is arguably increasing. These conditions seem to assure the continued salience of racial uplift ideology, though whether it assumes a liberal or conservative form depends on its larger sociopolitical context.[9]

Using the "uplift" framework, which I develop in greater detail in chapter 3, I argue that African American professional women who choose this approach to marriage and child rearing attempt to represent African American womanhood and motherhood as respectable. Black women of the early twentieth century were charged with not only being pious and neat in their homes but also contributing to reform efforts for the Black community. In addition, historian Victoria Wolcott asserts in her study of interwar Detroit that, although the politics of respectability's bourgeois focus often constrained Black women, it nevertheless gave expressive space and influence to Black women across class and gave them a clear role in racial pride and progress (Harley and Terborg-Penn 1997; McCluskey 1997; Schechter 2001; Wolcott 2001).

There are ways in which contemporary Black career women's strategic mothering practices do not line up perfectly with the politics of respectability. When Black women change their relationship with work, family, and community to focus more attention on their nuclear families, they challenge Higginbotham's notion of the politics of respectability through their seeming lack of commitment to racial uplift (leaving or modifying their relationships to their careers) and maintenance of white supremacist patriarchal norms (depending on men for financial stability) (McCluskey 1997; Perkins 1983; Wolcott 2001). This individuated focus on marriage and family, more in line with the nuclear/ companionate marriage ideal and harnessing the effects of neoliberal policies, complicates the early twentieth-century "uplift ideology." To be sure, the women in this study never identified themselves as operating in response to the politics of respectability. By developing the neo-politics of respectability as a framework, I show how Black career women continue the ongoing self-defense of respectability by presenting an image of Black women that is contrary to the high rates of nonmarital childbearing and disproportionate representation of the poor. Choosing to focus on their marriages and families by altering their relationship with work, these women recommit to the politics of respectability by offering a different representation of Black family life. Their choices certainly allow some degree of agency for Black career women and their families, yet their actions continue to be constrained by raced, classed, and gendered systems of oppression.

Constrained Choice

Like resistance and resilience, "choice" is a concept that comes with positive and negative interpretations and effects. In the lives of women, choice has been used to discuss sexual freedom, reproductive rights, and career preferences. For Black people generally, the primary concept considered in the literature on race and class and African Americans' increasing representation in the upper-middle and middle class has been the idea of opportunity (Jackson 2001; Lacy 2007; Landry 1988; Massey and Denton [1993] 2003; Pattillo-McCoy 1999; Weise 2004; Wilson 1987). It is important to note, however, that many of the choices afforded to the general population of women have been differently experienced when applied to Black women (Branch 2011). African American women have operated in and through a cultural system that makes them only appear to face the same choices and decisions as their white counterparts. Black women must perform significantly more cultural work to be perceived as middle class by mainstream America, and they must simultaneously maintain meaningful connections to the Black community. Black women of all social-class locations have had a long history in the paid labor force, as well as the labor force that should have been paid and was not (Harley 1997). Nevertheless, owing to the combination of a changed political economy and a focus on equal rights for women, people of color, and differently-abled individuals, more Americans have seen generational social mobility through greater occupational and educational opportunities than those allowed in previous generations (Biblarz et al. 1996).

Today, generational wealth inheritance is no longer the only predictor of social-class mobility. Cultural capital plays a significant role in the availability and perception of opportunities and the ensuing choices. Where social theorist Pierre Bourdieu sees these opportunities, made available through cultural capital, as routes to power and status within the mainstream, for Black women, the "cultural memory" of race, gender, and class oppressions creates a cultural contradiction in which class privilege disrupts racialized gender identity and vice versa. As bell hooks posited in her iconic *Ain't I a Woman* (1981), Black women and their families have long been devalued in American history and culture. And in her follow-up essay "Ain't She Still a Woman?" hooks recognizes that the devaluation continues across class:

> Black women face a culture where practically everyone wants us to stay in our place (i.e. be content to accept life on the bottom of this society's economic and social totem pole). Significantly, even when individual

Black women are able to advance professionally and acquire a degree of economic self-sufficiency, it is in the social realm that racist and sexist stereotypes are continually used both as defining Black women's identity and interpreting our behavior. (hooks 1999)[10]

Social class and cultural capital are shaped through Black women's raced and classed identity. Although their social class position comes with some gendered expectations, Black career women's racialized gender identity brings certain other expectations. Black career women are expected and encouraged to reach levels of education and career advancement that often place them in a higher social class than their families of origin. Their economic and social context then seemingly mimics that of middle-class and upper-middle-class whites. Most assume that the goal of upwardly mobile Blacks is to be able to access not only the economic advantages of whites but also the social advantages (housing choices, leisure choices, educational choices, and so on). Many Black people, however, "choose" either not to pursue these social and economic "advantages" or to pursue them selectively. For example, when given the choice, Gia, one of the women I interviewed for this study, decided to move her family from the majority white suburbs in North Atlanta to a majority Black suburb in South Fulton County/Atlanta. She saw this move as important to her family's well-being, but she nevertheless enrolled her son in a North Fulton County public middle school and cited the need for a good science program as her rationale.

There is a robust literature in which scholars have discussed the ways that choices are constrained by economic and political structures in our society and the disadvantages that result from these structures (Branch 2011; Darity et al. 1995; Wilson 1987). Although I acknowledge that there are many more opportunities for Black women and men and white women than there were in previous generations, I still recognize the opportunities now available in the African American community as embedded in *constrained choices*. Conceptualizing opportunity and choice in this way recognizes the convergence of growth in the opportunity structures that are available to individuals while simultaneously identifying continued social and structural barriers to those opportunities. For my purposes, *constrained choices* give the appearance of having been motivated by the actor's free rational will (see White and Klein's *Family Theories* [2008] for detailed discussion). Various factors, however, affect and/or impede the ability to make choices, which appear to be the choices the actor desires but are, in fact, constrained by other forces, often beyond one's control.

Choice has been a similarly important part of the discourse on women's negotiation of work and family. Much of the scholarship to-date has continued to create dichotomous relationships between women who choose to "work" outside the home and women who choose to "stay-at-home." The framework is so entrenched in our psyche around motherhood and parenting that a perceived "war" exists between the two isolated groups, until a parent event at school or a corporate reception at work brings both contingents out swinging.

Pamela Stone (2007) coins this work-family conundrum the "rhetoric of choice," which she says funnels all discourse into a conversation about culture and personal responsibility. She finds instead the "reality of constraints" wherein, even though the white professional women in her study were highly educated and affluent, their options were more limited than they seemed. Caught between the ideal mother and the ideal worker, the professional women in her study end up with a double bind in which they must reconcile "decisions" or "choices" they could have made about their careers in the absence of caregiving, especially mothering responsibilities, and the decisions they actually made to accommodate these responsibilities in light of the realities of their professions and those of their husbands (Stone 2007, 112).

But the discourse is different for Black women. Prior to my own research on Black career women who were choosing to stay-at-home or modify their relationship with work, Black women had been ignored in the literature (Barnes 2008). The focus on at-home Black women has historically been on Black mothers on welfare and their dependence on taxpayer (read: white) dollars. The politics of mothering and care play out most visibly along race and class lines where elite white women are expected to be "at-home" and poor white women, although expected to work, are given a pass if they do not. Elite Black women and poor Black women, however, receive disapproval from their families, the Black community, and the larger society when they are "at-home," but for different reasons: These constituencies find elite Black women are wasting their educations and success, while they chastise poor Black women for relying on public policies to bolster their unemployment (Davis 2006).

As a result, Black women who choose to be at-home moms have not been a part of the "mommy wars" for two primary reasons. First, their movement into the stay-at-home camp is relatively new and often temporary, especially given their understanding of the financial sacrifice and the keen awareness of the arrangement's likely temporariness. Second, and as the women in this study reveal, those who are "at-home" are often participating in the workforce in informal ways, difficult to quantify. They often modify their relationship with work to allow some flexibility in their schedules so they can be more "available" to their families. Accordingly, to divide these women into two groups, even though some may use this language, would be inaccurate. This study demonstrates how each participant employs strategic mothering to address the needs of her family according to her and her children's life stage. For each woman these strategies are impacted by marriage, family of origin, and community, and each operates within the raced, gendered, and classed systems that structure our society (Willie and Reddick 2003).

Intersectional Approaches to Work and Family Conflict

Most theoretical articulations on motherhood have focused on white women because white women and their decisions present the idealized norm and because whiteness continues to hold the privilege developed through capitalism and imperialism. This sentiment is made clear when E. Ann Kaplan explains her focus on white women in her study: "Because dominant forms privilege white, middle-class women, and because I believe dominant discourses inevitably impact minority ones, I have chosen to focus mainly on white, middle-class conflict" (E. Kaplan, 1990, 410).[11] Likewise, studies that use the intersection of race, class, and gender for understanding the linkages between family experiences and external structural processes begin with the fact that people of color and particularly women of color are disproportionately represented in the lowest economic groups and in occupations with the poorest pay.[12] Most of what we know about Black career women presents them through a fractured one-dimensional lens that in most instances ignores them. Thus, Black women's paid labor within the labor market and their unpaid labor for their families operate outside prevailing theories and debates about work and family. When mainstream feminist theoretical debates position Black professional women's emphasis on marriage and community, their decisions get lumped into a discussion on a "return to traditional gender roles"; for the majority of African American women, however, having part-time, flexible, or transient relationships with work has seldom been a useful, let alone viable, option.

This point is well illustrated when we look at the media attention given to high-profile white career women who have left or chosen to modify their careers ("opting out") versus media attention to the most high-profile African American woman, First Lady Michelle Obama, and the decisions she has made regarding her family and career. Following President Barack Obama's election, Mrs. Obama's image focused on promoting seemingly traditional gender roles as she took up the causes of combating childhood obesity, sustaining military families, and establishing the White House community garden. In the 2012 election, a *New York Times* article stated that critics had hoped she would use her historic position to move more deeply into politics, and *Politico* headlined an article calling her a "feminist nightmare." When Mrs. Obama responded to this criticism by focusing her speech at the Democratic National Convention in 2012 on being a mom and ended that speech by reasserting her identity as "mom-in-chief," most of mainstream feminism baulked. Given the history of race and gender in the United States, Mrs. Obama's stated focus on being a wife and mother illustrates the complexities faced by Black career women and the ways they must negotiate motherhood, marriage, and community.

According to Michelle Cottle's piece in *Politico*, when white women news pundits began deriding Mrs. Obama for backing away from a more politicized role in Washington politics, they were responding to the promise of her "Ivy League degrees, career success and general aura as an ass-kicking, do-it-all superwoman."[13] The expectation that a Black career woman must be an "ass-kicking, do-it-all superwoman" provides the backdrop that many Black professional women must wrestle with when making their decisions about work and family.

Tami Winfrey Harris, a news pundit responding to the white feminist backlash against Mrs. Obama, quoted Deesha Philyaw, a freelance writer for several on-line magazines:

> Of course, Black mothers are not endless founts of strength. Nor do they live charmed, guilt-free lives. Some Black at-home mothers are asked by family and friends to justify the decision to "waste" their educations. Professional Black mothers may have to forgo material comforts and greater financial security in exchange for more flexibility and time at home with their kids. But all this struggling and surviving happens in the context of our history. If a Black mother's household income is such that she can afford to stay at home with her kids or opt to pursue a career full time instead—either way, we've arrived at a profound historical moment. Either way, she is living a life her foremothers could only dream about.[14]

Harris, extending Philyaw's discussion to include Mrs. Obama, wrote, "Feminists who wish that Obama would strike a blow for feminism and against stereotyped roles of women, too easily forget that all women are not burdened by the same stereotypes. The way sexism visits white women and women of color, including Black women, is similar in its devastation but often unique in its practice."[15]

This public debate signaled what black feminist theorists have known and articulated for decades: race, class, and gender do not just orient and define our identities; instead, these relational concepts often stratify our society in a myriad of ways. They are historically related axes that create differential and hierarchical relationships with power, resources, and advantages. Using an intersectional approach that sees race, class, and gender as interlocking, interactive, multiplicative, and simultaneously understanding the differential practices and outcomes to Black and white women's decisions, requires us to view historical and contemporary processes in a larger context that makes clear the constraints on what appear to be voluntary choices (Andersen and Collins 2004; Brewer 1993; Brodkin 2000; Crenshaw 1991; King 1988).

Both Black and white women, who are able to make the decision to modify their careers, are obviously in a privileged, minority position. On the surface, socioeconomic class likens these Black women's and white women's experiences. Black and white elite women are college-educated, often with graduate and professional degrees, hold management, executive, and professional positions, and live in households with incomes commonly exceeding $100,000. In a *USA Today* report on a 2003 Census Bureau survey, Black and white women with four-year college degrees and master's degrees earned almost identical median incomes, with Blacks holding a slight advantage. In addition, Black women who held doctoral degrees reportedly earned more than white women, $72,743 and $65,278 respectively.[16] Yet, according to 2005 reports by both *USA Today* and the *Journal of Blacks in Higher Education*, sociologists and economists speculate that Black women's higher earnings are largely the result of the fact that Black women college graduates are far more likely to hold full-time jobs than white women college graduates and may even be employed at more than one place. In 2003, only 48 percent of white women college graduates held full-time, year-round jobs while nearly 68 percent of Black women college graduates worked full-time.[17] By 2007, white women's labor force participation rate had increased to 58.9 percent and remained constant through 2012. During the same period, however, Black women's participation rate showed little growth at 68.5 percent and remained relatively constant.[18] Since there have historically been very few sociological or anthropological studies that focused on middle, upper-middle, and elite Black women, we have census data that presents different information for Black and white women. With minimal qualitative detail, however, we are left with incomplete information. As a result, there are few examples of the effects of racism on Black women's upward social mobility.

Black feminists across disciplines have filled in many historic and literary gaps. Early works that focused on Black professional women have most often presented autobiographical success stories or described the ways in which Black women have overcome repeated assaults on their humanity, but, when Black women have succumbed to the pressures of their raced, classed, and gendered positions, their inability to overcome has been labeled weakness or mental illness, directly opposed to the image of the Strong Black Woman (Beaubouef-Lafontant 2009; McClain and Page 1986; Morgan 2000). When we take an intersectional approach, Leith Mullings's study in Central Harlem is again instructive because she investigated the health effects of the Sojourner Syndrome on Black women across class. Finding that many middle-income and professional women she surveyed chose to live in Harlem to minimize their experiences with racism, Mullings discovered that they experienced other racialized sources of stress:

> Middle-stratum African American women may experience unique sources of stress in managerial and professional occupations. Adding to the stress that may stem from well-documented constraints of discrimination based on race and gender in those positions, race and gender may interact to produce conditions in which professional women sometimes experience conflictive tensions between their status in the occupational and class hierarchy on the one hand, and race and gender solidarity on the other. (2005, 85)

Married Career Women with Children, in Atlanta, Georgia

Metropolitan Atlanta is a uniquely appropriate site to address the question of how African American professional wives negotiate and construct middle-class notions of motherhood and work,[19] especially given the area's historical and political legacy, the social, political, and economic prominence of African Americans, and the distribution of the Black population among the middle, working, and poorer classes (Bayor 1996). Atlanta, often referred to as the "Black Mecca" (Whitaker 2002) because of its long-standing history of being an economically, culturally, socially, and politically strong arena for African American life, is a place where Black people have made some of the more definitive political statements about themselves as Americans. It is home to six historically Black colleges and universities (HBCUs),[20] each of which have graduated African American notables such as Dr. Martin Luther King Jr., Marian Wright Edelman, Maynard Jackson, and Spike Lee. The African American communities of Atlanta have included well-known and sophisticated middle-class leaders who fought for political, economic, and civil rights (Harmon 1996; Stone 1989) as well as a strong grassroots, working-class base upon which much of their achievement depended.

In addition to its very rich tradition of African American middle-class professionals, Atlanta is also the product of its southern heritage; while it boasts one of the largest populations of African American residents, its Black and white residents continue to be divided on the basis of race and increasingly by class (Bayor 1996; Keating 2001; Pomerantz 1997; Stone 1989). Even with its wealth, the Black middle class in Atlanta has lived in segregated neighborhoods for most of the city's history. Despite newcomers moving to the more integrated and diverse outlying counties, a very large faction of the population "chooses" to live in African American neighborhoods.[21] South Fulton County, housing one of the largest populations of Black middle-class residents in the country and the geographic area where most of this study was conducted, has seen one of the largest growth spurts in the five-county metropolitan area of Atlanta. Housing developments have been approved for construction in the area during the past few years, and residents have benefited from new retail shopping and higher-priced planned communities and subdivisions.

According to the U.S. Census Bureau American Community Survey, African Americans in the metropolitan Atlanta area fare better than Blacks in the nation in educational attainment and income. The median household income for Black households in the United States in 2013 was $34,598,[22] But the median household income for Blacks in Fulton County was $35,600.[23] Similarly, 33.2 percent of metropolitan Atlanta's Black population (a ten-county region including Fulton, Cobb, Dekalb, and Clayton counties where study participants live) hold a professional, managerial, or related occupation as compared to 28.3 percent of African Americans nationally. Almost 20 percent of Black Americans nationally have a bachelor's degree or higher, compared to Atlanta's 26 percent,[24] many of whom graduated from the Atlanta University Center's colleges and universities. The twenty-three women and their families participating in this study have a reported median household income of $151,000, which places their incomes in the top 9 percent of all Americans.[25]

Going into the Field:
Black Middle-Class Households in Metro Atlanta

In recent decades, scholars have turned their attention to Black women's roles in the history of Atlanta. More specifically, they have detailed the work Black women have performed as strategic mothers and members of the Black women's club movement. Historian Tera Hunter (1997) detailed Black southern, and primarily Atlanta, women's strategies for survival as they faced discrimination postemancipation. Hunter states that despite deplorable conditions, Black women were "committed to balancing the need to earn a living with needs for emotional sustenance, personal growth, and collective cultural experiences" (3). Legal scholar Dorothy Roberts (2005), giving a more working-class history of how the Black women's club movement worked for the welfare of Black children, chronicled the work of Atlanta women like former slave Carrie Steele who founded an orphanage for Black children in 1890; she also studied the contributions of members of the Atlanta Neighborhood Union, which worked within communities to improve the living and education conditions of Black women and children. Providing historical context for the reform efforts of Atlanta's Black elite, Joseph Jewell (2007) and Karen Ferguson (2005) build on our understanding of the uplift movement and the politics of respectability, respectively. And anthropologist Harry Lefever details, in *Undaunted by the Fight: Spelman College and the Civil Rights Movement, 1957–1967*, the ways in which a select group of students and faculty at Atlanta's Spelman College shifted the institution's long-standing history of community service to a more active engagement in social justice (2005). Throughout each account it becomes clear that Black women, across social class, have historically been invested in resistance and resilience strategies, most of which rested on educating Black women and children.

This fact of engagement makes reconciling contemporary Black career women's decisions to leave or modify their relationships with work all the more interesting and ripe for investigation and analysis. Spending time with Denise and the other women at the library story time provided a preliminary focus group for the larger, more in-depth study. No ethnographic studies on Black career women and their relationships with work and family exist, nor have contemporary studies included Black career women's experiences of work and family conflict; thus, the research project began with an exploratory focus. Focusing on twenty-three women and their families is admittedly a nonprobability sample, but by focusing on a small sample size, this study helps to identify theoretically significant ideas that warrant further study (Marshall 1996; Small 2009). Moreover, according to H. Russell Bernard, nonprobability sampling aids in our understanding of internal validity (Bernard 2006, 195). In other words, we have a better understanding of what "goes on" in a particular population. In this case, it is an admittedly "hard to find" population with shared cultural competence. As such, by selecting African American, married, career women with children under the age of six, I used cultural model theory to select "domain-specific informants." Consequently, using in-depth ethnographic interviews results in an analysis that extends to people outside the sample (Bernard 2006, 208; Marshall 1996).

I determined that in order to work with women in a position to "choose" to modify their relationship with employment, I needed to identify women who were solid citizens of the professional and upper-middle class. I defined the professional class using markers developed by business and marketing executives where traditional definitions of professionals include people with advanced degrees in areas like law, medicine, or divinity, as well as teachers and nurses. The definition has expanded with the rise in the computer industry to include people in advertising, communications, engineering, and computer science (Dohm and Schniper 2007). Correspondingly, twenty-two of the twenty-three women hold a bachelor's degree, and one was in a management program at the bank where she worked (clearly well on her way to being a manager). Fourteen of the twenty-three women have a postgraduate degree, including six with master's degrees, two with MBAs, four MDs, one JD, and one DDS (see appendix).

All of the women I interviewed are married or heterosexually cohabitating and have at least one child under the age of six. They are between the ages of thirty-two and forty-seven, and they had their first child between the ages of nineteen and thirty-seven. I decided to focus on two-parent households to ensure the possibility that these women could modify their involvement in work with the support of a partner's income. Likewise, by focusing on mothers with pre-school-age children, I focused on a group likely to confront the need to make decisions about the relationship with work.

Because the study was controlled to create the "perfect" conditions for observing and analyzing Black women's choices concerning career and family, ethnographic observations were first conducted with three formal support groups for women who self-identified as "stay-at-home moms." I observed the support groups from 2003 to 2004 and took notes on my observations so I could develop the semistructured interview questions with both my research interests and questions in mind and to further elucidate patterns I picked up on during the observations phase.

By locating women in a controlled environment, I was able to identify women who fit the criteria. One support group had a predominantly white American membership, and two were composed of predominantly African American women, one of which was held at a church and included a strategy rooted in biblical principles. While completing the observations, I contacted women through the support groups and through a private school owned by African Americans and serving a primarily African American population where most parents are married and college graduates. I invited the women I met to participate in the study, and when they agreed, from 2004 to 2007 I met with each woman at least twice and often several more times (on average, about five visits with each woman), depending upon her schedule. Each mother was asked to participate in three phases of the project. First, I used a set of structured questions to ask each woman about her age, marital status, educational background, occupation, children's ages and birthdates, hometown, household tasks, professional and social memberships, time allocation, and financial status (which included a series of questions about income, expenditures, and savings). Second, I used a more open-ended list of questions to ask the women about their childhoods, family of origin, how they came to meet and marry their spouses, and experiences with education, career advancement, and family negotiation. Finally, I observed each family, either at home or while engaged in family activities (most often talking while transporting kids to different events or waiting for kids to be picked up after school or activities). I also observed the families and the mothers by accompanying them to appointments, on errands, and "hanging out" or "pitching in" when things needed to be done around the house while we were talking. I did not take notes during observations of family life as

I determined that would feel intrusive, but I recorded what I observed after I left each family observation. I also conducted twenty-three couple/family histories, including contextualized genealogy/kinship charts that helped to develop a narrative of each woman's family across at least three generations. In some cases the women helped me draw their genealogy charts so I was sure to transcribe the information correctly. The genealogy charts included names, birthdates, hometowns, any migration, education, professions, marriages, and children. This technique allowed me to see patterns across generations and to identify when such patterns had changed, a particularly enlightening exercise when considering migration patterns for education and professional development. I then returned to the field in 2012 to conduct follow-up interviews with the women to ascertain to what extent their work and family decisions had changed following the 2008 financial crisis. Atlanta was particularly hard hit when the housing bubble burst, and, recognizing that many of their strategic mothering decisions were temporary or fragile, I was interested in whether these women had been affected (see the epilogue).

To generate additional study participants, I employed snowball sampling where I relied on referrals from initial study participants. Recognizing the bias inherent in this model, I compensated by making sure I "selected" women who had some degree of diversity even within the group and attempted to keep them as anonymous to each other as to the reader. I use pseudonyms for the names of the women and their family members and blur any personal location identifiers they may have used over the course of their participation in the study.

Although Atlanta is a big city, one of the largest metropolitan areas in the country, few cities in the United States have such a historically strong Black middle-class in terms of wealth, prestige, and numbers. Likewise, the Black upper-middle class tends to occupy the same geographical and professional spaces; when they do not, the history of denied access and denied opportunity to particular spaces offers organizational and institutional structures to pull African Americans together. Indeed, when discussing the popular adage, "six degrees of separation," African Americans often find it's more like three degrees. Sixteen families lived in South Fulton County, and, as I got to know them better, I learned that many went to the same churches, sent their children to the same schools, and had the same pediatricians, among other points of connection. Although no participants were "best friends," there were several ways for their paths to cross. If I learned that they knew each other, I worked quite diligently over the course of our time together to make sure none of them knew I was interviewing the others.

To help with this process, when speaking generically about a particular location in the metro-Atlanta area, I use the proper name. For example, when the women could steal a few minutes away from their families to talk, I often met the women at the Starbucks on Cascade Road, a popular meeting location in southwest Atlanta, but when describing a particular subdivision or school they or their children attended I use a pseudonym. For instance, many families in my initial contact group had their children enrolled in the same school. To protect their identities and that of the school, I gave the school a pseudonym. In addition to changing their names and identifiable places, I also changed insignificant details about the women and their families to further camouflage their identities.

While all of the participants are married, professional mothers who live in the metropolitan Atlanta area, there are some geographical differences. These women reside in Cobb, Fulton, Douglas, and DeKalb counties and seven "cities"—Atlanta, College Park, East Point, Austell, Smyrna, Kennesaw, and Stone Mountain, which are all included in the twenty-eight-county Atlanta Metropolitan Statistical Area (MSA). There is also a good deal of diversity in the study group. Most of the participants are transplants to the Atlanta area. Only seven out of the twenty-three mothers and four out of the twenty-three fathers are native Atlantans. There were also some differences in educational attainment. I have already noted the high educational achievement of this group, but high levels of education were also reflected in the previous generation of their families. Thirteen (56 percent) of the participants' mothers held a bachelor's degree or more, and ten (43 percent) of the participants' fathers held a bachelor's degree or more.[26] Ten of the women's mothers-in-law (43 percent) and nine of their fathers-in-law (39 percent) completed a bachelor's degree or more. While this allows for an analysis of middle- and upper-middle-class social locations across generations, the other side of the coin includes ten women (43 percent) who are first-generation college graduates, one woman who was raised by her grandmother, and two who were raised by mothers who did not complete high school.

All of the participants' husbands, except one who is white, are Black men with at least a college degree. Of the twenty-three families that participated in the study, twelve of the husbands have advanced degrees. At the time of the study, nine of the husbands reportedly made over $100,000 per year, and only two made less than $50,000 per year, making most a part of the elite black middle or the stable core middle class (Lacy 2007). Of course, these statistics reflect not only the experiences of a small research group but also a very small segment of the American population in general, as only 6.25 percent of those over age twenty-five earn more than $100,000 per year.[27]

Research based on a small sample size often has mixed reviews. In general, researchers can learn a lot about that small group but will have difficulty expanding the research to reveal insights for others (Bernard 2006); however, small samples are necessary when trying to investigate in detail populations that have not been previously explored (Bernard 2006). The idea is that the "thick description" will give us ways to understand and build upon the nuances identified and presented—insights that would not be possible with a large comprehensive sociological survey (Geertz 1993). Additionally, a project focused on historical analysis would privilege past constructions of Black women's raced, classed, and gendered identities but would neither allow enough space for sufficient understanding of what is unique about the opportunities and constraints of the contemporary moment nor provide enough of an ethnographic record for future cross-cultural comparison. To answer this challenge I employed collective memory as a methodological tool for analysis.

Conducting intensive interviews and life histories gave me the opportunity to understand how the women in this study saw themselves. Their constructions and their everyday practices varied, most simply in their diverse approaches to work and family decisions. Most compelling was the way each conveyed the lessons passed on from their mothers and grandmothers, either through direct commands or observations. Each of the twenty-three women conveyed a collective memory of black women's experiences, which developed and fortified a worldview that taught Black women to be independent, strong, responsible for care of themselves and their children, and independent of men. Using collective memory as a methodological approach for each study participant, I learned what kind of Black woman they thought they were and what they thought their responsibilities were. I learned that they received much of their information from their mothers and grandmothers and some additional approved sites, including the Black church and historically Black colleges and universities. Additionally, their stories, which I recorded individually, did not occur in a social vacuum and were embedded in the collective memory of the social conditions that bore Black women in the Black community. For each study participant, the interviews were transcribed, and the texts were divided into broad categories and then reduced to smaller units for analysis. Using grounded theory, I employed open coding to determine clusters of categories. Texts went into more than one code when they were determined to have multiple perspectives. When the synthesis of the interviews was compared against one another, I was able to see multiple perspectives. I was also able to see where those perspectives were connected. This study allowed me the opportunity to maintain each participant's subjectivity while also recognizing the ways they were connected and integrated (Goodson and Choi 2008). In this way I am able to broaden my conclusions and develop theoretical perspectives of possible application outside the sample (Marshall 1996, 524).

Ultimately, this study is intended to address several gaps in the literature: first, the gap in women, work, and family literature that privileges the experiences of white women; second, the gap in Black family studies that has historically focused on the problems of poor and otherwise "dysfunctional" Black women and families; third, an analysis of the various ways Black women create their own agency and means of survival in their daily lives, regardless of their effectiveness, that connect them to the collective memory of Black women's strategic mothering practices. And finally, this study adds to the literature that seeks to close the gaps in public policy initiatives that take the onus off of Black women, and all women, for ensuring both the survival and accomplishment of their marriages, their children, their communities, and their careers with little support from our society.

Brief Overview

The following chapters illuminate the strategies Black women employ to negotiate their roles as mothers, wives, career women, and daughters. Each strategy privileges their stated goal of being available to their families and communities but situates that need within a raced, classed, and gendered perspective that sees availability as necessary for protecting the marriage, the children, and ultimately the community.

The first two chapters privilege the experiences of Black career women and the strategies the women practice. Chapter 1 discusses and analyzes the literature on Black motherhood, Black families, and Black women and work. I review previous studies and explain the inadequacy of scholarship on Black professional wives and mothers. After observing and interviewing each woman and asking her to define herself using terms within and outside the working/ stay-at-home mom model, I came up with terms that more adequately described the strategies the women were using. Chapter 2 explores each of these strategies, separating them for ease of analysis while highlighting their fluidity as it pertains to the ever-changing needs of Black career women's families and communities. I identify three categories that demonstrate the strategies Black women are using to navigate their lives, and I label them "modified-full-time career mom" (MFC), "modified stay-at-home mom" (MSH), and "available-flexible career mom" (AFC).

These three categories, although a bit rudimentary, clearly help in our understanding of the variation in action and perspective and present a clearer picture for analysis. I organize the women in this way because, while their decisions regarding career, family, and community are varied and best align across these three categories, some voices are stronger than others in expressing their perspectives. This organization allows multiple voices to be heard with depth across the various axes of investigation. Moving forward, I highlight each woman's relationship with work; however, I demonstrate that this relationship says or predicts very little about how they make decisions regarding work and family. Instead, it is just one strategy that supports the goal of privileging their marital and nuclear family.

The remaining chapters explore how Black career women develop and utilize various strategies for maintaining their families. Chapter 3 focuses on the ways African American professional and upper-middle-class married women privilege their roles as wives and redefine their relationship with marriage. Although their enactment of what I call the neo-politics of respectability implores them to get married and stay married for the good of their children, they also believe they are undoing generations of damage caused by a lack of emotional and financial trust in Black men. This lack of trust, reflected in the Black collective memory, is part of what families of origin use to counsel Black women against a primary focus on marriage. These women respond to this collective memory with a focus on the marriage that often results in a retreat from or modification with their careers. All three groups expressed a desire to privilege and maintain their marriages despite extended familial disagreement regarding their shifts away from work, and all attributed their struggles with this goal to being raised as independent women.

Chapter 4 explores the strategic focus on enculturating upper-middle-class Black children. The Black women in my study expressed the fact that some conflict with the demands of combining career and children lies in protecting children from the harsh realities of racism, while simultaneously preparing them to excel within the mainstream, majority white culture. These women implement what Karyn Lacy calls strategic assimilation (2007, 151): African American families privilege both mainstream, majority white practices that will help them navigate social structures and systems and African American culture so their children can "know where they come from" and feel connected to a sense of community.

Chapter 5 continues the discussion begun in chapter 4 by focusing on the growing class divides within the Black community and how Black professional women and their families are affected by these divisions. With the growth in Du Bois's "talented tenth," now closer to 20 percent (19.6 percent), many college-educated Black families have few reasons to interact with members of the community who are less educated and outside the Black professional class.[28] This chapter examines the growing disconnect between the Black professional and upper-middle class and the Black poor and working class and the resultant ideological conflicts. Similar to the climate at the turn of the twentieth century, a heightened focus on representations of respectable Blackness becomes the norm while the divide between the haves and the have-nots widens.

The conclusion revisits the neo-politics of respectability and the way professional Black women use strategic mothering, albeit through constrained choices, to ensure the success of their families and, by extension, the Black community. Analyzing professional Black women's reliance on the neo-politics of respectability to represent and advance the Black community illuminates contemporary Black career women's redefinition of marriage, motherhood, and community. This in turn helps those who are interested in gender equality to refocus efforts so that the onus of managing, negotiating, and sustaining marriage, career, and family does not fall solely on either women or nuclear or even extended families, and I suggest instead that the burden can be relieved through more definitive state-sponsored supports (Hansen 2005).

1

The Role of Black Women in Black Family Survival Strategies

When Cory's oldest daughter was born, she was working in the marketing department of a large multinational corporation, which required her to travel every week. She took three months off for maternity leave and then went back to work. Many of her coworkers expected that she would not return because most women in her position followed this model, but being a "stay-at-home mom" had never been part of Cory's self-concept. Cory, expecting to be like her mother and the women who were a part of her mother's cohort, noted, "My mom had a career in education, she did a lot of things she enjoyed doing, she never let having my brother and I disrupt her desires for herself." But Cory's busy work schedule was hard for her and her infant daughter. Cory explained her daughter's reactions: "She hated it. She would get so worked up when I left. My husband would pick her up from the babysitter when I was traveling, and it's like she knew when she saw him that Mommy was not home and she would basically cry and be upset the entire evening. Then if I still was not back when she woke up the next morning, she would give my husband a hard time. I knew I had to do something different." Cory further described the toll her travel schedule was taking on her daughter and her marriage: "Brian was returning to school to get his master's in divinity so I knew I couldn't quit my job. He was working, too, but we still needed my income and I loved what I did." Cory enjoyed her work and felt she would not like being a stay-at-home mom, yet she also wanted to support her husband's goals of completing his divinity program and becoming an ordained minister.

Cory responded to these challenges, not by leaving her career, but by locating a different employer with different expectations for employees. After months of putting out professional "feelers," Cory heard from a friend about a small Midwest-based, national marketing firm that was expanding and considering the Atlanta area. Cory's expertise with her current company was just what they were looking for. She joined the firm with a major contact already in place that could—given her track record with her previous employer—become a contract opportunity. Cory was clear that she was fortunate to find this opportunity. She said, "It all came together and fit perfectly in place. I knew it was God! I don't know how we would have managed without it."

Cory is part of a long tradition of Black women creating mothering strategies. In this chapter, I discuss and analyze the literature on Black motherhood and Black families that have centered the adaptive strategies Black women have employed for the survival of their families and communities. Highlighting the lived experiences of Black women like Cory, this chapter also expands the previous literature on Black mothers and their families with the goal of helping us understand how the race, class, and gender of professional Black women alongside communal expectations of Black educated women influence their decisions concerning marriage, motherhood, and community. Chapter 1 also engages the ways Black women's reliance on the collective memory of Black motherhood complicates their work and family decisions in a way that differs from white women who have traditionally faced the same choices. Finally, the chapter ends with my analysis of Black professional women's strategies and how they interrupt the pernicious discussions within mainstream discourse that continue to force a dichotomous relationship between "working" and "stay-at-home" moms.

Creating the Professional Black (Women's) Middle Class

Cory's decision to continue working while locating an alternative solution is part of the cultural model at the root of Black women's mothering strategies. According to sociologist Bart Landry (1988), not only have Black women historically had to work, but they have also wanted to work, particularly when they chose "meaningful" professions, far removed from domestic and service positions. In fact, historian Stephanie Shaw's seminal work *What a Woman Ought to Be and to Do* (1996) shows that during the late nineteenth and early twentieth centuries the Black community pushed young African American women to get educations and obtain jobs as teachers, lawyers, doctors, and professionals in other prestigious occupations. These occupations not only served the purpose of racial/community uplift but also protected women from domestic and low-skilled work, where they were vulnerable to economic and sexual exploitation.

Sociologist Elizabeth Higginbotham continues the historical trajectory but adds social analysis with her study of Black women living in northern states who entered college during the integrationist era of the North and the desegregation efforts of the civil rights movement in the South; that is, she conducted the study in the 1970s when these women were either enrolled in or recently graduated from college. In *Too Much to Ask* Higginbotham develops, conducts, and analyzes the research of her twenty-year project. The women in her study, although not actively fighting segregation, were often the first to integrate predominantly white colleges and universities in the late 1960s.

Higginbotham, like Shaw, details the struggles their families of origin endured in their pursuit of education for their daughters and reveals the fact that the parents of each of the fifty-six women she interviewed wanted their daughters to achieve their full potential. For most families, full potential meant having nontraditional postcollege goals, as compared to their white classmates, who envisioned lives primarily as wives, homemakers, and childcare-providers. When she asked the women about their postgraduation career and family goals Higginbotham found that 43 percent of the women she interviewed said they wanted to combine marriage, work, and family, and 23 percent envisioned marriage, children, and periodic or steady part-time work (Higginbotham 2001, 225). Landry grounds the discussion by asserting the importance of higher education and career in the lives of Black women with longitudinal statistical data in his study *Black Working Wives*. With the statistical analysis and the history of Black women in the workforce, Landry contends that a difference in ideology resulted in Black women's different practices: "Just as a particular ideology of white womanhood influences white wives' employment decisions, so too a particular ideology of Black womanhood, developed within the Black community shaped by Black wives' orientation to paid work. In the course of their activities for racial uplift, as they spoke their minds and lived out their lives, Black upper-middle-class wives developed and promulgated their own unique conception of true womanhood" (Landry 2000, 30–31). Developing a framework that included work—often featuring work at its core—meant that middle-class, working-class, and working-poor Black women's strategy historically focused on what was "best" for their families and the Black community.

As a professional class developed within the Black community around the turn of the twentieth century, two schools of thought, "saving" Black women and "uplifting" the race, converged. At the time, racism, articulated through gender and class, was exemplified, according to historian, Evelyn Brooks Higginbotham, through the trope of "the lady," signified by not merely gender but also class. In this vein, certain white women could be left out of the construct (namely prostitutes and poor or working-class women), but no Black woman, regardless of education, income, refinement, or character, could be conferred the status of "lady": "While law and public opinion idealized motherhood and enforced the protection of white women's bodies, the opposite held true for Black women" (Higginbotham 1992, 257). In response, Black women developed their own ideology. This ideology was clearly articulated by philosopher Anna Julia Cooper, an early twentieth-century Black scholar, who believed that elevating the status of Black women would uplift the entire race (Cooper 1892).

Then as now, attention to Black women's morality as a route to the Black community's liberation was fraught with critique. The politics of respectability was deemed elitist as middle-class (read: white) notions of culture, class, and deportment became the norm at the expense of "folkways" that might be attributed to rural (read: African) vestiges from the South (Wolcott 2001). In addition, many believed that a strategy supporting and articulating the dominant discourse about African Americans only reified, not dismantled, the racist, classist, and sexist hegemony (Gaines 1996). Instead of following the cult of domesticity that relegated white middle- and upper-class women to the private sphere, Black women of the nineteenth century championed a threefold commitment to family, community, and careers (Landry 2000). It is important to note that for them this strategy for survival, resistance, and advancement joined those strategies most prominently suggested by Black men of the day, including Booker T. Washington's call for self-determination and education in practical trades, W.E.B. Du Bois's desire for the "talented tenth" to gain higher education in the liberal arts, and Marcus Garvey's Back to Africa campaign (White 1999).

Lower-income women who were often not afforded the opportunity for higher education and financial security developed their own strategies. Their mothers and other female kin taught black women that they could not depend on either bourgeois practices or Black men to protect and support them. Discriminatory practices meant that the odds of Black men finding stable, consistent, well-paying employment were slim. Black men, frequently discouraged while searching for and being denied stable employment, often relieved their pain through abandonment, abuse, addiction, or adultery. Sociologist Bonnie Thornton Dill concurs: the American family has been defined, developed, and protected in a number of ways, but African American women and their families have never quite met the mark; Black women have historically been left far outside the articulation of women as wives and mothers (Dill 1988b).

The Problem with Marriage

The long-standing economic conditions in the Black community often made it difficult to begin or maintain marital unions if they did not provide enough economic support due to employment conditions for both Black men and women. Although the number of children growing up in married-couple homes mid-century was close to 75 percent (compared to barely 25 percent today), marriage was not considered a viable gender strategy, particularly in a patriarchal structure that privileged the male "breadwinner" model. Many scholars, notably E. Franklin Frazier, Daniel Patrick Moynihan, Carol Stack, Joyce Ladner, Linda Burton, Harriett Pipes McAdoo, Robert Staples, Robert Hill, Wade Nobles, and

Shirley Hill, have sought to explain both Black family life—its form, structure, and function—and the role of marriage.

Anthropologist Carol Stack's influential study of the economic and child-care networks of kin, fictive kin, and extended kin demonstrated the ways in which Black families worked together to provide economically and socially for their children (Stack [1974] 1997). While her ethnographic study focused on the life experiences of poor, marginalized, and disenfranchised primarily female-headed families,[1] she illustrated the fact that African American families' strategies for survival included relying on one another for the necessities in life, a strategy grounded in the historical communities created by slavery (Davis 1972).

Likewise, sociologist Joyce Ladner's study, which placed more emphasis on the effects of racism in the creation of an isolated Black community, illuminated how racism affected the development of Black womanhood. Focusing her attention on Black female adolescents in a housing project in St. Louis, Ladner suggested that the harsh realities of living in a racist and sexist society where there are few "protections" for Black girls and Black women required a certain type of "strength" to ensure survival; consequently, "Black girls are encouraged, in their quest for womanhood, to be the hardworking backbone of the family, and to have children" (Ladner [1971] 1995, 102). If these adolescents are to marry, then marriage follows later (Ladner [1971] 1995, 102).

More recent studies have further considered family patterns and interdependency within families. According to Carol Stack and Linda Burton (1993), kinscripts ensure family survival as members are assigned roles or scripts they must follow through the family life course. Family needs take precedence over individual needs. One hopes that both family needs and individual needs will be mutually beneficial, but in some cases kinscripts become more beneficial to those who hold the most familial power. For Black poor and working-class families, which tend to be multigenerational, that power usually rests with the oldest generation of women who consistently focus on family survival and reproduction.

These and other studies have sought to refute the images and myths about the pathology of the Black community and Black womanhood that developed as a part of public policy and public perception following the infamous 1965 Moynihan Report. Authored by sociologist Daniel Patrick Moynihan, the report follows in the theoretical footsteps of sociologist E. Franklin Frazier. Both began their analysis of African Americans by emphasizing the importance of unemployment as a cause of family disorganization among lower-class African Americans, and both confused the cause with the effect and thereby stigmatized the Black family and the Black community since the 1960s. According to Moynihan's controversial report, the deterioration of Black society is caused by the deterioration of the Black family. From his perspective, the culprit was the slave household, through which enslaved people developed a fatherless matrifocal/ matriarchal pattern that was carried through the generations because of the harsh effects of slavery on individuals and their children. Moreover, extreme urban and rural poverty meant that the Black family made little progress toward the "middle-class" pattern, and the migration to the North reinforced social and familial disorganization. Moynihan further asserted that the Black family was at the center of the pathology of the Black community, and he called for a national effort to strengthen the Black family. While Moynihan penned the report to garner support for structural solutions rooted in creating jobs programs in urban areas throughout the country, his focus on employing men and relegating women to the sidelines did not match the realities of African American economic and social life.

Marital conditions have worsened for the majority of African American families over time. Scholars have sought to understand the unprecedented persistent drop in Black marriage rates since the 1960s and the relationship between female-headed households and the rising rate of childhood poverty in the Black community. William Julius Wilson's controversial research pointed to a lack of "marriageable" Black men and the corresponding decline in Black marriage rates, and these findings led to public policy initiatives that have focused on getting poor and working-class parents married.[2] From the Clinton administration's "welfare reform" that used marriage as a way to both end welfare dependence and encourage the formation of two-parent families (1995) to President George W. Bush's 2004 initiative to promote "healthy marriage," particularly for low-income couples, to President Obama's "My Brother's Keeper" initiative,[3] which focuses on boys and men of color, the focus is clearly on marriage and men.

Scholars responding to Moynihan's report have provided much-needed corrections and nuance through quantitative and qualitative analysis, yet public perception and policy implementation continue to privilege the idea that Black families are deviant and correctable only through a heterosexual marriage model with men at the helm. For example, law professor Ralph Richard Banks's 2011 book *Is Marriage for White People?* offers a popular treatment of the topic of Black marriage. His overall analysis suggests that Black women, even professional Black women, are responsible for the decline in marriage rates because there are more college-educated Black women than Black men; therefore, Black men assert more power over the dating and marriage relationship than Black women, and Black women must exercise their power to date and marry outside the race to regain Black men's attention. Even though fewer women are getting married and more women are postponing marriage *across race and class*, primarily owing to shifts in the education and economic market,

Banks, by trying to "help" Black women, actually shifts responsibility for the health of Black marriage and family squarely onto the shoulders of Black women.

The impact of the Moynihan Report was and has been tremendous primarily because much of what he predicted for African American families seemingly came true (Hymowitz 2005). For Moynihan and many others, both then and today, the answer to all social ills related to the African American experience is the proper placement of the Black male in the Black community structure. The assumption is that Black men have been placed at a disadvantage; not only does the system discriminate against them in employment, promotion, and wages, but also Black women exercise reverse male-female roles, achieve higher rates of education, and often earn higher wages in white-collar professional and labor positions. These discrepancies purportedly leave the Black male feeling inadequate and alienated and encourage physical or mental desertion. Moynihan's attention to children being raised without a father in a society that saw the male head as normative and stable took center stage and worked to further demonize Black women as domineering and promiscuous, the root of impoverished conditions, low education rates, and high incarceration rates in the Black community. By describing these conditions as a "tangled web of pathology," Moynihan developed an argument that gained and maintained widespread currency. These "pathologies," all a result of the breakdown in Black families, were linked to an earlier categorization termed the "subculture of poverty" introduced by anthropologist Oscar Lewis (1959) and shortened to the "culture of poverty" in Moynihan's report.

Although the categorization received harsh criticism among social theorists, it has been consistently used to describe the persistence of poverty among certain groups despite active policies to eradicate poverty. According to historian Mimi Abramovitz, the culture of poverty thesis has been a prominent factor in upholding "the glorification of Anglo-American motherhood, the belief in childrearing as exclusively women's work, the narrow vision of proper single mothers as widows and the identification of worthiness with assimilation [into white-Anglo middle class society and] condemned other mothers who did not live up to these ideals as immoral and unworthy of aid" (Abramovitz 2000, 59).

Moynihan was not the first to criminalize Black family structure and Black women. This perspective developed during slavery and permeated the abolitionist and Reconstruction periods when white women and Black women were defined differently. A double standard of protections for Black and white women developed, one that continues into the "choice" debate. Protections for stay-at-home moms have been designated and enforced for white women both in the law and through the white male patriarchal system; for Black women, however, those same protections have been either nonexistent or accompanied by loss of privacy and constant surveillance. Alongside the lack of protections has been the development of a barrage of stereotypes to label Black women.

Sociologist Patricia Hill Collins has written extensively about these pernicious stereotypes that work to control Black women's bodies and ultimately their sense of self. Collins (2000) writes about four main controlling images that oppress Black women: the mammy, the matriarch, the welfare mother, and the jezebel. Each has been insidious in its presentation, and each affects Black women's decisions about marriage, work, and motherhood. According to Collins (5), Black women have been oppressed in three key ways—economically, politically, and ideologically. Beginning with slavery, the productive labors of both Black men and women were exploited, their rights as citizens rendered nonexistent, and racist and sexist ideologies justified their oppression. Collins writes, "From the mammies, Jezebels, and breeder women of slavery to the smiling Aunt Jemimas on pancake mix boxes, ubiquitous Black prostitutes and ever present welfare mothers of contemporary popular culture, the nexus of negative stereotypical images applied to African-American women has been fundamental to Black women's oppression" (Collins 2000, 5). Furthermore, Collins surmises that these stereotypical images "are designed to make racism, sexism, poverty, and other forms of social injustice appear to be natural, normal, and inevitable parts of everyday life" (Collins 2000, 69).

Black Women Rise to the Occasion

For Gail, married mother of three and former COO, the negative image of the welfare mother has had major impact on her and her decisions about career and family. Gail not only worried about what society might say or think about her decisions, but she also worried about her mother's reactions, which reinforced these notions. Gail explained: "My mom totally disagrees with my decision to be at home. She doesn't just disagree—she makes me feel bad; like I am not being a good mother by being at home. She thinks I am wasting my talents and spoiling my son and not contributing as I should be to my household. And she definitely thinks I am making a mistake by being dependent on my husband."

Gail's mother is a twice-divorced working-class woman who raised her five children as a single female-head for most of their lives in Cleveland. Her concern for Gail is rooted in her own experiences with her former husbands and her desire and need to protect herself and her children. Gail's experiences and critique from her "overbearing mother" provide a glimpse into the reality of Black, particularly working-class and poor, women's experiences and the strategies they have employed for the protection of themselves and their children.

Black women have always been both workers and mothers, but historically the relationship has been mutually supportive. A review of scholarship on Black women's productive and reproductive role in American history shows an unyielding commitment by Black women to do whatever was necessary to sustain their families and, by extension, their communities.[4] According to historian Jacqueline Jones, both productive and reproductive work has been important to Black women's identity formation.

> Black women's parental obligations, and affective relations more generally, played a key role in their struggle to combat oppression. Their attention to the duties of motherhood deprived whites of full control over them as field laborers, domestic servants, and "brood-sows." Indeed, the persistence with which enslaved women sought to define on their own terms "what a woman ought to be and to do" would ultimately have a profound impact on American history. (Jones [1985] 2010, 10)

Ironically, the ability of Black families to adapt to political, economic, and social conditions that were variously experienced because of racial inequalities have ensured their survival and simultaneously made them maladaptive in the eyes of the general American family ethos. Since E. Franklin Frazier's seminal analyses of the Black family (1939) and the Black middle class (1957), most scholars have sought to explain the "deviancy" and "dysfunctionality" of Black family life. While some scholars (Gutman 1976; Stack [1974] 1997; Sudarkasa 1996) have presented extensive research that explained the historical, social, and economic reasons for mother-centered households in the Black community, most of the country found the lack of male "head-ship" to be the reason for Black families' inability to adapt to American (read: white middle-class) ways of being and essentially believed their maladaptive family formations explained the Black community's inability to thrive and prosper (Moynihan 1965).

Disputing Moynihan and others, Black work and family scholar Bonnie Thornton Dill stated, "Black family life throughout the South preserved a belief in the importance of marriage as a long-term commitment . . . and acceptance of women who had children outside of marriage. Kinship networks were an important source of resistance to the organization of labor that treated the individual slave, and not the family, as the unit of labor" (Dill 1988b, 420).

Likewise, African Americans secured more rights and incurred more government surveillance, particularly in the form of seemingly progressive antipoverty policies (Moynihan 1965). Contrary to scholarly and public policy images, family structures like single-mother-headed households were never the ideal. In an effort to mitigate the damaging effects of growing up in a "stigmatized" family formation, Black educators, politicians, ministers, and community members constructed a cultural model that accepted single-family formations. Nevertheless, the community continued to recognize education and community engagement as key to "racial uplift" by allowing a new strategy that embraced some elements of the respectability era while merging with the necessary protectionism of independence. In other words, if Black women found themselves unable to depend on marriage, they and their children would be able to survive and in many instances thrive by relying on female kin and the larger Black community.

About half of the women in this study (eleven) were raised by either single mothers or grandmothers, and these young women attributed their ability to be successful in their careers to the women who raised them. Kalia, married mom of two and a social worker with a nonprofit agency, was raised by her single mom. Her mother was earning her Ph.D. while Kalia and her brother were growing up. Kalia asserted, "Really, people should commend Black families for having figured out how to raise healthy, vibrant, successful children given all we have experienced as a people. There have been many moments in our history in the United States where it would have been much easier to just keel over and die."

Following Kalia's assertion, it should be no wonder that Black women, once they have achieved a measure of financial security, often decide to change their relationship with work (or at least consider changing it). Indeed, Black women have been changing their relationship with work as it aligned with their goals for their families for centuries (in Africa as well as the Americas). Yet when social scientists posit that Black women on welfare need to go back to work or when editorials wonder why Black middle-class women are considering staying at home, historian Jacqueline Jones's explanation holds true: Black women define on their own terms, based on their familial and communal needs, how best to engage their struggle and combat persistent oppression (2010, 9–10).

The Effect of Race, Class, and Gender on Black Women's Career Strategies

Cory, who grew up in the Black middle class with two professional parents and a mother who was college-educated, expected the same for herself. Simultaneously, Cory's workplace expected mothers either to conform to their expectations, including extensive travel, or to resign. This combination created some challenges as Cory attempted to merge her personal expectations, familial expectations, and professional responsibilities. Additionally, Cory discussed her perception that each role had a different set of practices and outcomes, which depended upon whether you were white or Black.

Cory recounted an employer-sponsored meeting during which professional women received some tips on corporate culture. "They had a female executive speaker [at the conference], and I remember that she basically told us we could not have it all. She said we would have to make choices about our careers and our families. Something would have to give." Cory says that meeting changed her perspective on attaining corporate success and having a family. She said, "This woman was white, and she was saying you could not have it all. I knew it would be that much harder for a Black woman." Cory believes that because of the particular pressures on educated Black women, they are forced early in their careers to decide whether to climb to the top of the corporate ladder and become a corporate tycoon like Oprah or to seek a stable, healthy, family. For career women like Cory, while racism is neither as blatant nor as pervasive as it was during the Jim Crow era, there remains an understanding that the system has not changed completely for African Americans. Access to careers and opportunities, difficult for whites to achieve, is even more difficult for Blacks to gain.

In addition, it is not clear either how many Black women are financially able to change their relationship with work or how many Black career women would choose to alter their relationship with work if they could. For Black professional women, who have completed their education, established themselves in their careers, married, and had children, this career decision-making is uncharted territory with few precedents and enormous implications for how they view motherhood, marriage, and work. According to some, the stakes are higher than they once were because expectations have changed since their mothers' generation. Most women, however, said they had no idea they would experience such challenges while attempting to navigate marriage, career, and motherhood.

Jill, a surgeon and married mom of three who sold her shares in her private practice after the birth of her daughter, said, "You never think about how tough it is. It is work. I probably didn't appreciate the balance of work and family when my parents were doing it. You don't really appreciate it until you are in that setting. I never thought I would stop private practice. I just figured they [the kids] would fit in."

Gia, a former computer programmer, married with three children, agreed. "I thought I would be corporate," she said. "I thought I would be running my own business by forty-two. I am a stay-at-home mother. I never thought I would be a stay-at-home mother." She continued, "I dreamed of high power! I am high power right in my kitchen! I thought I would be more glamorous," she said laughing. "Now I just wish I could be a better mother, dynamic mother. I try to teach my kids about life. I teach the word of God, that they must triumph over adversity. I teach my kids to be successful. I say to them success in academics will be driven by success in your relationship with God."

Like most women, Jill and Gia could never have imagined what exactly went into combining career and family. Yet they articulate the particular position twenty-first-century Black career moms occupy as they navigate greater professional opportunity and a change in the pace of professional life that affects both career and family decisions.

Navigating Twenty-First-Century Shifts

The women in the study repeatedly cited the challenge of raising children in an increasingly competitive society where children have an abundance of access to mature content through media and technology and few consistent boundaries. Additionally, there is a lack of access to viable, affordable, support structures. According to Selena, a married mother of three who works in finance, "A lot of kids are raising themselves. People let their kids watch anything. There has been an erosion of values in our society. I teach my kids, but they get to school and get something different. It's not that parents don't care, but it's a reflection of the demands of society." Similarly Kya, former school administrator and married mother of two, said, "There is a busy-ness to our lifestyles, and there is no time to do the things we want to do. Also, it is increasingly difficult to have the resources you need. We try to work on our marriage, but it's expensive to go out. If we could afford a babysitter, we would spend more time together. Spending time with the kids is important, and trying to arrange play dates is difficult for everyone because everyone is managing so much." Natalie, middle-school teacher and married mom of three, concurred,

> There is way too much stuff to do. The kids have too much homework, we [she and her husband] have too much work, there is not enough time to play at school so we have to go out and find that. There is no dance or music at school so we have to go out and find that. Staying at home is a good option because one parent takes care of that stuff and the other works. If I had known ten years ago we could have stayed in a smaller house that Charles [her husband] could afford on his own. But as an only child myself, I had no idea how much work would be involved with multiple children.

Charlotte, former public relations manager turned children's book author and married mother of two, also commented on the pressures of combining career and family. She said, "Families today are not spending enough quality time together. There are too many activities and that leads to a lot of other things: problems. Parents are allowing the world to raise their children. There are conflicts between parents on how to juggle everything, and many families lack a spiritual foundation for a lot of it and how to manage it."

My interviews repeatedly revealed how professional upper-middle-class women were rethinking and redefining their relationship with their careers. In addition to discussing how society has changed and made it more difficult to live balanced lives, many women discussed how different things are in terms of work and family since their parents and grandparents were raising their families.

Richelle, housewife and mother of three, described her parent's generation:

They lived a slower life. They had fewer choices. They had financial burdens. We have so much to contend with. We do not have family helping
out with the kids. So for some of their basic problems yes, the problems
are the same. But we have to do so much more for basics. We have commute times that take away from time with family. They had more time
with us. The basic things are the same. 1. Marital—communication, marriage issues, and 2. Finances—they didn't have as much money as we
want to have. They felt to do the best you can with what you have. But
there weren't so many demands for career advancement. That puts on
a different type of pressure. My husband commutes thirty to thirty-five
minutes each way every day. If I had to do it too or had some other kinds
of demands from my job, what would be happening with our kids?

And the women described even more stark differences for grandparents.
"Theirs was different," said Keayba, physician and mother of three, speaking
about her maternal grandparents.

It was more related to migration and wanting a different life. Wanting
less racism. They moved from Alabama. My grandmother never talked
about her experiences there; it was very different. Their biggest stress-
ors were probably not having enough money. They didn't feel like they
had it, the financial piece is not a factor now but time is. They worked
for their children to have a good education. They had four girls, and
they sent all four to college. They really wanted to provide an education
for a different life, and they had the stress of racism. I know that was a
stressor.

For more than a century, scholars of Black life have discussed the fact that
Black people have to negotiate living in two Americas. Beginning with W.E.B. Du
Bois's theory of double-consciousness, we have been reminded that, because
of the harsh realities of racism, Black people have to guard their personal pride
in their Blackness while accepting the way they must maneuver through many
aspects of dominant white society. Du Bois called this a two-ness—"two war-
ring ideals in one dark body, whose strength alone keeps it from being torn
asunder" (Du Bois [1903] 1999, 8). Others, like Ulf Hannerz (1969) and Charles
Valentine (1971), have referred to it as biculturality; that is, two independent
processes of acculturation exist, one to the dominant culture and the other to
the culture of origin. Less attention has been given to how gender affects this
two-ness (Braxton 1989).

While intersectionality is useful in helping us to think about the multiple ways our identities can be viewed as a "problem" vis-à-vis dominant raced, gendered, and classed identities, it does not tell us how these identities are acculturated. In other words, research has demonstrated the various ways the Black community has acculturated its children to protect against racism, but there has been less scholarship on how Black girls are enculturated against racism and sexism within the Black community.[5]

Black women's "strength" as mothers and workers is one way that Black girls and women have been acculturated. The "strength" of Black women has been seen in the public imagination as a form of gender equity because Black women have not been portrayed as fragile and submissive dependents. Indeed, "being able to do" and "be it all" monikers have been badges of honor for many Black women. For Black mothers, teaching their daughters to be "strong Black women" has been more about basic survival than gender equality. Black mothers have traditionally felt that they must maintain a delicate balance of preparing their daughters to survive the interlocking structures of race, class, and gender oppression, while rejecting and transcending those same structures (Bell-Scott and Guy-Sheftall 1991; Carothers 1998; Lorde 1984, 2007).

Sociologist Tamara Beauboeuf-Lafontant discusses the effects of the myth of the strong Black woman in her multiyear study of African American women, ages nineteen to sixty-seven. She asserts that maintaining the myth of the strong Black woman is a "costly performance," which, while seemingly beneficial to Black women, works to maintain the patriarchal social order. Explaining the way it operates as both a constraint and a form of resistance, Beauboeuf-Lafontant connects the strong Black woman myth to both Du Bois's double consciousness and Darlene Clark Hine's dissemblance; instead of being "infuriatingly removed from the fully enfranchised life they could see around them," as was the case for Du Bois's double consciousness, "Clark Hine's use of dissemblance focuses on the agency of individual Black women to effect a 'self-imposed' visibility, as they intentionally veiled themselves to protect aspirations and feelings that could easily be shattered by members of white society, and by Black men" (Beaubouef-Lafontant 2009, 39).

Beauboeuf-Lafontant reports that dissemblance continues into the lives of contemporary Black women through what Charisse Jones and Kumea Shorter-Gooden refer to as "shifting." In their large-scale initiative, African American Women's Voices Project, Jones and Shorter-Gooden survey and interview Black women about their families, work, and personal responsibilities and find that they are reportedly "shifting" between Black men and white America to accommodate the expectations of each.

Redefining Career and Family

Exploring how African American women decide to change their relationship with work and how those decisions are affected by race and class allows us to probe for the cultural changes that have gone otherwise undetected. This exploration also allows us to locate the factors that have affected their decisions rather than provide a platform from which to judge them for making those decisions.

When Cory and I met, she had two children, and during the course of our interviews she became pregnant and had her third child. She had been working for the marketing firm that had allowed her to work from home for about five years. Unlike many companies that have tried flex-time and work-from-home opportunities, Cory's firm employs full-time marketing directors, with full-time salaries and benefits, but the directors travel 95 percent less than most marketing professionals because they handle local accounts; most of the business is conducted either over the phone via conference calls or in person after a reasonable drive, and the professionals set their own hours.

I met Cory through another family at the Monroe School, and when I asked her to participate in the study she easily fit me into her schedule. Cory is able to drop her infant and four-year-old off at daycare and preschool, respectively by 8:30 A.M., make it to a 9:30 A.M. step aerobics class, pick up her oldest daughter at 2:30 P.M. from her elementary school, and manage her successful $70,000-plus career where a major multinational company (not her previous employer) is one of her primary clients. Amazingly, for a couple of our interviews and observations I met her at her gym, participated in her step aerobics class, and conducted the interviews afterward at a local Starbucks.

Most women are not available in this way while working a full-time job. Cory's story is unusual. Each woman, however, defined her availability as finding some way to construct a nonstandard workday. Sociologist Anita Ilta Garey addressed similar frameworks in her discussion of "being there" (Garey 1999, 30). For the women in Garey's *Weaving Work and Motherhood*, "being there" existed on a scale where mothers could fall within a range from being physically present to physically absent but emotionally available. Garey discusses the insights of Lisa, one of her study participants: "Lisa may not always be there with her children, but she must always be there *for* her children, and what is important is that her children see her this way . . . being there means being there in her child's eyes" (Garey 1999, 33).

Garey's study participants were working class and lower-middle class, but their desires were similar to those of the women in my study. Even for those who were "stay-at-home" moms, being home with children under the age of five was less about intensive, structured learning for their small children and more about just being present, letting the child know that Mommy is there even if she is not actively engaged in the child's every activity. For the "working" moms, being available meant being able to be present when it mattered and not having to worry about taking time off from work if a child were sick, out of school, or involved in a special program at school. The mothers could be present when it mattered, and the children could rely on the fact that, though Mom and Dad were busy with work while they were at school, someone (usually Mom) would be there when they needed them.

The experiences of Cory and other moms seeking work/family flexibility so they can be "available" shed important light on intensive mothering and allow the idea of strategic mothering to operate as an intervention, particularly for Black women. Where sociologist Sharon Hays finds that most middle-class women are engaged in the culture of intensive mothering despite the economic, emotional, and financial costs, strategic mothering suggests being at home is less about focusing primarily on their children and more about meeting the broad needs of their families and their communities. By employing strategic mothering, they had either made decisions early in their careers to take a less demanding career track, or they were in a position to temporarily place less emphasis on their careers.

Creating a situation wherein mom can be available is trickier as our societal construction of work/life/family balance has not changed in any substantial way since the breadwinner/homemaker model was developed within the growth of the middle class. This constant construction prevails despite the fact that requirements to maintain a middle-class lifestyle have changed significantly since the economic downturn of the late 1970s, which made dual-worker/ career families much more prevalent. Simultaneously, while women have made tremendous strides in career advancement, studies still show that there are more women who graduate with professional degrees than there are women who reach the boardrooms.[6] The media generally explains the lack of women in executive positions and holding corporate board seats as the result of women's preferences; that is, they are more interested in being at home raising their children than engaging in career advancement. Countering this argument, recent popular press and scholarly discussions have cited the inhospitable, inflexible conditions women face in the workplace when they try to combine work and family.

Not only do policies (stated and unstated) make combining work and family less than ideal, but also frequent expectations from coworkers determine that women will not return, as demonstrated by Cory's interactions with her coworkers. Sociologist Pamela Stone's (2007) study has been the most prominent in refuting the idea that women are intentionally opting out. Through her interviews with college-educated attorneys and business women, whom she calls "the dream team," she notes that, while they say they have made a decision to stay at home with their children and focus on being moms, closer scrutiny reveals hostility in the workplace, especially when families include two individuals juggling and advancing their careers (Stone 2007).

Making Work and Family Work

As I began the study, I mused over the reasons one might pursue a more "relaxed" relationship with work. Perhaps those who opted to stay at home didn't like their jobs and wished they were doing something else. Or maybe they couldn't find good, affordable childcare. I thought maybe they had been laid off and decided to stay at home simply because they could. Perhaps their husbands had insisted. These "reasons" all ended up being part of these women's individual narratives, and my first impulse was to write them off as neo-traditional and outside Black women's collective focus on Black families and the Black community.[7] Upon closer inspection, however, it became clear that even as the history of Black women's work presents a different, more complex, picture of participation in the paid labor force, the contemporary moment finds a similar difference. At the root of their varied actions, both Black career women and Black stay-at-home moms are driven by what they perceive as best for the nuclear family. They assume that if the nuclear family is healthy and stable, the extended family and the larger Black community will follow suit. The women make decisions that ensure these goals, regardless of the potential problems inherent within the strategy. Scholars have named and discussed women's need to be "available" in various but similarly oriented ways. Most notable and recognizable are "intensive mothering" (Hays 1996), "work/family devotion schema" (Blair-Loy 2003), and "being there" (Garey 1999).

The history of motherhood as a social construction culminating in an ideology of intensive motherhood was articulated in sociologist Sharon Hays's influential work, *The Cultural Contradictions of Motherhood*. In it, Hays discusses intensive mothering as an ideology in which mothers are required to center their children and selflessly devote all of their energies to child-rearing. Not only do mothers invest their time and money at the expense of their own physical, emotional, and mental well-being, but they also use their ability to intensively mother to evaluate themselves as mothers (Hays 1996).

Sociologist Anita Ilta Garey's work with a racially and ethnically diverse group of women hospital workers collapses the heretofore need to separate mothers' commitment to work and mothers' commitment to family as separate units of analysis. She purposefully asks the women in her study to discuss their conceptualizations of being mothers who negotiate the meaning of work in their lives (Garey 1999, 13). Garey develops the metaphor "weaving" as "both a process (an activity—to weave something) and a product (an object—a weaving, something constituted from available materials)" (14) with the goal of merging two important parts of women's lives in the scholarly record. Garey argues the importance of investigating the intersection of work and family in women's lives so that we can rid ourselves of the idea that mothers, in particular, are either "family oriented" or "work oriented." She argues that this is not a true reflection of women's lives, and she finds that these cultural constructions reinforce and reproduce "cultural understandings of career or commitment to one's job as all-encompassing" (193).

Building on Garey (1999) but focusing on professional workers, Mary Blair-Loy theorizes that work devotion schema and family devotion schema are pitted against each other in historically gendered ways and chronicles the ways professional women have had to negotiate their attention to work and family to achieve and/or maintain advancement. Blair-Loy argues that the conflict between these two schemas was not disrupted for white women until the mid-1970s when legal gains as a result of the women's movement began to be institutionalized; college-educated, professional women were then able to gain access to career advancement. White women who gained access prior to this period generally had to choose the work devotion schema to achieve and/or maintain advancement. Blair-Loy (2003) finds that the youngest women in her study secured their careers before marriage and negotiated the contradictions between work devotion and family devotion by outsourcing the needs of their families. In this way they were able to either pay someone else or elicit the help of their mothers to perform care while they devoted their time to work. These women could thus move closer to an egalitarian schema or a distant-mothering schema with the assistance of paid, usually minority and/or lower-class, help.

Because work is such a strong part of Black women's constructions of motherhood, work/family devotion schema and, by extension, work/family conflict have not been at odds. Historical need for both partners to work has been understood, reinforced, and integrated into the cultural ethos in the Black community. To engage in what appears to be intensive mothering against the backdrop of traditional gender roles is unchartered territory that goes against what many professional Black women have learned from their families, primarily their mothers and grandmothers. Becoming stay-at-home moms or altering their relationship with work to place greater emphasis on their nuclear families seemingly asks these women to employ the perspective of middle- and upper-middle-class white women.

Although Blair-Loy's sample focused on white professional women whose cultural schema of devotion privileged marriage and children with ambivalence toward career advancement, the women presented in my study, while valuing this schema, described it is a dangerous prospect for African American women.

They were raised to focus on reaching higher education and professional positions, and they have done so; however, their location within the upper middle classes continues to be tenuous, particularly when they are asked to depend on the reliability of Black men's security in the marketplace. These professional Black women are trying to strategize maintaining the "family first" model (Hansen 2005) that has allowed for the survival of Black families while securing professional middle-class lives that demand career focus.

Black Mothers Have Always Worked: Redefining Work

Although I use the terms stay-at-home mom and working mom to denote each of the women's relationship with work, it was clear throughout the study that the women did not feel these ill-fitting terms adequately defined how they saw themselves. In an effort to find terms that would more adequately define their relationships with home and work, I created an interview question that sought to explore the stay-at-home/working mom dichotomy. Through my preliminary study with formal and informal support groups and my search through magazines and books geared toward readers who are mothers, I developed a list of terms that might describe how they saw themselves. I verbally asked each mother who participated in the study, "Which of the following terms would you use to describe yourself? (a) working mom, (b) homemaker, (c) stay-at-home mom, (d) part-time mom, (e) part-time-stay-at-home mom." Each mom listened to me read the list and then responded with the term she thought best fit her. Nine moms described themselves as working moms, one saw herself as a homemaker, four selected stay-at-home moms; seven chose part-time working mom, and two chose part-time stay-at-home mom.

The results were telling because, according to the stay-at-home/working mom dichotomy, only five moms would truly be considered stay-at-home moms (i.e., they were neither salaried nor wage earners). Even more telling, however, was the response to the follow-up series of open-ended questions. I asked the women what they thought of the categories in the survey. Despite my attempt at providing more options, most women felt the categories were too limiting and did not adequately define what they do on a day-to-day basis or how they prioritize their time. The women who would be considered stay-at-home moms do not consider themselves stay-at-home moms and do not identify with the images of stay-at-home moms. For example, Nancy, married mom of three and former internist, said she did not identify with women "who sat at home and ate bonbons. I am too busy to be a stay-at-home mom!" Nancy exclaimed. Moreover, even women who do adopt the title still see problems with its articulation. Gia, who identified herself as a stay-at-home mom, saw the term as too limiting. She said, "'Stay-at-home' mom is too simplified, it makes me think of la-la-world."

Likewise, Richelle, a self-proclaimed stay-at-home mother of three, stated, "Moms do work. Every woman is working. Those who have made homemaking their life, that's not real to me, it's commercial. Even though I build our business, it's not part-time. It's all or nothing. I don't know how you're a part-time stay-at-home mom. You're at home or you're not."

When asked if the categories in the survey adequately define who they are, only five of the twenty-three respondents felt the categories defined who they were, and it only felt that way for women who were primarily identifying themselves as working moms or part-time working moms. The other eighteen participants gave a resounding "No!" to the question; their explanations in most instances had to do with feeling like they were more than their work or career. Natalie, teacher and mother of three, replied, "No. I don't look at myself as defined by my work. It should have and has more to do with my overall purpose in life as opposed to the things I'm doing to get there." And Cara, a former school administrator who owns her own real estate business but self-identified as a part-time stay-at-home mom of three, exclaimed, "No! No! I don't like homemaker. My education does not allow me to be a homemaker. I can be a domestic engineer but not a homemaker." Cara and the other women demonstrated repeatedly that the terms we have traditionally used, "stay-at-home" and "working" mom, are not only flawed because they are social constructions that pit mothers against one another, but they are also inadequate tools of analysis because they artificially gloss over the myriad ways women organize their lives according to their gender and family ideologies.

Somewhere in the Middle

After observing and interviewing the women, watching them and their families navigate the complexities of their work, marital, and maternal lives, and asking them how these categories fit with the realities of their lives, I developed three categories that I use to analyze each woman's approach to her marriage, her career, her role as a mother, and her involvement with her extended family and the larger Black community. By creating three categories I not only remove the propensity to project artificial dichotomies between roles that are naturally fluid, but I also focus on the ways women define themselves.

Linda was clear that she was a full-time working mom, but upon closer inspection I found that Linda had made certain decisions that allowed her to pursue her career full-time and be available to her two children, a preschooler and a toddler. I call Linda and the other women who are employed full-time but have developed workplace structures that allow them to have greater flexibility *modified full-time career moms* (MFC). These women find greater flexibility either through working from home, creating flexible hours when workplaces are amenable, or following less ambitious career tracks. I met Linda, a dentist, through another family at the Monroe School. Her daughter was enrolled there in the three-year-old class, and her mother kept her younger son. Linda said, "One reason to be a dentist is I am not on call. I set my own hours per day. If someone calls to report a toothache I can call in scripts. There are really no emergencies, and I work less than forty hours per week. Some days I am off, or I have early days. I do not have a standard nine-to-five schedule, and I can find family time." Linda was able to structure her days in the office so she has "normal" working hours, and one day each week she works only three hours. She reported, "I have lenient/flexible hours. I work from ten to five, Monday through Thursday, and ten to one on Friday. I can drop Melissa off at school with no problem and pick Kenny Jr. up from Ms. Mary's house before six. And when my mom has them I can relieve her by six too even if I stop by the store or something first."

Denise, an attorney with two children, saw herself as a stay-at-home mom and explained that she was repeatedly asked to justify her decisions to her parents, but Denise repeatedly restructured her profession when her husband's career and her children's needs changed. In this case, Denise was an at-home mom when the children were first born, and her husband, who holds a Ph.D., had a steady, very lucrative job with a pharmaceutical company. When the children became school-age and her husband got a new job that included a lot of travel, instead of going back to work full-time as a practicing attorney, she received an opportunity to become a community liaison in the public defender's office. Although Denise is working, it is on a part-time basis; and, although it is in her field, she is not actually practicing law but performing on a legal public relations team. She says she enjoys this work because she is close to the law, "doing a good thing in the community, and [I] show my children that I am really making a difference in the community." While Denise is committed to the work she does, she is also committed to being available to her family. She says, "I am structuring my days so I do not have to use before and after care. I allow my children to recognize me as their mom. I take off from work to go to their school events, and I occasionally surprise them for lunch time."

Again, dispelling the dichotomous relationship between stay-at-home and working moms, Denise and the other women who are leaving or modifying their careers are categorized as *modified stay-at-home moms* (MSH). This category draws attention to the fact that women who no longer have a formal relationship with their careers or their employers are still working, not just at home but additionally in the more formal economy and their communities.

Lastly, Marilyn, an accounts manager for a state insurance agency with three children ages nine, seven, and four, described herself as the COO of her family while at the same time working part-time for a health insurance company. She and the other women who have created flexibility in their work and family lives are categorized as *available-flexible career moms* (AFC). Marilyn explained her role as family COO: "I handle everything. I plan everything. Every piece of paper, I organize. Every party, I plan. Everything that has to do with this family, I manage." Marilyn earned a master's in public health from one of the top five public health programs in the country. She has worked with her current employer off and on for eleven years and changed to a part-time schedule when she returned to work after having her last child. I asked her if she has been penalized professionally for her movement in and out of the company. "Absolutely!" she says, but she also says she is willing to take those setbacks as long as she can be available to her family. Marilyn is also the manager of her church's bookstore, vice president of the PTA at her children's school, a class parent for both of her sons' classrooms, and has been the basketball mom, the softball mom, and the soccer mom for her sons' sports teams. She adds,

> I like working. I like what I do. But I want to be available for my family. My biggest concern as a mother is instilling good values. So I try to be involved in their lives. I did stay home for a while, but that was not me. I hung out with some women who shopped a lot, and I just did not see myself living the way they did. I think as the kids get older I will come out again to be more available with their activities and stuff like that. Right now this works, and as long as it works I will do it like this. After that, I will make some more changes.

Marilyn's comments reflect the variability in strategic mothering. Her actions are not set in stone and change according to the needs of her family. This flexibility is rarely discussed in the studies and conversations on professional wives and mother's relationships with their careers. Studies show women and their families at one static moment in time and do not investigate or explain if and when there might be changes. Of course, studies acknowledge that mothers' relationships with careers necessarily change in the case of a divorce or a shift in the husband's employment, but rarely do studies discuss a shift motivated by the self-identified needs of the woman/wife/mother.

Marilyn, and the women like her who are enacting a combination of the *modified full-time career moms* (MFC) *and modified stay-at-home moms* (MSH) categories, are privileging availability and flexibility as keys to their success as mothers, wives, and career women. While all women seek this type of balance, where they can pursue their careers and take care of their families, without threat of penalty, most find that their career paths, employers, or financial circumstances will not allow it. For available-flexible career moms, the only strategies seemingly available are to reduce their work hours through part-time or flex-time schedules or change their career paths altogether so they line up more closely with their combined roles as mothers, wives, and career women.[8]

The strategies implemented that form these categories are not without ambiguity and ambivalence. While these women are embracing the flexibility in not only their careers but also their roles as mothers, they continue to be affected by the expectations of both the mainstream model of middle-class motherhood that prioritizes the nuclear family, male breadwinner/female homemaker model, and the African American model that prioritizes extended families (primarily mother's mother), including the responsibility for family and community advancement.

When I talked with Keayba, a thirty-six-year-old physician with one preschool child and one on the way (a total of three by the time I completed the study) and a husband in business for himself, she confessed she was battling feelings that her career was impeding her success as a wife and mother. For Keayba, however, it is difficult to leave her career as a physician because she has garnered considerable success and the accompanying income. With a family income of just under $200,000 and an individual income of $130,000, Keayba is the primary breadwinner in her family. Trained in family medicine, she is affiliated with the maternal and child health division with the medical school where she works. This means she is often on-call. Having completed her master's degree in research, she is also expected to write grants and research proposals. Her husband, Kareem, has his own law firm, and thus he is the more flexible parent in their relationship and is often responsible for picking up their three-year-old-son from childcare and starting their dinner. "I don't want that anymore," said Keayba. "One of my goals is for us to be able to eat dinner together as a family and not have to worry about work or time." The couple has talked about Keayba's leaving the medical school and the teaching hospital and either going into private practice or taking a position with a national health corporation. Keayba said, "I am hoping that I will be able to find a position where I can leave work there and not be on call."

According to Keayba, the desire to be more available to her family is rooted in the way she was raised. As the middle child and the oldest daughter born to actively engaged parents and community educators (both her mother and father hold doctorates), Keayba knows she benefited from the presence of and interaction with both of her parents in her formative years. She states her parents stressed education, and she learned its importance, which led her to graduate from prestigious institutions and become a celebrated medical doctor. She missed, however, the way they kept the family part going. "I wish I had been paying closer attention to take things away. I recognize that to provide the same quality [referring to what her parents did], it requires me to be more present physically and emotionally. Having a better balance is extremely important to me. They were my primary teachers. I want it to be the same for my children." Keayba also grew up with extended family nearby. She and her husband Kareem have no family nearby. "My parents are still in Michigan, my brother is in Virginia, and my sister is all over the place. Kareem's parents died before we married, and so our family [her extended family] is really all he has."

Most of the women in this study found various ways to stay connected to their careers while being "available" to their families, but their connections to their careers, while raising small children, was so permeable and fractious that most had to rely on their husbands' secure positions and high incomes to make and maintain their lifestyles. This puts them in a precarious position. One stay-at-home mom who had initially been a part of the story-time play group had to return to work as an accounts manager when her husband, a marketing director, lost his job.

For the women in this study, their roles as mothers are strategic and defined as multifold and multipurpose. This complicated approach to understanding mothering renders framework classifications like intensive mothering, work/family devotion schema, and work/family conflict inadequate in defining what Black women do as they strategically alter their relationships with work, family, marriage, extended family, and the larger Black community.

2

Black Professional Women, Careers, and Family "Choice"

Much of the work and family conflict debate has been rooted in the assumed contradiction of professional women's "return" to the traditional family ideal after all the gains that have allowed women to "have it all." When an intersectional analysis is applied we learn that Black women have always been in the workforce in greater numbers than white women, and, when given access to higher education, Black women have combined career and family much more frequently. Indeed, this combination of career and family has been an expectation for Black women whereas white women have often had to gain "permission" to do so. I draw attention to the fact that Black professional women have historically had a cultural ethos, which may be shifting, that combined work and family. It is also important to recognize the challenges in that combination. In this chapter, I ask if these professional women were raised with a gender strategy that focused on ambition, higher education, and careers with marriage and children to follow. And if so, how did they reconcile their decision away from that strategy to a strategy more in line with ideal traditional gender roles and family lives?

I asked the Black professional women in this study to tell me about their trajectory to college, their professional migration patterns, and their journeys within and without their careers. Their stories were repeatedly similar. In each instance they had been raised to get a higher education, be ambitious in their pursuits, and achieve career success, and each had also experienced some upheaval in their childcare strategies. Nothing, however, separated MFC (modified full-time career) moms, MSH (modified stay-at-home) moms, and AFC (available-flexible career) moms as issues that pertained to college and career ambitions. Only when I asked them specific questions about career and family conflict did they reveal the fact that they were often devising strategies to respond to the ever-changing needs of their families and communities, given the quickened pace of life and the shifts in the economy and the workplace. They asserted that some shifts were race and gender motivated, some were economic, and some were health related, but all required that they assess two primary issues: the benefit of working full time, staying-at-home, or combining the two; the flexibility of their careers and support structures to accommodate the challenges of family/career combinations.

I divide this chapter into two parts. First, I briefly discuss the educational and career aspirations of the women in this study and follow that discussion with an exploration of the challenges posed by professional migrations and shifts in access to childcare options traditionally available to Black mothers. Second, I continue the earlier conversation about the fallacy in the dichotomous relationship between stay-at-home moms and full-time career moms; instead, I study my three new categories of modified full-time career moms, modified stay-at-home moms, and available-flexible career moms. In each section I highlight the experiences of professional Black mothers and reveal one of the primary factors that has impacted their strategies concerning career and family—the workplace.

Becoming Black Professional Women

The Importance of HBCUs

Many Black professional women today are first- or second-generation college graduates. Even though educating young Black women has been an important part of the cultural ethos, until very recently, very few were able to complete college. Many in the Black community have historically turned to HBCUs to educate their children. In most instances, liberal philanthropic whites, white Christian denominations, or African American Christian denominations founded these schools, some of whose origins date to the early nineteenth century. Their purpose in each case was to "train" African Americans who were barred from admittance to historically white institutions.[1] Although the civil rights legislation of the 1960s banned segregation on the basis of race and gender, opening greater access to predominately white colleges and universities, historically Black institutions continued to flourish and were seen as places that would not only educate but also care for Black students. According to a study by Charles Willie, Richard Reddick, and Ronald Brown (2006), HBCUs are more diverse (when looking at race/ethnicity, class, gender, religion, and ability) than predominantly white colleges and universities (PWCU). They debunk stereotypes about African Americans by providing students with an opportunity to see the range of abilities people possess regardless of their race, class, or gender. Contrary to popular beliefs that question the practicality of HBCUs, they comprise only 3 percent of the nation's institutions of higher learning (105) but graduate almost 25 percent of African Americans earning undergraduate degrees. Additionally, nine of the top ten colleges that graduate the most African Americans who earn doctorates are HBCUs.[2] Fifty-seven percent of the women in this study earned their undergraduate degrees at HBCUs, and they planned for their children to attend one, too.

When I asked Cory, the marketing executive, what made her choose Tannerman,[3] Cory explained that her mom and dad had both graduated from a prestigious public university in the early 1960s. When it was time for Cory and her brother to head off to college, Cory expected to be shipped off to the same or another elite majority-white institution. Cory explained, "It was just understood that people thought you got a better education if you went to a white school." And Cory had been properly prepared for that: she had gone to one of the top independent schools in the city; she socialized with middle- and upper-middle-class Black and white peers; and she had excelled in academics and sports. But Cory's mother had other ideas. She told Cory to apply to some of the country's top historically Black colleges and universities, and Cory chose one of the oldest and most respected of the HBCUs. Cory explained, "When I was accepted I was still a little unsure because I did not know. Tannerman invited admitted students for an overnight weekend during their senior year of high school, and I remember calling my parents after a couple of days of being there and saying 'Just send me my stuff!' It was such a wonderful inviting place and I felt so comfortable and safe."

Kia, Linda, Keayba, and Sheri agreed that they really had no choice in attending an HBCU in the same way that they had no choice about whether to attend college. In each interview they laughed over the fact that their parents said something like, "I don't know where you are going to school, but my check is going to . . . ," and referred to whichever historically Black institution they had gone to or wanted their daughter to attend. "My mother always instilled 'Go to College!' There was no choice," said Sheri, thirty-seven-year-old mother of three and financial analyst for a major multinational firm based in Atlanta. Sheri holds an MBA, and she and her husband, a former school administrator with an EdD, run a real estate investment firm. Both Sheri and Kia have parents who graduated from college, which made the importance of education a fact in their households when they were growing up. Sheri beamed with pride when she talked about her mother, an assistant principal at an Atlanta area elementary school. "She went to Greer College, and we always went to their games. It was so cool meeting her old friends, hearing them reminisce. Sometimes we even got to meet her old professors. I wanted that kind of community away from home, and she always taught us to get our education. She got her PhD while we were kids, and that kind of stuck with me." Keayba had an older brother who went to an HBCU and in addition to his influence she had a number of cousins and community members who also encouraged her. "I knew I wanted to go into math and science, and when it was time to decide on colleges Reynolds made the most sense." Likewise, when Kia and her sisters decided where to attend college, Kia said her parents, who both hold advanced degrees, told them they could go to college anywhere as long as it was an HBCU outside their home state. The women in this study graduated from HBCUs like Clark-Atlanta University, Florida A&M University, Hampton University, Howard University, Morehouse College, Spelman College, and Xavier University in New Orleans, just to name a few. One woman, who was given the ultimatum by her parents, said, "I decided to go to North Carolina A&T because I wanted to be an engineer. It was the best decision I ever made."

Many of the parents, who were in college during the civil rights movement, did not want their children to experience the isolation and marginalization they experienced. "My mom said she did not want me to be the president of the Black student association," said Cory, when her mother tried to explain her desire for her children to attend an HBCU. "Having gone to an HBCU and knowing that it in no way limited my opportunities or options, I will choose that for my children, too."

Even for those women whose financial situation would have made attending any college difficult, there remained a need and desire not only to go to college but to go to one of the top HBCUs in the country. The mothers of both Gia and Nancy completed college after their children were born and then pushed their daughters to get their college education as well.

Gia, who grew up in a small midwestern city near Chicago where the gradual deindustrialization of the Northeast and Midwest have worsened living conditions for most of the city's population, knew she was going to college. It had been drilled into her head from a very young age as her family struggled to protect her from the influences that could lead her down another road. Gia was raised by her grandparents, not her mother and father, because her mother had become pregnant with her while in college and ended the relationship with her father. To ensure her mother's completion of college, Gia's grandparents and aunts and uncles rallied around her and decided that Gia's grandparents would raise the baby. Gia remained with her grandparents and did not really know her mother until she was five years old. "At first I saw college as my way out of Gary [Indiana]," said Gia. "My grandparents had very little education. They grew up during the Depression and then migrated from the South to Gary. They worked really hard to put all of their kids through college so I was actually second-generation college, even though I was being raised by my grandmother who had a sixth-grade education and my grandfather who had a third-grade education."

Gia was almost denied that opportunity when the Veteran's Affairs Administration changed the rules for dependents' educational assistance. The changes did not eradicate benefits to dependents but rather cut them significantly. Gia explained, "My uncle was an educator, and he saw what was happening to education benefits before the changes occurred. He came over our house one day and said we have to get you in college or you are going to lose your college benefits." While Gia's extended family could have supported her in college, the VA benefits made it much easier to support her in other ways. Gia went to the local junior college to avoid losing her benefits and completed her senior year of high school while she was there. This did not stop her from wanting to leave Gary so she applied and was accepted to Tannerman, and, thanks to her uncle, was funded via a combination of VA benefits, scholarships, and a small student loan.

In addition to having parents who instilled desire for higher education and stressed college because they "said so," many of these women also saw models of the benefits of higher education in their communities or through community members who acted as role models and mentors for particular careers. Gia's uncle helped her figure it out, but sometimes just a suggestion during the formative years struck a chord for a young person. In Keayba's case a friend of Keayba's parents was a dentist. Keayba, now a doctor, explained, "At first, because of Mr. Ben, I thought I wanted to be a dentist. I eventually learned I did not want to be a dentist, but I knew as early as kindergarten that I wanted to go to college because I knew I had to go to college to be a dentist."

The Importance of Minority Scholarships at PWCUs

Not all of the women attended HBCUs. Many were the benefactors of minority scholarship programs offered by predominantly white institutions. In the late 1980s and early 1990s, private funding became available from large corporations and foundations who sponsored scholarship programs for a few promising minorities at private institutions that had earlier been beyond most African Americans' financial reach. Selena, Richelle, and Natalie were a few of the women who received full or partial scholarships from private colleges and universities that were directing their admission efforts at promising African American high school students. Indeed, many of the women interviewed recounted being able to attend college with no loans or very few loans because of generous scholarship programs set aside for the Black community's top high school students. Bart Landry and Karyn Lacy write about this period as the time in which the "New Black Middle Class" grew in stature, prominence, and numbers (Lacy 2007; Landry 1988).

For Selena, who grew up in Atlanta, being "courted" by one of the prestigious predominantly white institutions in New England got her out of Atlanta and away from her friends who were choosing HBCUs. "I went to a college fair," said Selena, "and they invited me to apply. When I was accepted and my parents got the scholarship information, they were relieved by the offer and so

smitten with the prestige of the school they were ready to ship me off then."
While Selena feels incredibly fortunate to have attended and especially to have
finished with minimal school loans, she feels similarly to Cory's parents. "I am
not sure if I want my kids to have that kind of experience. The Black kids felt like
we were all lured there and then left to figure it out on our own. It was pretty
isolating and I haven't been back since." Selena did well in college, graduating
with a BA in economics, and completed her MBA in finance. She says her mother
had always pushed her to go to college because she herself had not gone and
wanted her daughter to have options.

Likewise, Richelle, whose mother never completed college but wanted
higher education for her children, said she knows she would not have gone
to college without the scholarship offered by the small midwestern college
not too far from home. "I wasn't even sure about the college application process," she said. "My guidance counselor, seeing that I was doing well in my
courses and on my SAT scores, suggested I apply. I really didn't know much
about the HBCUs since no one in my family had gone to college, and I knew I
had to go wherever they gave me money." Richelle's story especially resonated
with many of the women who had grown up in single-parent or working-class
households.

Similarly, Natalie was awarded a full scholarship to a private PWCU in the
South, thanks to her cousin's help with the college application process. When I
talked with Natalie about her preparation and decision making for college, she
recalled knowing very little about applying for college. Her mother and stepfather had not gone to college and could not direct her. Her stepfather's younger
sister, only a few years older than Natalie, helped her through the application
process and recognized that her niece was extremely bright and just needed
guidance. "I don't know where I would be without Shelley," said Natalie. "I knew
a lot of people were talking about college, and I had friends who were applying. I
was even in the magnet program so teachers and counselors were talking to me
about it, but no one was sitting down with me and helping me do it." She continued, "I don't blame them, though, there were like four people in the counsel-
or's office, one person assigned to seniors, and there were about four hundred
seniors. There was no way he [the seniors' counselor] was going to have time to
help me. He probably didn't even know I needed help." Natalie draws attention
to one of the deterrents Black youth face when preparing for college admission.
Even extremely smart students like Natalie, who earned a National Achievement Scholarship for her PSAT scores,[4] often had difficulty navigating the college terrain. In most instances, students must depend on family to help them
with college decisions.

When College Isn't an Option

Those women, who were unable to capitalize on the legacy of HBCUs, the scholarships being offered by predominantly white institutions, or family members' help in navigating admissions, found themselves trying to figure out how and where they would go to college and how they would pay for it. Like Gia, Gail and Kathy were born in the deindustrializing Midwest in the late 1960s and early 1970s. But unlike Gia, Gail and Kathy did not have mothers who had completed college or grandmothers who were insistent that their granddaughters would attend college. Kathy's mother had only an eleventh-grade education and raised six children on her own, and Gail's mother finished high school but, as a single mother with five children, found it difficult to fathom a viable route to college. For both moms, education was very important but survival took precedence. Kathy said of her mother, "You could not live in her house and not work. She really stressed responsibility." All of Kathy's sisters went to college, but only she and her youngest sister finished. "We really didn't have any models for how to do education. We knew it was important, and people were telling us to apply but then what? I think that's what happened to my sisters. I had some friends who were going so I applied and got accepted that way I felt like I knew someone there. It helped to keep me there." Kathy ended up getting a degree in business administration and got an internship in the hotel industry while she was in college. The internship not only helped her work her way through college but also "launched a career I never even thought about. I knew nothing about the hospitality industry before college."

Similarly, Gail knew her only way out of the declining industrial Midwest was to go to college, but there was no way for her to do so. An average student, Gail attended a mediocre public school and knew nothing about how to get scholarships, but "I knew I wanted more. I had been working since I could look like I had a work-permit." The oldest of five children, with a single mother who worked all the time, Gail was seven years older than the next oldest child and worked to get everything for herself as well as her siblings' necessities. "I decided to go into the military. I knew that if I went in the military, I could get a skill, and then I could get the GI Bill to go to school. It seemed like the only way." But Gail's mother did not want her to go into the military and would not sign her consent. Gail explained, "I was so frustrated with her. I felt like I took care of myself. I took care of her kids. And all I was asking was that she let me go. I had never asked her for anything else, and she would not sign the papers." Gail's mother wanted her to go to college but could not find a way to make that happen; she thought Gail should work and save to go to college later. Gail resented her mother's resistance, but she had another plan. When she turned eighteen, she no longer needed her mother's consent. "Going in to sign up was

the best day of my life. I remember feeling so free!" Gail did her basic training, completed her tour, and received training in ambulatory medicine. She
then went on to get an emergency medical technician (EMT) certification and
worked in the reserves and as an EMT until she could get things in order to
go to college. She moved to the Atlanta area in the early 1990s, having heard
about all of the opportunities for young professionals, and enrolled in a small
university in the Georgia state system for a degree in business management.
Upon finishing her degree with honors, she took a position as a consultant,
which allowed her to travel, something she really loved to do. In retrospect,
Gail understands her mother's perspective: "While I don't agree, I can respect
the fact that she was focused on our family's survival, and that model has helped
me even though I took a different route."

Black Professional Women Respond to Communal Shifts

Each of the women in this study, like most Black professional women, began as
children with an understanding that they would go to college, do well in college,
and have careers. They were expected to be ambitious (see chapter 3) and realized they had to have this type of focus—driven by parents, community members,
and even themselves—or their trajectories risk derailment. They understood, as
Keayba articulated, that they had to go to college to have a career. Accordingly,
once they were married they continued to work and pursue their careers. None
of the women in this study became housewives or modified their careers immediately after they got married. As studies have shown, married Black women
with children have higher rates of employment than white women. The contemporary moment, however, finds a visible shift in this pattern; more Black
professional women are choosing to alter their relationship with work following
childbirth. Some have articulated it as a new opportunity for Black women; they
can now afford to stay at home or work part-time, so they do. Some media outlets have suggested that, like white women, they feel a need to be at home with
their babies. Yet few Black professional women grew up with this model. Indeed,
only two of the mothers of women in this study were housewives or stay-at-
home moms. Of these two mothers, one went back to work when her daughter
started grade school, and the other, after learning her daughter was choosing to
stay at home, begged her not to leave her career.

    Two important social shifts have affected the Black community in new and
important ways: there is a delay in the birth of a first child; and many families are
far from extended kin and fictive kin due to educational and professional migration. Most professional Americans have been affected by these shifts. Because
women are pursuing not only college degrees but also advanced degrees and
careers, they are delaying marriage and children. In 2013, "The average age of

first marriage was 27 for women and 29 for men, up from 23 for women and 26 for men in 1990 and 20 and 22 in 1960" (Barkhorn 2013). The effect on white families is nominal because the middle-class nuclear family model stressed parental independence, but, for African American families, the impact has been significant. First, delayed first births means grandparents, particularly grandmothers, are older. As Burton and Stack found in their study of kinscripts, grandmothers begin to feel they are too old to keep up with babies and small children (1993). Because people are living longer, women who delay childbirth may also find themselves sandwiched between generations as they have childcare and eldercare responsibilities, sometimes for both parents and grandparents. Additionally, because of shifts in retirement options, many seniors are working past retirement age or enjoying their retirement age. Therefore, they are less available to support childcare than previous generations had been.

Migrations due to educational and professional opportunities have also impacted African American families in important ways, and migrations not only impede support by extended kin but fragment communal support as well. When Black women have grown up in particular communities, neighborhoods, and churches where they have developed friendship and support ties, often across generations, movement away from those networks can force a self-reliance that Black families have never previously needed (Stack [1974] 1997). These factors coupled with shifts in workplace culture make "staying at home" or altering their relationship with work necessary.

Navigating Childcare

Only six of the women and four of the men are from Atlanta; two of these are couples. The others migrated either for school and never left or for work. While they have made their lives in Atlanta, both educationally and professionally, they are challenged by lack of proximity to their families of origin. Being away from family often meant they had to rely on paid help or people they didn't know as well to help care for their children. For some it meant bringing their parents to them. Kia moved her parents to Atlanta when her executive position required that she be less available than she would have liked. Selena's in-laws moved to Atlanta from Detroit when they retired and often picked the children up from school or "filled in" on the sidelines at Saturday afternoon soccer games when Selena and her husband couldn't be there. Most women described times when their families had come to "help" with the kids. These prolonged visits were usually when the children were first born, when they had a pressing deadline, or when both parents had to be out of town for an extended period of time.

While some have suggested that members of the professional class would rather utilize professional childcare agencies for their children's needs (Murray

1998; Wrigley 1999), recent scholarship has challenged these notions by citing the difficulties parents have in locating and negotiating childcare (Hart and Kelley 2006; Hertz 1997; Hertz and Ferguson 1996; Macdonald 1998, 2010; Uttal 1997; Uttal and Tuominen 1999) and considering the poor conditions childcare practitioners work under (often low pay, no benefits, and inability to afford childcare for their own children). One issue for parents is placing their children in childcare provided by co-ethnics (Uttal 1997). In addition, sociologists have drawn attention to the hidden problems found in expensive nanny and au pair agencies (Brown 2011; Romero 2001). Given the literature, both popular and scholarly, it makes sense that many women said they felt hesitant with locating spaces that would be convenient, affordable, safe, nurturing, and consistent. As a result, nine of the women used a family member for childcare, usually their mother or their husband's mother, or a home-based center independently run by a church-member, friend of the family, or referred by a friend for childcare. Even for babysitting needs, most of the women relied on family or very close friends for short-term care.

Kin-Care

Only three women in the study used their own mothers for full-time childcare when their children were small. Each of these mothers was employed full-time, and each was an Atlanta native so their mothers were not only available but also present. Kalia, a human services manager who works a flex-time schedule, reported depending on her mother until her son was able to go to preschool. According to Kalia, "I didn't have any problems with childcare because I was lucky enough to have my Mom so he [her son] never went to outside care outside family until he went to preschool. He had never been with a stranger." Kalia was able to take advantage of her mother's availability because her mother is disabled. Kalia's mother, a PhD in biology, suffers with fibromyalgia, a chronic disease characterized by widespread pain, fatigue, and some cognitive dysfunction, and, although a fully functioning person, she is unable to work full-time. Her availability to her daughter and grandson comes naturally, especially since she remembers having a community of support when she was raising her own children.

Kalia was very aware of how her mother's illness, though giving her a few "bad" days here and there, ended up being a blessing for her young family. Additionally, since Kalia's family was one with the least amount of household income and net worth, having her mother provide childcare produced benefits beyond caregiving. "It's funny," Kalia said, "if my mom wasn't disabled we would not have had that. We would not have had her to keep Khalid. The drawback was she was not the most dependable to be able to come every day, and that some-times caused a problem." Kalia had to figure out another plan.

> Sometimes mom's rough days fell on my day off or the day I got off early.
> A few times I was able to ask Booth's [Kalia's husband] parents. His mom
> had a flexible schedule because she was in grad school. Sometimes I just
> needed to piece something together until I could get out of a meeting or
> something. It was stressful sometimes, but it was worth it because Kha-
> lid got to know both of his grandmothers, and I loved having him being
> taken care of by people who loved him.

Selena, employed in financial services, said her mother kept her first two children when they were first born. "I didn't have any problems with daycare centers and homecare centers, I just knew I wanted my mom to keep them." Like Kalia's situation, it wasn't always storybook simple. Selena said,

> When Mom was keeping both of the kids that was hard. Mom was retired,
> but it was hard for her to keep both of them, and she would get tired.
> Then it got really hard because Mom would like to take off from keeping
> them so she and my dad could have little vacations, and I would have
> to find a sub. We used to have temporary childcare that we would use
> when my mom just couldn't do it, but they lost their funding. After that I
> started depending on family for sub back-ups. If that didn't work, I would
> have to take off [from work].

Linda, also from Atlanta, figured out early on that her mother needed breaks, and she rearranged her schedule and found part-time care for her two children. "My mom had retired so I knew she would want to keep Melissa when I had her. Then once I had Kenny Jr. Mom just took him too." But Linda, a dentist, also arranged her schedule so she could have a bit more flexibility and spend more time at home. Linda's mom picks her daughter up from school in the afternoon and keeps her son four days a week. Linda expounded, "Someone recommended Ms. Mary to me and she has been a godsend. She keeps five other kids so Kenny sees going to her house like we used to see going to visit our cousins. He's with me or my mom most of the time and then he has Aunt Mary's house where he goes to play with his 'cousins.'"

In each instance, mothers who were Atlanta natives found it much easier to manage their careers and their family because their parents, particularly their mothers, were nearby. Indeed, five of the six women who were from Atlanta were modified full-time career moms and understood their ability to combine their roles as resting on help from their mothers.

"Just-Like-Kin" Care

Not having family, particularly mothers, around or available to help had a tremendous impact on professional Black mothers' ability to combine their careers and the needs of their families. Only one native Atlantan was a stay-at-home mom, and she lived in the suburbs of Atlanta where it took approximately forty minutes, without traffic, to get to her parents' house. For many mothers, the solution was locating people "just-like kin" to help out. This approach differs from Stack's study because those participants discussed "child-keeping" among kin and fictive kin through negotiated reciprocal arrangements that usually did not include monetary payment (Stack [1974] 1997, 63). For the women in my study, their "just-like-kin" childcare givers received monetary payment. Yet their approach to childcare was to treat the children they kept, and their parents, like family. Typically these in-home childcare givers were licensed by the state to keep small groups of children, no more than six, depending on their ages, in their homes. Many of the working women preferred this form of childcare to formal day-care centers and nannies because it was cheaper with similarly individualized care. Because the care was in the person's home, it felt (as Linda said about her son's preschool) like they were going to visit with a family member or close family friend rather than a paid childcare center.[5]

Kya said her in-home childcare giver was a lifesaver. With the hours Kya had as a school administrator she needed someone whom she could trust. Kya employed an older church member who would occasionally keep children in her home. When Kya was ready to look for childcare, Ms. Bridgette wasn't taking care of any other children and could take care of both of her children when Kya was working. Her son went after school, and her toddler daughter went all day. Kya left her job as a school administrator when her youngest was three. Since leaving her job, Kya uses Ms. Bridgette for occasional babysitting when she and her husband want to have time alone. "It is great having that kind of continuity," Kya said. "They have known Ms. Bridgette their entire lives, and since I am not from here she has been like a mother to me as well." Kya grew up in South Carolina around a tight-knit family and the church. "We went to my dad's side of the family twice a month for visits and saw my mom's side for dinner every week after church." When Kya began thinking of where she wanted her children to get their early childhood care, she wanted it to be her family, her husband's family, or just like family. Her husband, Timothy, is from Atlanta and was raised by his mother, a teacher, and his father, who had a PhD in physics.

When Kya and Timothy started their family, Timothy's father had passed away, and his mother had not retired.

> My mom wasn't here, his mom was still working. . . . The next best option was Ms. Bridgette. Since we go to the same church, I had known Ms. Bridgette for a long time, and I was friends with her daughter. We were able to work out an arrangement where I would drop Sean off at her house along with Laura, she would give them both breakfast and then take Sean to school. At the end of the day she would pick Sean up from school and bring him to her house, and once he got older help him with whatever homework. She would give them dinner, and then Tim would pick them both up at around six. I worked long hours and didn't get home sometimes until eight or sometimes later. Tim being able to pick them up already fed meant all he had to do was get them bathed once he got home, and sometimes he left it for me.

Kya said she didn't mind him leaving the baths for her. "It was the only time I really had with them all day. Sometimes I was actually mad if he did it without me even though I was exhausted when I came in the house." Kya depended on Ms. Bridgette because she made everything so easy (Uttal 2002). But Kya decided to leave her position as a school administrator because of the hours and the stress of the work. She said, "I would have kept working with a less stressful job." Kya, now an educational consultant, often works on contract, which means she is more available to her family but still able to work in her field without the overwhelming stress.

Jill, who was sandwiched between three generations, was not able to rely on her mother for help with childcare. Jill, a surgeon, was forty-one when she had her first child. Before she had children, she and another surgeon had started their own private practice. When I met Jill she had sold her shares in the practice and was working for a government-supported program in hopes of alleviating some of the stress of taking care of her two children (she now has three) and two elderly, ill family members, her mother and her grandmother. Jill's mother had been taking care of her elderly grandmother when her mother started showing signs of dementia. Jill felt she had no choice but to bring them both to live with her. Shortly after her grandmother passed, Jill found that it was all too much for her to handle and continue in private practice. "I had antici-pated having my mom take care of the kids," said Jill. "She was retired. I thought with my mom helping I could have a nanny and keep my private practice, but I wanted to take care of the kids myself." Once Jill's mom got sick, Jill had to change her plan. She said, "I didn't want the outrageously late hours being in private practice requires and with Mom being sick, I did not want to rely on a full-time nanny." Jill says she was saved by a family friend who referred her to an in-home care-giver. "I called her, and she had an opening, and I was like, thank the Lord."

Mixed-Methods Childcare

For busy professionals, locating childcare that fits their schedules can also be a problem when they do not have available family members nearby. Cara was in Chicago when she decided not to return to her career. But even once she moved back to Atlanta, where she and her husband had been raised, she did not rely on their parents and reported not feeling comfortable with childcare. Because her father was significantly older than her mother, when he passed away her mother was ready to live a little. "She was really still young when they got married, and they were really old school so now when I call my mom, she is busy." Because of the inheritance she received when her father passed away, Cara was able to consider other childcare options. "I decided to stay at home, but I also hired a nanny. I knew since I was managing my father's business I needed help at home, my mom wanted to have her own life, and I did not want a daycare center." Cara said that doesn't mean she doesn't use her mother and her husband's parents for childcare. "If we are going out they are the first people we call. We are very particular about babysitters and prefer family first, then a few select friends." Although Cara had issues with childcare and saw that as a primary reason to stay at home with her daughter, the inheritance she received from her father made her truly comfortable with being her daughter's primary caregiver.

Charlotte, a children's book author and former public relations director, had difficulty with the lack of flexibility in formal childcare centers. Trying her hand at authorship when she had her children, Charlotte was not going into an office every day but still needed blocks of time to complete her work. "Childcare is definitely a challenge of working at home. It is very difficult to find part-time childcare." At one point Charlotte was in a bit of a bind and tried to bring family members in to help out when absolutely necessary. "I am trying to meet a deadline right now and have a lot to do so my mom is here to help out." Charlotte's parents live in rural northeast Georgia, just a couple of hours from Charlotte and her family, so they can come in for the weekend or when Charlotte has a deadline. "It's great having them close enough to work with my schedule. Having someone [paid help] come to the house is sometimes difficult and unconventional so I haven't been able to do it."

Karen, a pediatrician who had relied on her family and a host of family friendships for childcare when she lived in New Orleans, found that the problems accompanying migration became very apparent following her move. Karen and her family moved to Atlanta following Hurricane Katrina. While

Karen's move was motivated by a natural disaster, the effect is similar for families who move for careers. Karen said, "When we were in New Orleans we had family, and they kept the children. We had more family friends. Here [in Atlanta] we had a sitter through the church, and she moved. Our other sitter is graduating and leaving. We have a new babysitter referral now, and we don't know her as well." When Karen and I talked she had already made some changes to her work schedule to accommodate her desire to have more control over her time and be available to her family, but childcare was still an issue when she needed to go to work. What Karen identifies here and what is echoed through the conversation of many of the women is an insecurity and discomfort with the childcare centers and the care options they present. While very few found locating childcare to be the sole reason for leaving the workplace, it was definitely a point of concern for all of the women, whether they were in the workplace full time, part time, from home, or not at all.

Black Professional Women Redefining Work

Most of the women, even when they have not completely exited the workforce or altered their professional positions, feel they have placed less emphasis on their careers than on their families. This shift in focus was often prompted by a change in the needs of the family and the workplace's inadequate response, either directly or indirectly. As a result, the women, unsure how to name their decisions, simply stated they are trying to be more "available," a persistent and driving theme.

Regardless of each mother's relationship with her career, she is reportedly the primary childcare-giver when her children are at home: she provides most of the housekeeping and meal preparation in her home, and she continues to be the family planner and organizer (and sometimes manager of the household income/budget). The career women in this study refer to themselves as "command central," COO (Chief Operating Officer), and family manager, and they pride themselves on being available to their children and their husbands. Marketing executive Cory articulated her feelings about her work and her family and sees the benefit in committing to both. "I enjoy working. I like what I do. I think Black women make adjustments to their professional goals before they get high enough for there to be an impact. I think it is good for my daughters to see me working and to see me being involved in our family financially, but I do not want my work to interfere to the point that I cannot be available to them."

For modified full-time career moms, being more available in Jill's case meant selling her medical practice and going to work for a public hospital when, within a two-year span, she faced the passing of her grandmother, the juggling of two small children, and the deteriorating health of her mother. For modified stay-at-home moms, such as Kya, it means leaving her dream of being a school administrator so she could see her children before bath time. For available-flexible career moms like Kalia being more available meant working a flextime schedule so she could relieve her chronically ill mother who was helping her by taking care of her son.

It is clear then that Black professional women have followed a mothering strategy that privileges survival of the family. Once they have children, often delayed by their educational pursuits, they also have to respond to other facts: they are not near kin who can supply childcare, their mothers and other family members are elderly and need care, and the demands of the workplace do not support the demands of navigating family life.

Having it All? Modified Full-Time Career Mom

For the women who continued to be employed full-time, their decision to continue working full time was usually impacted by three factors: (a) they really enjoyed their careers, (b) they had reliable, affordable childcare, and (c) their households needed their incomes to maintain their lifestyle as they either provided the primary income or the most stable income and benefits. Additionally, their life course strategy was usually modeled on that of their mother, friends, and other women they admired. The professional Black womanhood model that historically combined marriage, motherhood, and career fit their reality. These women were ambitious, they believed they could have successful careers and families, and no life events had altered that perception (Gerson 1986). These women followed the uplift model; they attended some of the nations' most well-respected colleges (seven out of nine went to HBCUs) and followed their mothers' and grandmothers' advice not to depend on a man. They also achieved career success, and while they encountered some setbacks in their careers they describe them as choices meant to allow them to be more available.

When I asked Natalie, married mom of three, about any potential work/family conflicts in her position as a middle-school teacher at a well-known and prestigious Atlanta private school, she said the conflict was mild, expected, and had very little to do with her.

> They made it clear that a teacher being pregnant is an imposition on the school. After the initial notification it's all celebration. But going to tell the principal is different because you want them to hold your job. The "guess what" is always "you're pregnant." A lot of teachers give a certain time period and then do not come back, so the school feels like they are left in a lurch because you are probably not coming back but they have to hold your job.

Natalie, who had worked at three other private schools before coming to her current position, discussed how this was the typical trajectory for white women. "A lot of times they don't come back because they go into teaching so they can be home with their kids. They teach until they get pregnant, then they stay home until their kids go to school, and then they come back. It's different for Black women." Natalie saw her role as a teacher as a career, not a work and family choice, and she also never saw herself as a stay-at-home mom. She adamantly insisted that she was raised to be independent. At one point in our many conversations Natalie said, "My expectation of my life was that I would work. I had never known anything else." Natalie did consider staying at home after her second pregnancy, but it wasn't because of a desire to be a stay-at-home mom. She almost died after her second pregnancy when she had uterine bleeding that physicians had a hard time locating and stopping.

> With my second pregnancy . . . I had a big bleed from my uterus. I fell and I thought that was what caused it but I was told it just happens. I lost a lot of blood and would not take a blood transfusion [because it was against her religious beliefs]. Since I was near death when all of that happened Charles was scared and wanted to feel like I would be safe and be here. He was really afraid I was going to die. I think both Moms [her mother and mother-in-law] wanted me to stay home. But I couldn't. I went back to work five weeks after she [her second child] was born. It was too soon. Doctors said wait six to eight weeks. But it was not part of my experience that women did not work. After I had Cameron [her last child] I might have considered staying home because I had been exposed to the idea, but by then we were accustomed to a particular lifestyle that required two incomes, and we were not willing to make the sacrifice. The power dynamic in our relationship had not changed either, and I did not want to be dependent on him [her husband].

Natalie said it was her desire to get back to work and "make a difference" alongside her desire to "take care of herself" that made her go back. These are two hallmarks of Black women's thinking on work and family that challenge the very idea of staying "at home." Natalie's husband makes close to $150,000 per year as a sales associate with an IBM subsidiary. That is not counting the couple's rental properties that bring in a profit of about $20,000 per year or Natalie's almost $50,000 per year income.

As a lead teacher at a middle school international baccalaureate program, Natalie has been able to maintain some flexibility while being employed full time. Additionally, the fact that her children are now school-age makes things a lot easier to negotiate. While Natalie isn't making as much money as she would like, her children get a discount at the private school where she teaches, and at the time of the interview she was thinking of moving her middle and youngest children there. "I often have a lot of work that I bring home," said Natalie, "and that conflicts with the kids' activity schedules but having Cam and Chelsea [her two youngest children] at the same school would help a lot. We would at least be on the same schedule." Here Natalie was referring to the fact that having three children in different schools meant three different holiday, vacation, and planning-day schedules: "It turns out that unless your kids are in your exact same school, you will often have different schedules, which means being a teacher presents other family conflict issues you really don't think about." "Even pick-up and drop-off can be difficult since I have to be to school earlier than they do and I leave later. If they are at my school, they can wait for me to get done and we can leave together. And . . . we get the same breaks," she said with excitement. The only thing that prevents Natalie and Charles from making the decision is the tuition. Natalie would get a small discount for her kids because she is a teacher at the school, but tuition for two children, even with the discount, would strain their finances.

In previous generations, being a teacher meant mothers were available to school-age children. Children went to their mother's schools or in the same school district and therefore had the same breaks. When there were conflicts due to meetings teachers might have outside school hours, they were minimal, and family members, friends, and neighbors provided childcare. Careers that previously seemed to offer the perfect fit for balancing work and family life increasingly require some negotiation. As a result, Natalie and the other MFC moms are constantly looking for ways to make the pieces of their lives fit together.

Selena, who works in the government sector of the banking industry, said her position has been great for someone with kids because it is flexible, but she complained about the difficulty she had when she was pregnant. "There was no maternity leave policy," she said. "Pregnancy was considered an illness. I had to use all of my sick time and vacation before they would sign me up for unpaid leave. So when I came back I had no time. They have since changed it, and there is a maternity leave for pregnant moms now. But for me, with the kids, it is flexible to leave when I need to but it depends on my manager." Although Selena had never planned to be a stay-at-home mom, when she encountered some difficulties with her manager she considered it. "I thought about going part-time and my manager told me if I went part-time I wasn't serious about work and I wouldn't be in line for promotions. I felt like she was telling me I had to make a choice between being at-home and continuing my career." Selena's mother was a stay-at-home mom, but she had always told Selena not to stay at home. "She told me I needed a job to take care of myself. She always said you have to have your own money. That always stuck with me. I have fear of somebody controlling me. That is what I have internalized. She always had a cloud I associate with her not being employed. I didn't want that cloud." Selena's decision to continue full-time employment was influenced by both her manager and her mother. They both made it clear that the best way for her to be in control of her own destiny was to demonstrate commitment to her career.

Selena could have taken time off or reduced her hours with very little effect on her family's financial stability. Selena's husband is an attorney with the public defender's office, and the couple owns two rental properties. If Selena had left her position or changed her hours, the couple had already decided that her husband John would go into the private sector for better income and benefits. But Selena said she and John like what they do, and she didn't want to change that. "My mom also said you should like what you do, and I like my job a lot. I just didn't like the way my manager acted when I was having my kids and went out on maternity leave. When I went to talk to her she said these are the choices you made. But when her [Selena's manager's] father got sick she had to leave to take care of her own responsibilities. When she came back she apologized." Selena speculated that some of her manager's animosity was racially motivated: her former manager was white; her current manager is Black, and things are much better. "This manager is a mentor to me and she looks for opportunities to assist us. She is overall flexible if you try to balance things. She tells us to 'work hard so you can make up for when you are away.' I like that philosophy, and it works well for my desire to be a working mom."

As Natalie and Selena demonstrate, the workplace can be inhospitable to women with families, who are forced to locate ways to manage their careers and their families while trying to make sure neither suffers. They also have to consider how their changes in the workplace may affect family finances. Natalie thought enrolling her children in her school would make things easier for her to manage, but two private school tuitions would greatly influence her family's financial stability. Selena considered reducing her hours or staying home all together because of workplace inflexibility, but that decision also had unintended consequences. In the end, Selena experienced some relief through an understanding manager, and Natalie was still sorting out the best plan. It is clear that individual solutions, the order of the day, place a good deal of pressure on families to resolve problems themselves. Even for those who have not had to manage inflexibility in their corporate environment, "side" jobs have become major factors in their financial status as couples attempt to fund their lifestyles, retirement, and wealth portfolios. When asked if they had any additional income outside their place of employment, all but two of the study participants stated that they or their husbands had another source of income, ranging from cottage industry crafts to computer servicing.

Jill and her husband Paul have both tried their hand at entrepreneurship. Paul has his own computer installation and computer hardware firm, and, until 1998, Jill was a co-owner in her surgical medical practice. It made sense to the couple for Jill to leave her practice while they maintained Paul's business. "I could still make the most money, and I have the health benefits, and with Paul having his own business, we could work to support his business and I could still practice medicine." The plan has worked for the most part. Paul, self-employed for fifteen years, makes approximately $70,000 annually. Although Jill lost a considerable amount of earning potential when she sold her practice, her reduced income and increased flexibility still produce a combined household income of about $190,000. "I am very family oriented and the Medical Center allows for my family in ways private practice did not. It allows me to keep my family first and not sacrifice."

Surviving significantly past the uncertainties of the first five years when start-up companies are their weakest, the couple has been able to build their family and their business but not much else. Paul dabbles in refurbishing antique cars for shows and resells them, but, according to Jill, the hobby does not always generate enough income to justify the cash expenditures. The family now has three children, with two in private school, and they pay $900 per month combined for their tuition (with a sibling discount). As far as investments go, they have a few mutual funds but no college funds. Jill laments the fact that they are not able to build a whole lot financially right now, but she realizes she has the type of balance most dream of. Paul's business keeps him involved with the family and household, and Jill's job provides enough flexibility and income to balance it all. Nevertheless, the needs of their families are constantly shifting. As Jill stated, "This is working for now. Who knows where we'll be in five years."

Many of the moms discussed this type of uncertainty with their career and family plans. Using strategic mothering as a lens allows us to make sense of this ambiguity because it considers the life course of the mother and the child(ren). Just as Jill had to navigate her life course and her mother's life course simultaneously, when her circumstances suddenly included both a baby and a dependent mother, the combination of which compelled her to sell her medical practice, Jill will likely have to reconfigure things when her youngest child begins grade school and again when her oldest child begins college.

Kia, a woman I met at the Monroe School where her two oldest children were enrolled, decided to create some new strategies for her family by not depending solely on her job for her family's financial stability. She planned to implement a new strategy once she learned she was pregnant with her fourth child. Kia and her husband Trevor, both thirty-six, met in college where they were getting bachelor's degrees in engineering. After graduation they both accepted engineering positions with a top firm, got married, and moved a few times until they landed in Atlanta, where they moved into one of the city's premier African American swim/tennis communities. The homes in their subdivision range upward of $400,000 with well-manicured lawns and luxury cars to match. The two currently earn more than $200,000 per year from the engineering firm where they are both employed, and they both have even greater earning and leadership potential. To add a little financial flexibility to their lifestyle, the two began investing in real estate and a multilevel marketing firm. Taken together, these investments give the couple assets worth $1.2 million, not including their investment holdings in the form of stocks. Kia was raised not to depend on a paycheck for your family's security, especially as a Black family. Kia said, "I come from a long line of entrepreneurs. My parents are business owners. They own real estate, a florist shop, and they have printed newspapers." Kia's parents also taught her and her sisters that having an education and a career would give them certain options as well, and Kia has combined them both.

Kia, a career mom, had been working full-time and managing the couple's real estate and multilevel marketing firm when she learned she was pregnant with her fourth child. Despite the fact that she enjoyed her job and had never seen herself as a stay-at-home mom, she planned to leave her position after the child's birth, but Kia said her decision had very little to do with being home with the child. It was an opportunity to change direction. Having been successful in corporate America, she saw an opportunity to leave her job and focus on the family-owned businesses. Kia said, "I want to do a lot more for myself and my family than for this corporation. I have seen the light, and I believe the answer is to be in self-employment, not using all of my talents and skills on this corporation." The couple decided Trevor would stay at the corporation, at least for a while longer, for the health benefits and his opportunities for promotion, but as Kia surmised, "putting all of their eggs in one basket didn't seem like a good idea." Kia and Trevor are not alone in their understanding of the current financial picture, particularly for families of color. Being a highly educated, high-earning family does not guarantee the ability to maintain future financial stability for oneself or one's children.

Similar to Kia and Trevor, Sheri and Clarence decided to take a stab at entrepreneurship and found their niche in real estate. Clarence left his job as an administrator in the Atlanta public school system to invest full-time in real estate. He had been dabbling in real estate investments for a number of years, and, once the investing income began to replace a large percentage of his teaching/administrator income, he decided to leave his education career of thirteen years and begin a full-time business in buying, remodeling, and reselling real estate. The couple talked about Sheri's leaving her career as a financial analyst for a major corporation headquartered in Atlanta, but they knew they needed to wait until the real estate business was also replacing her income of $75,000 per year. With the birth of their third child, Sheri's strategy was to be pragmatic. "I would love to be home with the kids, especially because of my work hours, but we need the benefits." For both couples, Kia and Trevor and Sheri and Clarence, their ability to rely on one person for the stable income and health benefits guaranteed through an employer while the other person developed and grew a business opportunity worked well. It is important, however, to note that each of the families with modified full-time career moms discussed having another way to bring in additional income. They all seemed to agree that they could increase their wealth portfolios, a factor that has been very important for the continued stability of upper-middle class and professional African American families, while also allowing some flexibility for one or both spouses to be able to leave their careers and protect the family's finances from unexpected dismissals and lay-offs (Bradford 2003; Conley 1999; Marshall 2001; Shapiro 2004).

Pushed and Pulled: Modified Stay-at-Home Moms

The media and private-sector pundits would like us to believe women are choosing to leave their careers because of an "innate" desire to be at home. Social science research clearly demonstrates, however, that women are often making the choice to be at home or modify their careers because of challenges in the workplace. Sometimes the challenges simply make managing work and family difficult, as in Selena's case or, like Kya, the environment makes the workplace too unbearable, especially when there are other options. For others, the constrained choice to be at home is motivated by the loss of a job, and when scholars and pundits focus on those who have "opted-out" they often miss what led to the "decision" and how women reinvent the reasons for their departures. The role that the structure of the workplace could have on women's "decisions" about work and family requires close attention (Williams et al. 2006). While many of the studies drawing attention to the ways the workplace has turned the "opt-out revolution" into the "pushed-out" reality (Stone 2007), there is scant conversation about the impact of this trend according to race (Williams 2010).

This study fills this gap because understanding the circumstances under which Black women choose, when placed in the framework of women being "pushed-out," becomes necessary for understanding the intersectional impact of race and gender. The women who are categorized as "modified stay-at-home moms" identified themselves to me as professional women who left their careers and became "stay-at-home moms." Even if they were involved in other income-earning activities, if they told me they were "at-home-moms" I viewed them as such. I categorize them as MSH moms for several reasons: they are their child(ren)'s primary caregiver; in many instances their "decision" to leave their careers was not wholly their own, building on the concept of constrained choice; and in most instances they are involved in some income-earning activities. These activities range from supporting a family-owned business (usually started by their husbands), to working by contract, to building their own businesses.

Nancy embodies this position best. She left her career as an internist at a community health center when her twelve-hour workdays took a serious toll on her health and the stability of her family. After several pregnancy complications (her first was stillborn, and during her second pregnancy she miscarried one of a set of twins), Nancy came to the realization that with two small children at home she could no longer combine her work as a physician and a mother. "It was coming at too great a cost to all of us." Nancy altered her working life. First, she tried to reduce her hours, but that made her feel even more frazzled. Shortly after having her second child, she decided to leave the health center and become the full-time manager of the household and her husband's construction firm. The couple has struggled to establish the cushion they dreamed of when they came together as high-powered, high-earning professionals, yet they know their family is better off since Nancy came home. "We would be done with our student loans at this point if I had stayed," said Nancy. "Now I just work to keep my credentials and certifications up." When I asked Nancy what she meant by this, she explained that she occasionally works as an internist filling in for other physicians when they take vacations or have to be out for extended periods of time. This allows Nancy to continue being board certified without having the hours and responsibilities of an on-call physician. The couple has discussed Nancy returning to work full-time to take some pressure off of their mounting expenses because they have two of their three children in private school and a part-time nanny who does some cooking and cleaning. But Nancy says they are able to keep things as they are for now by garnering additional income through a few rental properties, including an apartment that is attached to their home and a vacation home in Florida that they frequent for long weekends and school breaks.

Some professional women, like Nancy, are forced to reduce their hours or commitment to their careers due to stressful workplace conditions that make it difficult to successfully combine the two. Others, like Gia, Gail, and Monica, are "pushed-out" because of shifts in the workplace. When I initially asked all nine of these women about the decision to leave the workplace, they attributed the move to focus more time on family; when asked to recount the specific events that led to the decision, Gia, Gail, and Monica discussed being laid-off either just before or just after their pregnancies, thus essentially being forced to "decide" to stay at home.

Gia had been out on maternity leave with her third child when her company, a major telecommunications firm for which she was an information technology (IT) specialist, went through a major restructuring. "I came back from maternity leave, and the next day they laid me off," Gia said. "They knew they could not do it while I was out on maternity leave so they waited until I got back." Gia said she and her husband decided she would stay at home for a while with their three children and maybe she would go back to work later.

> The timing was good. We had just bought a new house, my husband was diagnosed with multiple sclerosis, and we had two small children in child-care. We just felt like I needed to be home. We would not have been bold enough otherwise. After I was laid off Ben said, "Stay home for a while." I could see the benefits to my children and my family from my being home so I wasn't in a hurry. I honestly felt like I need to do this for my kids. To see them be better people. After a while Ben was riding me to get a job, and I was looking, but nothing was coming about, and I thought maybe there's something else God wants me to do. Recently Ben doesn't men-tion it. We're spiritual; we know maybe God wants me to do something else. As African Americans sometimes we see dollar signs, and we think we need the money more than what being at home provides. I would not have been bold enough to leave if I had not been laid off though. And I do not think I would have wanted to. Being at home is not so glamorous. There is no reward. At your job you get promotions and increases . . . no one says thank you every day for clean clothes and ironed clothes.

Ben brings home about $135,000 annually. The family also owns a rental property that nets about $300 per month. The couples' mortgage and house-hold expenses come to approximately $3,500 per month. The couple also reports owning stock, investing in an IRA, and opening a college fund for their children. They also pay tuition for their three children to be in private school. Gia reported, "Sometimes we feel strapped. It's hard to go on vaca-tion or to get another car. But those things are extra, and we weigh what we are able to accomplish with one pay check against what we would lose with two." Gia discusses her decision in cost-benefit terms and sees her time at home, following the loss of her job and her unsuccessful search for a new one, as something the family needed.

Although she did not make the decision to be at home initially, her family's situation makes the decision easier to accept. Gia still shows signs of ambiva-lence when she discusses the family's financial position, her reliance on her husband's paycheck, and her desire to be acknowledged at home like she would be if she were still working (indeed, she believes this is the best thing for her family and even sees it as something God wants her to do).

Gail and Monica experienced similar setbacks when they began having children and they lost their jobs. When Gail was laid off from her position with a business solutions firm, she was five months pregnant with her first child, which was not terribly disruptive to the couple's projected schedule: "We were thinking I would stay home until the baby was about eighteen months." Lawrence was an accounting manager at a major multinational corporation headquartered in Atlanta. He brought home more than $100,000 per year. He was on the fast track to management, and the couple lived considerably below their means. Their first home cost them $180,000. Gail was at home so there were no school costs. Grandparents lived nearby so there were no babysitting costs, and the couple bought an inexpensive Kia minivan instead of the fancier and more popular Honda and Toyota versions. "We could definitely afford for me to be at home, and once Keith was two we decided I would stay home until we couldn't afford it anymore." Now, with two more children, Gail is still at home . . . kind of.

> At first I was cool with being at home. I started getting bored, but I didn't want to go back to work. I wanted more time on my own and to be able to have my own schedule. I got involved with the homeowners' association, and Lawrence and I were doing neighborhood watch with some of our friends in the community. Then there was a member of the community who was running for county election, and I started working on his campaign. I would take Keith with me, and he'd sit through meetings in his baby seat. Once Don was elected I started doing more with the homeowners' association and started taking classes for property management. That was fun! I really enjoyed it, and it seemed like I could manage my own time.

Gail decided to get her property management license. She worked from home for the firm that managed her subdivision for a while and then went into business for herself garnering the support of her community and subdivisions nearby. Gail stated, "I really enjoy what I do, and I have control over my schedule. But I never would have found this work and started my business if I had not been at home first."

Being a stay-at-home mom does not always mean one is focused "intensively" on the child(ren). Women make modifications based on their needs and the needs of their families. When Gail says she never would have found that she enjoyed being a property manager without being at home she is correct, but her position as a "modified stay-at-home mom" allowed the flexibility to pursue a career change to property management and entrepreneur. Because she was locked into neither a full-time career role nor a full-time stay-at-home mom role, Gail was able to make changes that better fit her own needs as an ambitious woman and her family's needs as a flexible and available woman. However, these are still individualized solutions, and the constrained choice offered by her being laid off and having a husband who could support the family with ease financially ultimately created the space for Gail to find and pursue her passion.

Monica, married mom of three and formerly in the computer technology industry, was laid off when her second child was an infant. Monica and her husband, Will, worked for the same computer technology firm, and both were laid off when the company went through a major restructuring. As with Gia, who was laid off from her IT position, the shifts in the computer industry in the late 1990s took their toll on both households. Unlike Gia and Gail, Monica did not have a spouse whose income could support the family. Before Will was laid off, he was not making enough money to "bring" Monica home full-time. Monica already held a real estate license and showed properties on the weekends before she was laid off. After she lost her job, she turned to real estate full-time and cobbled together a few other ventures including Avon sales and a direct-sale baby's supply company. Will got his mortgage broker's license, and he opened his own mortgage broker's firm. Monica stated she planned to get her broker's license as well so they could bring in a bit more business.

By her own admission, they were struggling; the couple's earnings were cut in half—from $100,000 per year to just over $50,000 per year. The couple felt like they had few options. "There wasn't really a conflict with work and family," Monica stated when I asked about how she managed it all. "Really the problem came when I was laid off because we really couldn't afford the care we wanted. Then it seemed like if I could do real estate from home, I could also be at home. I believe God has me here to be a nurturer as my kids are growing up. I might have to return to support us financially, but if independent work [working from home] was good I could maintain flexibility."

Monica's experience highlights the primary question that is on the minds of many African American women who have the means to "stay-at-home" but ultimately struggle with the idea: Can I depend on my husband? Gia and Gail were fortunate to have husbands with high incomes in growing positions, in very stable fields with stable employers. Monica wasn't as fortunate. Her husband had a mid-range income in IT, and when the dot.com bubble burst both he and Monica were forced home.[6] In addition to making rapid career changes into real estate, Monica was forced to continue her marginal position in the workplace because of childcare constraints. She was simultaneously "pushed" and "pulled" out of the workplace. She was "pushed-out" by shifts in the economy that took their toll on IT specialists during the late 1990s and early 2000s. Similarly, Monica was "pulled-out" by the lack of quality childcare available once their family income was cut in half. Monica talked about her concerns over how much nurturing her kids were getting at the daycare center and the high level of turnover.

I was at home with Justin for five months, and then I started looking for care. We tried a place that had such high turnover I was afraid none of the employees really wanted to be there or weren't being paid enough to be there. For me that meant they might not be giving my children a high level of care. . . . I know being at home is good for the kids but I wanted to go back to work for financial reasons but it was so hard to find good childcare that we could afford. It started to make more sense for me to be at home. Not just for the cost but also for the level of care.

Monica's decision to be at home was constrained and ultimately had more to do with accessing affordable quality childcare than with really wanting to be a full-time stay-at-home mother. By modifying her relationship with work she could do real estate and other side jobs from home and also be her children's primary caregiver.

Kathy is another mom who was "pulled-out" of her career with the birth of her child. She worked in hospitality, a stable and growing field in Atlanta. Her work hours, however, did not line up with daycare center hours, a conflict that ultimately made both continuing her career and taking care of her son impossible. Initially, Kathy thought she would go back to work after her son was born. With her degree in hospitality, she worked in the events management department of a five-star downtown hotel and enjoyed it. But Kathy's husband asked her to consider staying at home once their son was born. Kathy stated, "I took three months off from work. I was thinking the whole time that I would go back. After three months I thought I would be happy to go back. But once I had him and I was getting close to the three months, I thought I would like to stay home and decided that if we could afford it I would love that." Kathy and Ronald, who also worked in the hospitality industry as a chef, started looking for daycare centers. "Ron didn't want to find a place anyway so it was hard for him to be impartial when we went to visit places. But I had references from friends and thought if they were happy then I would likely be happy as well." Kathy reported going to some of the higher-end daycare centers and liking them. "They had cameras in the rooms so you could check in on your child, and they had people they called chefs preparing the kids' food. Being in the hospitality industry this was right up my alley." Kathy even reported visiting one place that immersed toddlers in a foreign language so they could become bilingual at an earlier age, but the cost of these recommended places helped to make her decision. "When we started figuring out the budget and how much it would cost for Terrance to go to one of these places, we realized most of my salary would go towards childcare. When we added in the fact that Ron and I often have odd hours when there are special events at the hotel and we would have to pay for extended care or find an after-hours daycare center, it just didn't work."

Kathy continued, "I figured I would have to work like crazy to keep him in day-care. It seemed better for all of us if I just came home." Kathy and Ron thought losing Kathy's salary would be unaffordable, but, after investigating the child-care they wanted and needed, they realized it was much more cost-effective if Kathy stayed at home. The couple decided that with Kathy home they could also look into starting their own catering and events-planning business. Kathy said, "For now, we can afford for me to be at home, and my trying to be in corporate America while we try to build our own thing would be futile."

When investigating the circumstances surrounding professional Black women's decisions to be "stay-at-home" moms, two things are clear: first, most are not at home intensively mothering their children; second, most did not "choose" to be at home. The choice was constrained even when mothers, like Kathy, say they chose to be at-home. Of course, the same could be said for women of all races and ethnicities, but for professional Black women, the choice to stay home further demonstrates the conflict and ambivalence experienced when the decision, forced or not, is made.

Given the cultural ethos that says take care of yourself and never depend on a man, modified stay-at-home moms have to figure out how they will explain and make sense of their decisions for themselves, their extended family, and their communities. For some mothers, who find it difficult either to completely leave their careers or to be completely focused on their careers, modifying work and family so they can combine the two seems to be the best strategy.

Trying to Make It All Happen: Available-Flexible Career Moms

Charlotte was one mom who was able to combine both career and family. When I asked Charlotte if she considered herself a stay-at-home mom she said no, and when I asked her if she was employed full-time she said no. Following her dream, Charlotte had already self-published one book and had a book contract in hand when she left her public relations position. She wasn't a mom quite yet at that time, but she was definitely getting ready. Charlotte and her husband had decided to adopt when they were unable to conceive on their own after several tests and fertility treatments. Once they adopted their son and daughter, Char-lotte continued to be "employed," through her book contract, which included advances and real deadlines but allowed her a lot of flexibility.

I consider the women like Charlotte, who are enacting a combination of the roles of full-time-career moms, modified stay-at-home moms, and available-flexible career moms. These women privilege availability and flexibility as the keys to their success as mothers, wives, and career women. However, having the ability to combine work and family responsibilities in this way is very rare despite the fact that it is a relationship most employees would like to have with their employers. Indeed, a study by Joan Williams found that although scholars have long held that flexible schedules are good for employees and employers because they increase productivity and decrease turnover, few professionals can actually achieve flexibility without the threat of serious reprisal from their workplace (Williams 2000). Women anticipate "paying" for their apparent lack of drive and ambition when they "choose" opportunities that make being a working mom and wife more sustainable. The alternative is often rigorous marginalization in which women experience fewer opportunities for advancement, slower pay increases, and a marginal relationship with their careers (Williams 2000). For African American women these costs can be even more detrimental to the financial stability of the family because their positions in the professional and upper-middle class is often precarious. Most women who employ this strategy say it is most ideal for combining their desire and need to work, parent, and partner. But this temporary strategy allows them time and space to privilege the needs of their nuclear family while anticipating reentering the full-time career track once their modifications are no longer necessary.

Several professional Black women in this study either concluded their employment to begin a new venture or continued with their employer but modified their hours and commitment; thus, they were developing the necessary and important flexibility in their day-to-day work lives to ensure their availability to their families. Workplace structures had some effect on these strategies. For example, Karen found it nearly impossible to work full-time as a hospitalist pediatrician and manage her family.[7] Although she contemplated staying at home for a while, the structure of the medical field does not include on/off ramps for moms who are physicians. Because moms who choose to "stay-at-home" can't always really be at home, Nancy had to continue working on a contract basis and periodically take her board exams to maintain the option of being a practicing physician. As a pediatric hospital doctor Karen worked part-time since she had her first child. She said, "I went back part-time after Genesis, and I was home with her but would work a couple days a month. I didn't want to work then. I wanted to be at home with her. With the other two I worked part-time but would move around a bit. After the third I stayed home four months and went back part-time and then went full time. I worked full time for the benefits and the steady income while Steven [her husband] was building his law firm."

Karen and Steven's experiences were similar to Nancy and Aaron's (Nancy's husband). Both couples included a hospital doctor wife and an attorney husband. Steven, like Aaron, was starting his own business but as an attorney in private practice. And, like Nancy and Aaron, Karen and Steven experienced pregnancy complications that made the idea of Karen being at home important for their family's health and Karen's health in particular.

When I met Karen, she had recently moved to Atlanta from New Orleans following Hurricane Katrina. Karen had three children when I met her but had experienced two miscarriages between the births of her first and second child. Although Karen stated that she wanted to be at home, especially when her children were babies, in many ways her health difficulties made her feel like she needed to focus more on home than on work, which was causing her a great deal of the stress she was looking to reduce (Jackson et al. 2001; Mullings 2005; Mullings and Wali 2001). "There was the workload that made it difficult, and then there was also some racism in the system that made things difficult," said Karen. She mentioned several incidents that she said were "mildly racist that had to do with how the 'good old boys' network" works in the South, but she remembered one incident in particular that occurred when she was pregnant with her second child that she couldn't decide if it was sexist or racist and had a tremendous impact on her. Karen said, "A guy I worked with who was in a supervisory role wanted to know when I was going to be through having children. He actually asked me that. When he changed positions and moved into another department, two other colleagues got together and decided I should move. They didn't want to work with me anymore." When Karen returned from maternity leave after she had her second child, her new supervisor told her she was on a new rotation. "It was frustrating more than anything. I am a good doctor, and to have colleagues do these things is frustrating and demeaning. . . . It makes you doubt yourself and I definitely considered leaving altogether at that point." Karen decided to stay and feels working part-time is the best of all worlds. She said, "When I was choosing my career I had no family goals. Now we do things to try to make it work . . . trying to find the balance. Something always suffers, and it is usually the path of least resistance, which is usually the children. I personally prefer to avoid a lot of it." Karen and Steven's solution to this work-family conflict is to work part time. "We each have either worked part-time or stayed home since we had the kids. We don't like for the kids to be in care from 6 A.M. to 6 P.M. We work mostly holidays and weekends. Right now I work one or two weekends and as needed."

Now that her children are in school she feels her schedule gives her time to work and spend time with her family, but it is definitely at a financial cost. Her husband started his own law firm only a couple of years before Hurricane Katrina so, while he was doing well, he wasn't bringing in enough business to sustain the family yet. And because she was a part-time hospital doctor she wasn't bringing in as much money as her earning potential suggested she could. Once the couple relocated to Atlanta they faced even more financial hardship. Her income dropped from about $60,000 a year to about $30,000 a year. Steven had been self-employed making about $100,000 and dropped to $30,000 working for the Fulton County Solicitor General as a law clerk. Additionally, the four apartment buildings they owned in New Orleans that netted approximately $30,000 a month before the flood weren't bringing in much of anything after the flood as people were displaced and the city was busy with cleanup. "People have been great, but we hope to go back home as soon as we can," Karen said when discussing the jobs they were fortunate to find and the way people helped to get their kids enrolled in school and set up with the things they needed to create a new home. "It's been hard to put everything back together here."

Karen's story is unique in that she had to deal with a major natural disaster that spurred its own debate about race and class in America. However, the inflexibility of the medical industry was a better predictor of her desire to work part-time as a physician rather than either the desire to "opt-out" or the result of the unanticipated move to Atlanta. She had already been combining her career and her family life by being a part-time hospitalist for almost ten years before moving to Atlanta. The other factor that affected Karen's relationship with work was the subtle "racism or sexism" she experienced with her coworkers. Karen never articulated that these mildly racist or sexist environments impacted her decisions to work part-time, but it was clear they had an effect on how she felt about the workplace. Scholars have discussed these ambiguous raced and gendered verbal assaults as microaggressions, the new form of workplace bigotry where small nonphysical slights work to undermine a person's humanity, value, worth and confidence (see McCabe 2009; Pierce 1995; Pittman 2012; Solorzano et al. 2000; Sue et al. 2008).

Cara, a former school administrator, had a similar experience. Like Karen, she thought some of her challenges with her employers might have been caused by her race or her sex, but she wasn't sure.

> We were in Chicago at the time. Towards the end of my pregnancy everything changed. I had been in the school for seven years and had never received an unsatisfactory. In one year I received an unsatisfactory, and it seemed that everything was related to my pregnancy. I don't know if they were trying to get rid of me because I was Black and one of very few Black administrators or because I was a woman starting a family. It didn't make sense, but I could see the writing on the wall. I figured if I stayed they couldn't fire me, but they could make life really difficult.

Like Karen, Cara's position at work was made uncomfortable by her race or gender identity; she wasn't sure, and she had no way to find out. She just knew that if she stayed, even if her position was not in jeopardy, her ability to be an effective administrator might be undermined. Additionally, according to Chester Pierce, who first introduced microaggressions as a conceptual concept, "in and of itself a microaggression may seem harmless, but the cumulative burden of a lifetime of microaggressions can theoretically contribute to diminished mortality, augmented morbidity, and flattened confidence" (Pierce 1995, 281).

In a bittersweet turn of events, Cara had a way out. At the time, Cara's father had been fatally ill, and when he passed away he left Cara a significant amount of inheritance from his real estate investments, including several rental properties. Cara and her husband, Anthony, who was also a school administrator in Chicago, took his death and the inheritance as their time to leave Chicago and move back to Atlanta where they had both grown up. Cara said, "Dad's gift gave me the freedom to choose not to go back to the school system and to move back to Atlanta. My daughter being born was the reason to be an entrepreneur. Once I had her I never went back."

Cara's dad, who had only completed two years of college, developed a substantial real estate portfolio over the course of his life. Her mother, who was considerably younger than her father, was trained and worked as a nurse. Since Cara's dad was self-employed, managing his real estate business, Cara spent most of her time with him while her mother worked long hours at a high-stress job as a nurse. Cara's dad emphasized the importance of education, and Cara graduated at the top of her class in the magnet program at one of Atlanta's best public high schools and then graduated from Dodd University with a bachelor's degree in psychology. Cara then decided to enter the education field and completed her master's degree in teaching and school counseling.

Cara and her husband, Anthony, met in a graduate school class while she was completing her degree in school counseling and he in school administration. A few years later the two married and moved to the suburbs of Chicago to take administrative positions. Cara had not only experienced plenty of success in her career of choice, but she also learned through her father that real estate was a lucrative investment. When he died he left her one million dollars cash and the remainder of his real estate portfolio including five properties worth a total of $500,000. Cara was thirty-one-years old, had been married four years, and had just had her first child. She was disillusioned with the impact she could have on the school system and decided to leave education. Cara initially took some of the properties and sold them to catch up on taxes and began rehabbing them for sale. Now, Cara spends her time raising her three children while also managing a portfolio that includes residential and commercial real estate that on average nets about $350,000 per year. Cara's husband also left school administration and is now a consultant for federally funded tutorial and after-school programs. His income also tops six figures, and the two reported making approximately $600,000 per year including interest from investments in stocks, bonds, annuities, mutual funds, and hedge funds. Cara is also an owner in a multilevel marketing distributorship where she self-discloses making approximately $10,000 per year. They own their home, paid $31,000 cash for a car, pay $975 per month combined for their two oldest children who attend a private preschool and grade school respectively, and have a live-in nanny whom they pay $2,000 per month. From Cara's perspective she is living the life, and, while she sees the value in her father stressing her higher education, she also understands the value of generational wealth (Conley 1999).

Cara is able to make decisions Karen was unable to make when she encountered workplace microaggressions because her father left her in a great financial position. Cara said, "My father was a real estate investor. I want to be able to take and build on that. He also led my studies, and he spent a lot of time with me, and I try to emulate that with my kids." Conversations with Cara revealed that she spends a lot of time thinking about generational wealth. Similar to what Kia said about her family's financial future, Cara said, "I want to be the master of my own destiny, and I want that for my children." When I asked Cara if she thought race played a role in the decisions she was making for her children, she said yes. "I remember learning in college that Black women were the mules of the world," said Cara referring to the infamous statement made by Nanny in Zora Neale Hurston's *Their Eyes Were Watching God*. "When I think of Black women I think of suffering, and it should not have to be that way. Why should we have to suffer?" Cara and Anthony are very determined not to allow suffering in their family tree from their generation forward. Nor do they want anyone they know to suffer. It is instructive that Cara chose this particular passage as her mantra. Just like Janie in *Their Eyes Were Watching God*, Cara is looking for and establishing her own resistance strategies. Cara was looking for the same thing Hurston's Janie was looking for, self-determination. While the novel's Janie married to gain the respectability Nanny thought she should have and divorced and, later, established a relationship with Tea Cake that led her to an affirmation of her own womanhood, Cara found it in her ability to take care of her family.

Cara says she is drawn to the multilevel marketing industry because it provides opportunities and opens doors for anyone regardless of their education or income. She said, "I was able to make certain decisions based on my income and professional status and education. But my goal is to be like Trisha and Darrel White. They are owners in 'PlantRemedies' and net about $900,000 per year. They are Black, and I think about Trisha every day. She makes $20,000 to $30,000 per month residually."[8]

Cara said she and her husband are hard on themselves. They constantly want to improve themselves and help others improve themselves. "That's the draw for me," said Cara. "I was lucky to have my dad leave me this wealth and also educate me and train me in how to take care of it. Not everyone has that. Multilevel marketing gives everyone a shot at building wealth, not just an income."

Cara was able to parlay the inheritance she received from her father into a very lucrative business enterprise for herself so, while she "chooses" to be at home, she is combining it with "working" as a real estate investor. Building on her earlier comment about being a "domestic engineer," Cara said, "I have a very unique role. I've never seen this on TV. It's very confusing. My role is not traditional. I'm sure others do it. I just haven't seen it. I am having difficulty defining myself and what I do. I have never seen anyone do this. I guess I am an 'entrepreneur stay-at-home mom' a 'trying to make it all happen Mom.'"

All of the women in this study grew up believing they are supposed to have it all, but they feel pushed and pulled in myriad ways and find themselves just trying to make it all happen—do it all. Given the expectations of their parents, previous generations, and the larger Black community, they feel a responsibility to stay engaged in their careers in some form. Additionally, because most have a tenuous position in the upper-middle class, their finances often dictate they continue with their careers or some type of work. Yet they are not freed from their responsibilities as caregivers and homemakers, and, regardless of their position as MSH moms, MFC moms, or AFC moms, they still feel the majority of household and childcare related activities fall on their shoulders.

3

"Just in Case He Acts Crazy"

Strategic Mothering and the Collective Memory of Black Marriage and Family

Charlotte, whom I met through one of the moms at the Monroe School, poignantly described one challenge facing Black career women, raised to be ambitious, when they modify their relationship with work: "My mom always taught me to be able to take care of myself just in case he acts crazy." Charlotte and I laughed when she explained the outlook, but her statement was not new in the context of the study participants. Charlotte's mother was not speaking specifically about Charlotte's husband, who holds a master's degree in computer science and is a senior manager at a telecommunications company, nor was she speaking about Charlotte's father, to whom she had been married for almost forty years at the time of the interview. Charlotte's mother was talking about the collective memory of Black male and female relationships, and she cautioned Charlotte long before she was even dating her husband James. The statement has taken various forms, but the sentiment has been repeated to each of the women in the study by their mothers, grandmothers, aunts, extended family, or close fictive kin. Although Charlotte's mother had not experienced her man acting "crazy," many Black women have, and the collective memory is a strategy Black mothers have used to protect their daughters, especially from race, gender, and class oppression.

Karen said she grew up with the adage "mama's baby, papa's maybe," and she knew what it meant: if anything happened, her children were her responsibility. "That stuck with me despite the fact that I am married. I know if anything goes down those three are my responsibility. I can try to get him to do more, take him to court, whatever, but everybody is going to look at me and say 'where's the momma?'" Kya expressed exasperation when she remembered that, as she was preparing for her wedding, her mother encouraged her to keep her birth name. When she told her mother she didn't want to because she wanted her family to have the same last name, Kya said, "My mom actually told me it would be difficult and expensive to change my name back if I were to get a divorce." From Kya's perspective, planning for a divorce before you were married was not a good sign.

Scholars of Black motherhood have noted that "many Black women live with a collective memory of their children who were sold away, raped, lynched, denied an education, and ghettoized in urban America. This memory serves as a reverberating consciousness which reminds Black mothers of their importance in fostering strong children who will survive and survive whole" (Brown-Guillory [1996] 2010, 201).

The Power of Black Women's Collective Memory

Collective memory is increasingly a part of the discussion about large group behavior. It works by reconstructing; that is, it always relates its knowledge to an actual and contemporary situation (Assmann and Czaplicka 1995). The trauma of slavery and the enduring effects of anti-Black segregation and discrimination make African Americans an important group through which to understand collective memory and cultural identity. Black mothers have been responsible not only for caring for families but also for preserving cultures and collective memories (Moras et al. 2007). Gloria Joseph and Jill Lewis (1981) wrote, in their study of Black and white mother-daughter relationships, that Black daughters are meant to respect their mothers and that Black mothers are called upon to teach survival and independence. They were to be taught to "survive in and for the community" (106). Joseph and Lewis state, "Black daughters are actually taught to hold the Black community together" (106). In Andrea O'Reilly's book-length treatment of what she calls Toni Morrison's Politics of the Heart, she engages the ways several black feminist scholars have understood Black motherhood as different from the dominant view of motherhood. In sum, according to O'Reilly, Black mothers' insistence upon independence for their daughters includes a critique of marriage, particularly dependence within the role of wife and an articulation that daughters must be strong (O'Reilly 2004, 13).

According to anthropologist David Scott, drawing from the work of Maurice Halbwachs, generations recollect or remember their pasts within distinct frameworks of collective experiences and collective hopes; however, generations can have different relationships with those memories. The experiences and hopes of the contemporary moment shape each generation's memories. Determining how each younger generation connects to or disconnects from the collective memories of an older generation, especially when entrenched memories elicit a connection and simultaneous desire to do something different, is at the root of this study (Scott 2008).

In addition to the collective memory passed on to Black women from the elder women in their families, one major influence on Black women's perception of their family lives has historically been the representation of Black women and their families in the scholarly press, popular press, and news media. Black women have long had to counter stereotypical images about themselves and their children, not only because they are negative but also because they have detrimental effects on their everyday lived experiences. Recognizing the damage, Black middle-class women of the early twentieth century developed the politics of respectability that sought to demonstrate a different image and, more important, to protect them from the ways these stereotypes justified the sexual improprieties Black women experienced at the hand of white employers (Higginbotham [1993] 2006; Shaw 1996). Today, white employers are able to justify harmful workplace practices through many of these same, but modified, stereotypes. Sociologist Patricia Hill Collins refers to them as controlling images and explains that they change names and depictions according to the needs of the period, but ultimately they have the same power (Collins [1990] 2000).

Recent advertising campaigns targeting Black women and Black mothers have continued to reinforce stereotypical ideas that Black families are dysfunctional. One campaign that received the most public debate in recent years called upon the controlling image of the welfare queen and pictured young Black children who were improperly raised and unprotected by their mothers. A young Black girl declared "the most dangerous place for an African American is in the womb."[1] In another advertisement a Black child stated, "Honestly mom . . . chances are he won't stay with you. What happens to me?"[2] Posted on the sides of buildings, inside subways, and at bus stops, these billboards target Black and primarily poor Black women and are problematic on their own, but, because Black families are most often depicted as poor or working class at best, these images are easily transferred to all Black women and their families.

To analyze the impact of these advertisements on public perception, one must study statistical data from the Census Bureau: the annual median income of Black households in 2011 was $32,229, a decline of 2.7 percent from 2010; 27.6 percent of Black households were in poverty; 43.4 percent of Black households lived in owner-occupied homes; and of Black families 45.2 percent were married couples.[3] The Black middle class and in particular Black middle-class women once again feel that they have something to prove and seek to incorporate the neo-politics of respectability into their strategies for survival. Even Black media outlets that target the Black middle class are susceptible to these images and feel a need to address them and offer a different perspective. This was demonstrated in the special issue of *Essence* magazine, following the first-term election of President Barack Obama in 2008. In it, the editorial staff wrote about the Obamas,

Our dreams about the future of the Black family had been nearly
extinguished—now the fires of hope burn bright. They represent the best
of who we are. They're the graceful family we see in church. They inspire
us with their family values. Their extended family tree of grandparents,
siblings, cousins, and friends remind us of our powerful familial bonds.
And they assure us of our endless and extraordinary possibilities. ("The
Obamas, Portrait of America's New First Family," *Essence*, 2009, 75)

This image of the Obamas as representing "the best of who we are" demonstrates the focus on respectable representations of the Black community
from the magazine that purports it is "the voice of today's dynamic African
American women."[4] The magazine tells us that we should not only be proud
of President Obama for having been elected as the first Black president of the
United States, but we must also celebrate his accomplished family life, for
"inspiring our family values" and "assur[ing] us of our endless and extraordinary possibilities."

In chapter 3 I explore the ambiguity and ambivalence Black career women
experience when respectability is demonstrated not only through their college educations, professional accomplishments, and career successes but also
through their ability to maintain stable marriages and families. Because collective memory admonishes a Black woman never to depend on a man, the women
in this study discussed how vulnerable they felt if they decided to become
stay-at-home moms, to reduce their hours, to work part-time, or to work from
home. The vulnerability manifested itself in their relationships with not only
their husbands but also their matrifocal families and the Black community as
a whole. When we remember Gail's mother's sentiments suggesting that good
Black mothers are either supposed to work or they must be on welfare, we see
that professional Black women can feel they are letting the entire Black community down when they do not manage to succeed at combining mothering,
marriage, and career.

Correspondingly, in addition to the very public stereotype of the "welfare
mother," Black women's collective memory suggests Black men do often "act
crazy." These are certainly not the only men who lose their jobs, abandon their
families, turn to adultery, addiction, or abuse, but the stories relayed to or experienced by Black women often have long-term effects, as Black women dependent on men have nowhere else to go when things don't turn out as expected.

As demonstrated in chapter 2, Black career women report they have been
raised by their families of origin, namely their mothers and grandmothers, to be
ambitious and pursue higher education, to be independent, and to focus their
pursuits on their careers. Because they have been raised to be independent,
these Black career women have had to learn to be submissive as wives, which

they see as key to marital success, and thus ensure the stability and survival of their families.

Likewise, the professional Black women in this study express a desire to privilege the concerns of their husbands rather than the wishes of their mothers and grandmothers. In so doing, these career women feel ambivalent without role models in extended, secure Black families for either marital stability or cultural representations. Instead, these professionals turn to women like themselves for advice and support, through both formal and informal friend groups. These women have decided to focus on their nuclear families, and they now have to figure out how to navigate the consequences.

The shift away from a focus on careers and toward marriage and specifically their role as wives demonstrates what I consider a new take on the early twentieth-century "politics of respectability," which required that Black women demonstrate achievement in both the private and public spheres (Higginbotham 1993). This portrayal of "true virtuous Black womanhood" demonstrated to whites and the Black community that the Black community held a certain set of standards for itself. These standards, when followed, opened doors among the white establishment and created representations and pathways for upward social mobility for the poor and working-class members of the Black community known as "racial uplift." In the new millennium, the "neo-politics of respectability" finds Black women placing less focus on achievement in the public sphere and more focus on achievement in the private sphere. Black middle- and upper-middle-class women potentially garner even more notoriety in the public sphere for being women who have focused their efforts on their families, something perceived to be sorely needed in the Black community. The women who participated in this study did not refer to themselves as performing a twenty-first-century neo-politics of respectability. Like the women of the early twentieth century, they had no reason to conceptualize their actions in this way. They did express repeatedly, however, the importance of maintaining their families with a marriage-focused resolve meant to benefit not only themselves but also the entire Black community. Yet even this resolve is couched in ambivalence, given the women's matrifocal, independent upbringing.

Too Much "I" and "Me": Raised to Be Independent, Learning to Be Wives

When asked if they were raised by their parents (or guardians) to be more career women, wives, or equal parts both, all twenty-three women in this study responded that career trumped all else in their upbringing. Some thought their parents had tried to provide them with some balance for navigating career and family, and a few made a point of saying they felt they had not been prepared to be wives. The idea of preparation to be a wife had nothing to do with proficiency in caring for a home. All felt they had been taught to do homemaking things with ease, most often with the belief that their mothers and grandmothers taught these skills as essentials to ensure their independence. These Black career women, however, had something else in mind when referring to wifely preparation: they were talking about learning to be submissive and learning to compromise with and trust their husbands. The role of being a wife (far more than their roles as professionals, mothers, daughters, and sister-friends) was the one they felt affected their decisions about career and family most and the one that created the most conflict between them and their families of origin.

Myra, thirty-eight-year-old mother of two, felt her parents had not raised her to be a wife or, at the least, had not emphasized what it took to be a wife. She said, "Both of my parents wanted me to have a good education; to have a strong career and be independent." Myra is from New Orleans, and her husband is from Maryland. They met in Washington, DC, when they were both completing advanced degrees. The couple later moved to Atlanta, and, once they started having children, she became the primary caretaker for her two children during the week while her husband, a private attorney for a major development firm, was at work. On the weekends, Myra worked as an occupational therapist while her husband tended to the children. The "partnership" worked primarily because he wanted her to "stay-at-home" with their children.

Myra, who holds an associate's degree in science technology, a bachelor's degree in health sciences, and a master's degree in occupational therapy, dreams of returning to school for her doctorate. She said she never thought she would be an "at-home-mom." But when her husband, who was raised by his grandmother while his mother pursued her education and career, asked her to stay at home and "just try it," she felt she could not say no and reported that she actually enjoys it. Because his salary exceeds $225,000, Myra felt their finances could handle it, and she could always return to work if she wanted.

Myra stayed home full-time until her second child was born. When she was ready, getting back to work did not take long at all; she was able to locate a part-time position that would only have her work some weekends. "It was a perfect scenario, although I do miss all of us being together on the weekends to do things with the kids. But it is only until they are both in school, then we can have a more 'normal' schedule." Relying on a gender strategy that privileges the desires of her spouse and her spouse's career (Stone 2007), Myra has reconciled the difference in the life she envisioned and the family life she has (Gerson 1986). "I expected to be a career woman," she said. "My mom worked and took care of us and I thought I would do the same. It took a lot for me to decide to be at home just because he wanted me to, especially since I had no desire on my own." Myra said she appreciated that he wasn't making any demands and simply asked her to "try it." "If he had said I had to, that probably would have been the end of us," she continued. "I don't think my ego, my education, or my upbringing would have allowed me to be completely dependent on him because he told me to."

For Myra, his request suggested something more than his desire for her to be at home with the children as their primary caregiver. She said she also had to be sure he was not trying to control her, limit her desires, or make her dependent on him. For Robert, controlling her was not the issue; instead, he valued the fact that his grandmother had raised him while his mother pursued her own goals, and his grandmother provided a stability that was valuable to him. I talked briefly with Robert about his thinking when he asked Myra to stay at home; he said, "I could afford it, and so I wanted to be able to provide that for my kids and not just my kids but for her, too. It seemed important, and I kind of felt like why not? Why can't we try this? It will only be for a short while, and then we can pursue whatever else we want professionally and financially."

Myra, Robert, and their two children live in a subdivision where homes are priced between $400,000 and $600,000. Her children receive private swimming lessons in the subdivision's private pool, and her family's investment portfolio includes rental properties that net a total of $2,000 per month, IRAs, stocks, and a well-funded 529B plan for the children's education. "I work because I want to," Myra said of her weekend work. "I love what I do, and so I did not want to leave it completely. We were fortunate that I had the type of profession that could be flexible so I could have the best of both worlds." According to Myra, her family back in New Orleans was primarily confused. "Being an at-home mom was not a common construct for my mother, aunts, and family members." Myra said her family was very close, and she reported speaking to her mother, aunts, and several cousins regularly even though her family was still primarily in New Orleans, other parts of Louisiana, and Texas. "I think they got it or explained my decision as having to do with being so far away from home and family." Essentially, according to Myra, the decision made sense to Robert and her because they would have to rely on professional daycare without the extended family who had always provided the care and support for geographically close family members.

Nancy's family, primarily her mother and maternal grandmother, felt similarly to Myra's family about Nancy being at home with her three children because they were in Texas and Nancy was in Atlanta, but, according to Nancy, they weren't quite so understanding once they felt that she had been home a little too long. When Nancy first left her position as a physician, her family was very supportive, and her mother, a recent fan of Dr. Laura Schlessinger, often quoted the popular radio personality's famous motto, "I am my kid's mom."[5] When Nancy had her second child, after the first was stillborn, and decided to stay at home, Nancy's mother supported her. The family thought it was a good idea, given that Nancy lived so many miles away from her extended family and they certainly did not want a stranger taking care of the first grandchild. When one year at home turned into three, then the women in her family decided Nancy had been home long enough: "I can remember being home for Christmas, and I was taking care of the kids, and it was difficult because the baby was really small. My grandmother walked by and said, 'I don't know why you doing all that, they ain't gonna appreciate it.'" Nancy continued, "It hurt a lot when she said that, and I decided that, even though I appreciated my mother and both of my grandmothers and all that they had done for me, I did not want to raise my family the way they had raised theirs and I battle with that every day."

Nancy was raised by both sets of grandparents when her mother and father got pregnant with her as teenagers. Nancy, always a bright, ambitious child, became both her maternal and paternal grandmothers' joy. She was raised primarily by her maternal grandmother in her early childhood while her mother finished her high school education, went to nursing school, and later, when Nancy was seven, married her father, George. With parents and grandparents actively engaged in her education and well-being, it was no surprise that Nancy graduated with honors from her high school, obtained a full scholarship to Reynolds, and completed a program at an Ivy League medical school. She said of her upbringing,

> I was raised around strong Black women as an only child for a while with just my grandparents, my mother, and me. My grandmother, even though she did not have a lot of education, was a pillar in the community. I remember people coming to her for advice or asking her to hold their money. It was clear that she was in charge. I was raised like that. I think they wanted to give me an easier life in terms of work so they stressed education, but they also wanted me to be strong and be able to take care of myself.

Nancy greatly respected all the women in her family, not only because of the sacrifices they made on her behalf but also because she was raised in a strong, supportive, rural Black community where her successes were considered the community's successes.

When I probed Nancy about what she meant by not wanting to raise her family the way the other women in her family had raised theirs, she elaborated: although both sets of her grandparents were married and her parents later married and established a home for her and her siblings, she had watched both her grandmothers and her mother interact with their husbands in ways that were often conflicted, argumentative, and stern. "There is no love," said Nancy. "I mean there is. I know my grandmother loved my grandfather and my mother loves my father, but you cannot see their love in how they interact and how they treat their husbands. There is no respect. I do not want that kind of relationship with my husband."

Again, probing some of her thoughts, Nancy alluded to biblical submission as one type of respect and included unconditional trust and compromise as other essential features. Like Myra's husband, Nancy's husband Aaron could afford to have her stay at home. Also an attorney, Aaron started his own development and contracting firm. "We could afford it, and I trusted him enough to know I could depend on him, and even though my mom and grandmother loved and trusted him and had no reason not to trust him, they could not understand why I would give up my career and 'depend' on a man. I don't think it was necessarily Aaron they didn't trust, but a man." Despite the older generation's criticism, clearly rooted in the Black women's collective memory of tenuous Black male and female relationships, Nancy's decision to be "at-home" was what she felt was best for her family. The decision, however, was not just for the kids.

According to Nancy, once Aaron's business began earning enough money to provide his income the couple set up an office near their home, and she and the children could easily walk to the office. Nancy managed the appointments, the orders, and the accounting. "I think it gave both of us a huge peace of mind to know that I was managing the business. That way he could focus on making the deals and doing what needed to be done to grow the business, and I could focus on the bookkeeping and management . . . and of course the kids," she added after a pause.

Most of the time Nancy and I met at her home to discuss how she was making it all work; we sat at her kitchen table as she was feeding one of the children or watching one play. She occasionally hired a nanny to watch the children while she took care of things at the office. I met her at the office for one of our meetings, and it was full of Aaron's construction models, invoices, and children's toys. I asked Nancy if she had regrets about leaving her career. "Absolutely not," she exclaimed. I was a bit surprised, expecting her to feel she had wasted her time through medical school, residency, and fellowships, so I asked her to explain. I was even more surprised by her response. "I don't agree with my mom and my grandmother, but I do listen to them," she said. Seeing the confusion on my face, she continued, "I make sure I keep up with my Boards . . . you never know what will happen." We both laughed a bit, but it was clear that Nancy respected her mother and her grandmother. Nancy realized that their relationships with their husbands and their advice regarding care of herself and her children was directly related to their strength to maintain their families.

Nancy learned this same strength when she saw her mother work days and nights to earn her license as a registered nurse. Nancy saw it when she worked as a volunteer at her mother's hospital and saw her mother take orders from doctors while her mother did all the work. That convinced Nancy that she would be a physician. But she also knew her mother and grandmother provided the encouragement and finances for her to go to college and become a doctor, not a nurse. And Nancy knew that they expected her to exhibit the strength they thought they had passed on to her. For Nancy's mother and grandmother, Nancy's decision to stay home did not demonstrate that strength; it seemed that she had forsaken all their support and dreams when she left full-time medical practice to help her husband manage his business and take care of their children.

In some ways, Nancy was listening to her family when she decided to "keep up with her Boards." To her mother and grandmother she was ensuring her independence and her ability to take care of her children herself "just in case he acts crazy." But Nancy said she heeded their advice for different reasons. She saw it as a smart strategy to ensure her family's survival—not just her own survival and that of her children but also Aaron's survival. Nancy saw herself as preparing for unfortunate possibilities: if something happened to Aaron or if something happened to the business, it might become difficult for him to take care of them. Nancy wanted to make sure that she could find stable employment as a physician and that would keep them from losing everything. Nancy surmised,

> Coming home showed Aaron that I trusted him; keeping up with my licensing and taking part-time work showed him I had his back. This is a positive approach to the same things my mom and grandmother were asking of me. It has the same result but comes from a different place. That's what I mean by doing things differently. I am preparing for if the bottom falls out because I love him, not because I can't depend on him.

Kalia, thirty years old, with one son, struggles with the idea of depending on her husband in part because her mother was not able to depend on her father. Kalia has a master's degree in social work and has worked in management for several social service agencies since completing her degree. She settled into a position where she could do job-sharing once she had her son but confessed the part-time employment was less for her son and more for her marriage.[6] She said, "I could not do it all, primarily because Booth [her husband] was barely doing anything. I considered leaving because if I had to do it all, work, take care of the house and take care of Khalid, I figured I might as well do it without having to worry about somebody else." Kalia admired her mother's strength and her ability to raise her and her brother on her own (and with a community of friends and family Kalia calls "Aunties"), but she recognized the fact that it was difficult and not a path her mom had chosen for herself. "My mom and dad dated in school. They were both working on their doctorates. She got pregnant. They tried to make it work for a while, had my brother in the meantime, and later decided they should part ways. My mom never disparaged him for leaving. He was Nigerian, and I think they loved each other, but their cultural backgrounds made it difficult for them to be together." While Kalia can see how well she and her brother turned out despite the fact that her mother was a single mother, she said, "I don't really know him [her father], and I know I don't want that for my kids." Kalia, like Nancy, expressed a desire to do things differently. Growing up without her father and seeing how hard it was for her mother to raise her and her brother by herself made Kalia want to make sure Khalid has his father in his life. She said, "We are working through not separating. We are making adjustments and trying to find common ground, but it is difficult. Sometimes I feel like I do not really need to cater to him. I can take care of Khalid. Booth is an adult; he can take care of himself. I think we just remember how much we love each other and how long we have loved each other, and we try to make it work."

Kalia and Booth have dated since high school so their shared history makes her want to try to work it out. But her work-family model thus far suggests to her that she does not "need" him. Kalia's attitude is similar to the many professional Black women who were raised to be independent individuals. For Kalia and many others, being a wife was desirable, especially in regard to raising children, but they had no real training in how to maintain a marriage, a career, and children simultaneously. Most of the women in this study realized that they have to work at their family lives just as much or even more than they work at their professional lives. Kalia says that ultimately she stays in her marriage because she wants something different for her son and because she loves her husband. Like Nancy, Kalia values the companionate marriage model that depends on the loving relationships between spouses to sustain the marriage. According to Jennifer Hirsch and Holly Wardlaw, this model transforms other aspects of marital and family relationships to fit a Western model built on romantic love. Instead of older marital models built on economic partnerships or communal arrangements, contemporary individuals usually expect their emotional, physical, and financial needs to be met by and with their partners (Hirsch and Wardlaw 2006).

Marilyn, the daughter of a dentist and an educator, said she too was raised to be an independent career woman and was ambivalent about marriage and family until she met her husband. "I never daydreamed about my wedding day or what my husband and kids would be like," she said in a matter-of-fact manner. But then she met her husband. "We had been dating for a couple of years, I loved him, and he asked so it seemed like a good time to get married. Then a few years later it seemed like a good time to start having kids." But Marilyn and her husband separated after their seventh year of marriage. Marilyn attributed their separation to having too much "I" and "me" in their relationship. Marilyn said, "I was going through a point where I was redefining who I was, and we hit a point where he did not connect with me at all. I felt exasperated. We learned valuable lessons during that period. We learned we needed to grow and change but stay connected to each other. Too much 'I' and 'me' makes it hard on a marriage."

Marilyn is a very achievement-oriented woman, but she reduced her hours as an account executive for a national health insurance firm several times so she could be more available to the needs of her family and her husband in particular.

> It became clear that I was always putting Jonathan [her husband] last, and that was not sustainable for our relationship and ultimately for our family. When I was working full time everything revolved around work and the kids. Whatever I had left went to Jonathan, and it wasn't much. The difference now is I am more present for him, and I get seven hours of sleep per night instead of five, and we are not rushing around as much. Just by reducing my hours I changed the way I thought about work and my career. It wasn't everything anymore. I no longer felt like it was me trying to climb this elusive ladder to make things better for my kids. Just clearing that focus from my mind freed up space for my husband and our marriage.

Gia and Ben met in college just before he started his fraternity pledge process. She said, "I helped him through his process, and I just kind of knew [they would get married] then. But I wasn't focused on my 'Mrs.' degree.[7] I just knew I wanted to be successful." When asked about her family life, Gia said she looks to her grandmother as a role model for how to be a mother but feels it is difficult to rely on her grandmother for clues on how to be a good wife. "I am half the mother my grandmother was, but my grandmother had to be a different type of wife because my grandfather was an alcoholic, and she had to take more control in the household." She continued, "I was controlling initially because of it." Gia discussed some of their initial difficulties. "It's not that he wanted to control me and I wanted to control him, but rather I was unwilling to compromise. It was like I had something to prove and couldn't allow him to be over me, but he wasn't trying to be over me. It was a crazy mess." Gia said she realized in time that she was responding to "stuff" she expected to happen. She said she was defensive and protective. "I couldn't let go. I couldn't just be free and comfortable in our relationship, and I realized in time that's what marriage is." While Gia's decision to be at-home was precipitated by her lay-off from her IT position, she said she chose to leave her career. "I knew it was risky business to let go. It was the hardest thing I ever had to do. But I knew I had to do it if I wanted my marriage to survive." Now Gia wouldn't have it any other way. Not just because she is the full-time caretaker of her children but because Ben was diagnosed with multiple sclerosis. She explained, "If I was still in corporate America, I would not be able to take care of us. One of the key factors in controlling multiple sclerosis is limiting stress and eating a healthy diet. By being at home, I am able to do that. I am able to limit his stress, and I am able to prepare our meals, and not be stressed myself. I am able to take care of all of us."

Selena is still in corporate America's finance industry. She and her husband, an attorney, had been married nine years at the time of the study, and they have three children. Selena said, "My image for being a wife comes from my spiritual beliefs and books that I read. My mother set an example but taught something different. She modeled being a submissive and supportive wife. My dad was definitely in charge. But she taught me to be independent." Like Gia and Ben, Selena and John also met in college, and much of their dating life was long distance. John was in college in Atlanta, and Selena was in New England: "We didn't know if we would get married. We figured once we were in the same place at the same time we would either split up or get married. . . . We got married." Selena was raised in a two-parent household, but she said her parents shielded her from the realities of marriage. "I did not understand what it took to maintain a household," she said. "I thought it would be la-la land, but it's not. It is a lot harder than I thought it would be." When asked who she looks to for guidance on family issues she said, "I look to my mother for images of motherhood, but there was some contradiction between what my mother taught and how she actually modeled being a wife." Selena's mom was one of the few homemakers in the study. "She was home until I was about five or six, then she became a seamstress fulltime. Even though she was working, my dad was still in charge." Selena talked a lot about her father being "in charge" and her mother being "submissive." She clearly did not want that model for herself, but she struggled with how to avoid it while she wasn't working.

Selena took time off after she had each of her three children and reduced her time to three days a week for about five years in between her second and third child, but she never considered staying home full time, primarily because her mother taught her not to become dependent. Because Selena's mom did not attend college, she never felt like being a homemaker was really her choice. Selena's father completed college and had some graduate school so they never really needed her mother to work. Selena says she thinks her mother felt stuck, and thus she taught Selena to focus on her education and her career and never depend on a man for her financial stability. That maternal advice caused some friction early in her marriage. Selena said it took her a while to achieve a balance in her relationship with her husband:

At first we had separate [bank] accounts because my mom always said, "make sure you have your own money . . ." even though she didn't. One day John said why do we have separate accounts? I'm like uh . . . All I had was, "because my Mom said to have my own money." I didn't have a good answer, and I knew that sounded dumb. He hadn't done anything to make me think I needed my own account. I wasn't dependent on him. So we opened a new account together. We still have our own play money [discretionary funds that they each can use how they please], but we pay the bills and all of the other family stuff from one account. I think that helps.

While Selena looks to Bible reading and prayer to help her sort through some of the contradictions between what her mother modeled and what she taught, Selena, like Gia, also understands that being submissive does not mean "laying down like a rug to be walked over." Rather, it means a bit of give and a bit of take, especially when both spouses are responsible to and for each other and their children.

All these achievement-oriented women decided on their employment status: full-time, "stay-at-home," or a combined model. They all went through high school knowing there would be college, went through college knowing there would be a career, and started their careers knowing they wanted a family, most often with kids in mind. But often they weren't sure about marriage. As Marilyn suggested, it just kind of happened.

The Costs of Marriage?

Many members of today's Black community believe in and support marriage, if not in reality, then definitely through the ideal. For some, however, not marrying has been a strategy, a means of protection, and a way to save oneself from the pain of the relationship, the abandonment, or the loss of independence. As a young woman growing up in the deindustrializing Midwest in the early 1970s, Gail's perception of marriage was negative at best. She said she always knew she would be successful; at least that was her desire. She was very driven and describes herself as having a type-A personality, but she was raised in a working-class family where her mother never married her father, worked all of the time, and had very little time to interact with her five children. When Gail's mother remarried and that relationship proved to be rocky, Gail concluded that marriage was not a good idea, and her mother and stepfather's subsequent divorce sealed the deal. "There just weren't any good models of how to do marriage and family," Gail stated. The only other married person she knew was her aunt who, in her estimation, was a religious zealot and explained marriage as being submissive to a man. Gail said, "While I understand what that means now, as a kid I did not get it, and I knew I did not want what she had. . . . I was totally against being married." Gail saw herself as an independent ambitious woman and, prior to meeting her husband, felt companionship would do; marriage was not worth the risk. Gail described her initial interactions with her husband:

> We met at a party being thrown by a mutual friend. I had just ended an unhealthy relationship, and I was not interested in starting another. But he was so persistent, a real gentleman, and really cute. But I was so independent because of my upbringing and because of my time in the military. I remember Lawrence would laugh at me sometimes because I carried a registered weapon, and he would call sometimes and ask what I was doing. I'm like, "oh, I just got back from the firing range." I know I come off as really tough, but now that I feel safe I translate that energy into my family and making sure everything I do benefits them. But I can definitely come off like a mama bear.

The couple married two years after they met. Gail was thirty-nine years old, and Lawrence was thirty-seven. They now have three children, and, although it's taken some negotiating, she feels it's a pretty good fit; moreover, she finally has some models for her own marriage, and her marriage provides a model for other people. "If I had known us back then [when she was younger], I think I would not have been so resistant and given him such a hard time."

Richelle also grew up affected by the fact that her parent's marital relationship was neither stable nor healthy. Instead of choosing not to marry, Richelle wanted marriage for herself. Knowing the outcome of marriage, however, particularly when one is trapped in economic instability, Richelle's mother encouraged her to focus on her studies so she could go to college and improve her life chances and her future children's life chances, whether she had a marriage partner or not. This notion had an impact on Richelle, a thirty-five-year-old married mom of three, who had aspirations to become a medical doctor but getting married right after college meant making a choice. Richelle explained,

> Mom had all four of us before she got married. They [her mom and dad] were married seven years and then got a divorce, but they had been together five or six years before they got married. Growing up in my house, my father was not around, but my mother put a lot of energy into us. Everything was about us—anything else was secondary. I wanted that, but I wanted to be married. I wanted to have children. I met my husband in college. We got married in '98, had our son in '99, and I knew I could not pursue medicine then.

Richelle grew up poor in a small town in Indiana on Lake Michigan. Her parents divorced when she was ten, and she was raised in a single-parent home with the help of her grandmother (who was also a single parent) and two uncles (her mother's brothers). Richelle's father was in and out of the workforce and often drank a lot. He was affected by his environment, which afforded him few opportunities and no models for success. Richelle said her mother always told her that "if they had been able to move, their marriage would have survived." Richelle said her father did not associate with married people or other people who were committed to family goals. Richelle recalls, "The guys he hung out with saw no reason to come home after work, or consistently contribute their pay to their families." Richelle knew she wanted something different.

> I was taught to get married, but, having experienced what she had, my mother emphasized me doing well in school and going to college. So I could take care of myself and any children I had first. Marriage was on the backburner. I focus on being a mother. That is what I know. That is the example I had. The example she [my mother] gave me. But I also knew it was important for me to get my education and to get married. But I did not know what to expect in marriage. Because my mother put so much time into us, working most of the time as a daycare worker and often part-time so she could be with us, I feel the same way. I am committed to spending time with my kids. My sister was home with her kids too, but now she is working as a nurse only on the weekends. She picked a field where she could have flexible hours. We both worked our schedules for the needs of our family. How we were raised affects that.

Kathy said she had a pretty good life as a child, but she alluded to the fact that growing up in deindustrializing Detroit in a poor, female-headed household with five other children had its share of struggle. Kathy became pregnant at the age of sixteen, and, although she really admired her mom, she was afraid of a life that mirrored hers.

> I knew my mom would help me. Her mom had helped her with us. But I wanted more, and I knew she wanted more for me. I was sixteen, and I had an abortion. I felt horrible, disgraceful. I felt like I had disappointed my mom. She had us young, and she did not want that for us. She wanted us to get an education and move on. She wanted us to have a chance. So she said, "This is what we're going to do," and she took me to get an abortion.

Growing up one of six children and born to an unwed mother with only an eleventh-grade education, Kathy said, "I yearned for a normal family. My parents were together 'sort-of.' They sometimes lived together but never got married. We somehow had enough most of the time. But I knew it was hard for my mom, especially when my dad wasn't around. He would get a job and be around, but when the job dried up, he would leave for a while. It took its toll on my mom." Her father's employment instability affected her parents' ability to have a solid marriage. When I asked Kathy to describe her family of origin she said, "wonderful, typical, all got along, and all still get along." But I could tell she was conflicted. She wanted to make the best out of her situation growing up, but she wanted something more for herself.

Kathy had a big, warm smile on her face when I asked her to describe her current family. I was interested in how she saw her companionate family as compared to her consanguineous family. She replied, "Wonderful! I never experienced anything like this. I have love from my husband, love from my child. It is a feeling everyone should have." Kathy's nuclear or companionate family life is extremely different from the matrifocal/female-headed family she grew up in. She understands that a large part of that difference stems from her mother's economic hardships raising her family essentially by herself; as a result, Kathy vowed to herself that she would plan a different situation.

Many of the women, particularly those who grew up in female-headed households or family situations that did not line up with traditional family forms, demonstrate how conditions of the poor urban environment have an impact on family stability. Richelle's mother's statement that her marriage could have made it had she and Richelle's father moved away from the negative influences associated with poverty focuses much-needed attention on the conditions under which marriages exist. Contrary to current social policies that emphasize marriage as a key to eradicating poverty, it was clear to Kathy's and Richelle's mothers that their partners' inability to nurture and maintain their marriages had less to do with whether they valued marriage as an institution and more to do with the social and economic constraints under which they had to support a family. Contrary to popular belief, the high rates of never-married and divorced, particularly among the poor, working class, and lower middle class, do not demonstrate defects in personal or cultural character. Instead, the prevalence of single-mother households demonstrates the impact of long-established inequalities in education, the job market, housing, and basic opportunities; in fact, the rise of both poverty and financial instability corresponds to a decline in marriage rates for most of Black America (Clarke 2011).

Staying Married

Throughout this study, participants discussed at length their desire to maintain their marriages and find ways to be successful wives and mothers. They rely on their religious views, their families and friends, and their own resolve to rationalize why they work so hard toward maintaining their unions, despite the difficulties. Black women's conflict, embedded in the "mother wit" cues from their families of origin,[8] alongside recent scholarship with titles such as *Is Marriage for Black People? How the African American Marriage Decline Affects Everyone* (Banks 2011) and *Inequalities of Love: College-Educated Black Women and the Barriers to Romance and Family* (Clarke 2011), leave professional Black women with little hope for getting or staying married and suggest Black marriages are not expected to last. As a result, marriage prospects concern not only Black women but also the entire country. One longitudinal study found that after three years, 17 percent of African American families were divorced or separated, three times the white percentage (Veroff et al. 1995). Given this, Black women often feel they are damned if they do and damned if they don't.

An eminent Black feminist theorist and I engaged in a casual conversation; she suggested that many Black feminist colleagues who wrote about Black women's rights at work and at home in the 1970s and 1980s are perplexed by the emphasis young Black women are putting on their desire to be married and the amount of "stuff" they will "put up with" to stay married.[9] Although white feminists balk at the fact that white women are "choosing" to be home with their children rather than pursue careers recently opened to women, it is interesting to note that Black feminists are concerned that Black career women who are experiencing unprecedented professional opportunities are pandering a bit too much to Black men.

Averil Clarke's study of college-educated Black women and their barriers to romance may explain why, much to Black feminists' chagrin, Black professional women are focusing their energies on maintaining marriages. While much literature on Black college-educated career women suggests they sacrifice or postpone romantic interests for their education and career pursuits until it is too late, Clarke explains that her study of college-educated Black women found that their low likelihood of marriage is conditioned by "the low value of their options rather than the low prioritization that they give to romance" (Clarke 2011, 157–158). In her savvy assessment of inequalities embedded in romantic relationships, she says Black women are repeatedly constructed as undesirable romantic partners. Realizing that they are viewed as undesirable, they develop strategic responses that deemphasize unfulfilled romantic and family formation desires and instead emphasize career advancement and temporary dating relationships. Although the response is effective in helping women to achieve success in other areas of their lives, the strategy is predicated on the fact that racist and sexist arenas offer limited power to address unfulfilled romantic and family formation desires (Clarke 2011, 155). The women in my study are married and have the romantic commitment that the women in Clarke's study seek, but my study's professionals still contend with the idea that they, as a group, are undesirable; their status as wives is much more precarious than their status as mothers and career women, and therefore all, or at least the majority, of their efforts must go into maintaining the marriage.

Each woman I interviewed saw a commitment to the marriage as essential to the well-being of the family unit, and each was pledged to its success. They made adjustments to their careers and to their relationships with their families of origin and even reconciled their upbringing as independent women with their desire for marriage and family. Toward that end, they attempted to be flexible and to seek compromise. Marriage and family therapists usually advise people to draw the line at the three As—adultery, abuse, and addiction—but, for some women, even these can be worked through. I found this area of inquiry difficult to hear and refrain from giving my opinion, but to maintain the essential open and honest lines of communication between us I did not offer my commentary. Thus, this discussion reports on what I learned from the women who trusted me enough to share marital details.

As Linda and I talked at her dining room table late one evening, she offered a very compelling case in point. She and Kenny met through mutual friends when they were both building their careers. He was establishing his own insurance office, and she was an orthodontist: "We started off really well. We got married. We had our son. I don't really know what happened. I don't know if it was the stress of everything with our careers. At the time I was opening my own office. I don't know, we never really figured it out, but we're still working through it." Linda explained that she and Kenny had separated for a short time because they had both been involved in relationships outside their marriage. "It wasn't sexual for either one of us. I think we were both looking for some void to be filled." Linda was aware that those were sometimes the most dangerous forms of adultery. The ones where you are trying to fill a void, she said, "You realize your partner isn't giving you something you need, and that's hard." While Linda was matter-of-fact in her explanation, I could tell she was feeling some distress as she tried to explain what had happened and why. She continued with quiet resolve,

> I know how this is supposed to work, though. I was prepared for this, I think. People married and divorced before I married so I was schooled on what to expect and what to do. I know I'm not doing what most people expect. I know I was supposed to leave. Or maybe he was supposed to leave me. I don't know. We are still getting through it with prayer and building trust. But we believe what we stood up for when we got married, and we believe that mistakes do happen. We're working from that point.

Linda explained that she wasn't able to talk with a lot of people about it because few were supportive of her decision to stay. Because both Linda and her husband had committed adultery, her mother approached her decision with some empathy and understood why she would want to work through his mistake. Linda said, "I looked at the situation, and I had to admit my role in why he would step out, and he had to admit his. We're in counseling now, and it's not easy, but I think we can make it."

Linda's statements were a testament to what I heard repeatedly from the women in this study. They earnestly wanted to maintain their marriages against all odds. They believed they could work around and through many problems and setbacks, no matter how dire they seemed. In Linda's case of dual adultery, her family and friends were somewhat willing to accept her choice.

Gia's experience was a little different. During our third conversation, after Gia had given me the impression that since college all had been well between her husband and her, she told me that she and Ben almost separated a few years ago. When I asked her what prompted her to consider separation, she said, "I suspected an affair. I didn't have any proof, I didn't find anything, and I didn't catch him in a lie or any of that stuff you see on television. I just felt it. I think it was somebody at work." Gia threatened a separation, and Ben's behaviors changed. "I decided to let it go," she said. "I got what I wanted, which was for him to focus back on me and the kids. I don't know what he was doing. I don't want to know. Things got better, and we moved on." Gia's ability to allow Ben time to correct his behavior and move on as if nothing had happened was directly related to her focus on her family. She said, "It's supposed to be for better or worse, right? That's what I kept telling myself. If he hadn't changed his behavior I might have taken some other action, but he changed. He let me know that we were okay. So I decided we were okay." Gia's ability to reconcile Ben's behavior and focus on her marriage had a lot to do with how she was raised. Gia was raised by her grandparents, and she saw her grandmother make sacrifices to tolerate things her grandfather, a functioning alcoholic, did. Gia said, "They only had a ninth-grade education between the two of them, but my grandmother knew staying with him allowed her to put five children and a grandchild through college."

> It's true. I did have to consider the fact that I was dependent on him. I mean I still have my degrees and my skills so I can go get a job, and I would have if he hadn't changed. I would have started figuring out how to put myself in a position to take care of myself and the kids. But I had to ask myself what I wanted for my family. What kind of life I wanted for my kids. I still love him, and since he was willing to change, I was willing to keep our family together.

Gia said she had friends who had divorced because of adultery and other indiscretions, and they were trying to put their lives back together. "It's really hard on everyone, especially the kids. But I know it depends on the situation. It's hard to let it go, but I decided I had to." Gia's decision to stay was a strategy she learned from her grandmother, but by all accounts it's one her grandmother thought she had prepared Gia not to need. Gia explained, "I'm not sure how my grandmother would feel about my decision." Gia's grandparents are now deceased, and Gia took a long pause as she thought about what her grandmother might say. "I think she might be okay with my decision to stay, but she would tell me to go back to work. She wouldn't want me to be in a position where I couldn't leave if he did it again." Gia was raised to be independent. She graduated from college, she had a viable career, and, even though the shifts in the economy led to her being laid off, she had her degrees and her skills so she could get another job. Gia reconciled her decision because of its importance for maintaining her family, a form of strategic mothering that, while different from what her grandmother would have wanted, came from the same sense of strategy her grandmother used to sustain her marriage and educate her children.

Some women were also reconciling abusive relationships. None were reported as physically abusive, but a couple of accounts told of verbal abuse. Kalia's husband Booth has a quick temper, and that, coupled with the inappropriate language with which he grew up, makes the couple's disagreements and arguments particularly stressful for Kalia.

> He grew up in a house where they yell and curse at each other. The way that we speak to each other is our boundary. His dad called me a "bitch" before. Booth says they're words; they don't mean anything. But I didn't grow up like that so it does not feel like a comfortable and safe environment with his family. He won't take anger management classes. But he is working on it. He's not trying to hurt me, he just thinks you can be yourself and be comfortable with your wife, with each other, so you should be able to say what you want. He's working on it. Now he blows up like that maybe two or three times per year, and most of the time it's when we have issues but never in front of Khalid.

Kalia said any outbursts in front of Khalid or directed toward him would lead to their separation. "I won't bring him up in that environment, and I have told Booth that so he knows, that's a deal breaker for me." Kalia works in social services, and she knows the dangers of verbally abusive relationships on children: "Words most certainly do hurt, and it's the sentiment that goes with them that can be really damaging."

Frances, whom I met at one of the support groups for stay-at-home moms, discussed how her husband's verbal abuse was accompanied by controlling behaviors. Frances lived in a quiet subdivision in Duluth, Georgia, in East Gwinnett County about thirty minutes north of Atlanta. We'd met a few times after the meetings and also at her home. Frances lived in a two-story home about an hour's drive from her southwest Atlanta community of origin. Because of her relationship with her husband, she felt pretty isolated, and that seemed to be the way he wanted it. Frances said she decided to be at home when her first child was three and her second child was eight months. When we met she had not been home full-time for very long, and she was definitely still getting used to it. Staying at home was something she and her husband decided she would do after she had her second child. The decision had caused some discord in her marriage because she really didn't want to stay home. Frances told me of her rocky relationship with her husband whom she described as controlling, primarily verbally, and she thought he wanted her to be at home so he could have better control of her. "It's just the way he did it." Frances explained. "I was working, and everything was going well at work. We had Nina in a good childcare center, and I was making progress at work. Then Jason [her husband] started complaining that I was coming home too late or bringing too much work home. . . . 'That's not what he signed up for,' he would say. Once I had Stacey that was it. He basically insisted that I come home." Frances said she left her husband when he started being verbally abusive.

> I'd been home [at-home mom] for a little while so I already felt a bit vulnerable. He complained about everything I did. He was upset if dinner wasn't ready when he walked in the door. He called a few times during the day to make sure I was keeping the girls on their schedule. It wasn't just that he was concerned, and I could understand that. It was his tone. He just seemed angry, like I was in the process of doing something wrong all of the time. It was like I was stupid. It made me nervous.

After a while Frances decided to leave. "I went home [her parents' house]. I didn't know what else to do." Frances said she returned to their home only after Jason promised to get counseling. "Things got considerably better. It's better, but it's not perfect. I still want to go back to work. My being at home [stay-at-home mom] makes me feel too dependent. It makes me feel defensive. But I'm trying to work with him on this, and I figure I can go back once the girls go to school." Frances was the only mom in the study who left her job and stayed at home because her husband asked/told her to. In other instances where husbands played a role, they made the suggestion, and the wives decided for themselves if they wanted to comply (remember Myra). Frances confided, "I never wanted to be an at-home mom, and I really do not enjoy it." Frances's story was very compelling. After months of sitting in on the group meetings I knew from Frances's discussions that she was struggling to do the "right" thing. She often talked about what "God" wanted her to do and questioned if she was doing the right thing. When I probed to find out what prompted her to make some of the decisions she had made regarding work and home, she said it had a lot to do with her upbringing.

According to Frances, her parents thought she was the wayward child. Her sister, an unmarried physician with no children, was the star of the family. She was demonstrating the independent upbringing her parents taught her. According to Frances her parents wanted her sister to get married and have kids, too, but, in the meantime, being able to take care of herself satisfied them. But Frances had barely made it out of community college. Her parents saw marriage and motherhood as the way to keep her in line. "I have talked to my mom about it. I talk with her about my frustrations. But my mom tells me to stick with it [the marriage]. When I left Jason I went home. My parents said I had to go back. My dad said it was okay to separate, but my mom is status quo; she told me I had to go back. You stay, no matter what. That's what my mom believes." Frances thinks her parents see her husband as providing a financially secure life for her and her children so she should not need to work. She is expected to be content, especially because she did not follow the education path they laid out for her.

> They [Frances's parents] don't understand what I complain about because he makes so much money. I'm supposed to be satisfied because we have things and I don't have to work. They [her parents] did very well financially; better than their own parents, with a nice house and nice cars. They wanted the same for me—for me to do better than they did. They don't realize, times have changed, I want to work, and I did not get married to raise my family by myself.

Frances believed her mother wanted to be an at-home mom, but the couple could not afford it. "My mother thinks I have it made, and she really thinks I'm about to screw this up." But Frances struggles with the ambiguity of being raised to be independent alongside the expectation that she will give up that independence to be at home. Frances said, "My mom seems to believe you should have a career and be independent but only to a point. After that, family comes first. I struggle with what that means in my relationship, but I try to trust him and trust my mom." Of the twenty-three women in the study, Frances's mother was the only one who encouraged her daughter to stay at home. Even if their mothers had been stay-at-home moms themselves, most did not want their daughters to be dependent. Frances's story is a little different from the others because she was the self-proclaimed wayward daughter who struggled to find her professional footing. She tried her hand at nursing school before getting a degree in business administration, and she quit her nursing program with only six clinical hours left. "My parents aren't exactly confident that if I were to leave Jason I would know how to take care of myself and my girls. They don't want me to move home. That would look bad. And they don't want me to have to struggle with the girls, especially if Jason and I can figure out how to make it work. I think with God's help we're trying."

Becoming Respectable Wives and Mothers

A circular interstate highway, known locally as "the Perimeter," goes around Atlanta and many of its neighboring cities. Just inside the Perimeter, on the southwest side, as you pass one of the city's most prestigious Black land-owning areas, sits a large church. The church was established in 1927, but this location just inside the Perimeter is new. Built in 1994, the new location mirrors the church's ascendance from a middle-class white congregation to an upwardly mobile, professional, middle-class Black congregation. This church was home to one of the stay-at-home mom support groups observed for this study. The group called themselves Moms After God's Heart, and their mission, posted on the church's website, stated they had "a biblical focus for women who were transitioning from professional careers to being stay-at-home mothers."

Nancy invited me to the group. As we talked about some of the things that had encouraged her to choose to leave her position in internal medicine, she told me about the support group she went to on Wednesdays, and we agreed to meet there. Over the course of the study, I went to many of the meetings on my own, often when Nancy wasn't there. Like all of the women in the study I was interested in why the Moms After God's Heart decided to stay at home, return to work, or modify their relationship with work. With these women, I was also interested in what brought them to a church support group whose mission was religious instruction for mothers transitioning from careers to be stay-at-home moms.

I attended the meetings for several weeks. At one point the group was moving chapter-by-chapter through the book *Beautiful in God's Eyes: The Treasures of the Proverbs 31 Woman*. It is a text based upon Proverbs 31: 10–31, in which King Lemuel's mother admonishes him to look for a wife who is a "virtuous woman, a rare treasure." Seven to twelve women gathered at the meeting each week to discuss the book. Among them was a former physician, a fund-raising manager for a national nonprofit research center, a hotel management executive, two teachers, a small business owner, and a cosmetologist. All the members were college graduates, married, and considered themselves stay-at-home moms, although

I eventually discovered that most had issues with what the term conjured. As an ad hoc member of the group, I purchased and read the book so that I could join the discussion. Looking through the book, I was amazed at the fact that the author, Elizabeth George, offers words of encouragement in the first chapter for women who may think it is too hard to meet this standard. "First of all," she says, "Proverbs 31 was spoken by a woman" (George 1998, 12). This statement is meant to dispel any idea that the pursuit to become a virtuous woman is the "personal and unrealistic fantasy of a man" (12). Second, the quest to become a virtuous woman is attainable (13).

When I talked to these educated women about the book and its goals, it was clear that they believed the focus on biblical understandings of marriage and motherhood was meant to provide models for women who had none. Only two of the women who attended the meetings had been raised in married-couple households during their entire formative years. Focusing on the stability of their own marriages and family lives became of even greater concern to those who had not grown up that way. This focus had a tremendous impact on ambitious career women with few, if any, role models for positive marital relationships. In addition, these women saw their relationship to the church and their commitment to marriage as emblematic of a stable respectable middle-class lifestyle that few had known as children. They saw the Moms After God's Heart support group similarly to the women who participated in the workshops and meetings of the Black women's club movement of the late nineteenth and early twentieth centuries; all were simultaneously creating, influencing, and demonstrating respectable Black womanhood (Carby 1987; Higginbotham [1993] 2006). Facing the uncertainty and ambiguity of their position as newly minted respectable ladies, the women of the Moms After God's Heart support group reflected on what God had to say about their roles as mothers and wives at their weekly meetings and often critiqued the ways in which they were raised.

At one meeting in particular, following the opening pleasantries and an update on "the kids," the meeting began with the topic for the day. Still following the outline of the book *Beautiful in God's Eyes,* the group leader (a member volunteer) began the meeting with the topic "friendship." The biblically based study guide that accompanied the book introduced the story of Naomi and Ruth and the friendship that developed between mother-in-law and daughter-in-law. As the respondents talked about the text (Ruth 1:6–2:23) and explored all that Ruth had given up for her mother-in-law, the conversation quickly turned to a more personal discussion of the relationships the women had with their mothers-in-law, which in turn moved to the fragile relationships some of them had with their own mothers. They discussed how they had been raised to think of family life in one particular way, but they were working hard as wives in their own marriages and as mothers to do something different. Nancy had been attending the support group meetings for more than a year and felt the women helped her reconcile her upbringing with her desire for a stable, peaceful family. It was clear that Nancy felt safe in this space as she discussed how her mother made her feel. She said, "It's like my mom does not want me to be happy, or she thinks I am an idiot. She thinks my husband is taking advantage of me or something because I try to be the type of wife God wants me to be, and she does not understand that . . . to her it is about being in charge with my dad . . . for me it is about being submissive and letting my husband do what he needs to do for our family and supporting him."

Some of the other women suggested that generational differences account for the variance in how they and their mothers understood their roles as mothers and wives. Kathy said, "Our mothers did not know how to be wives. They were focused on their work and their children, but they did not realize that not having a supportive model of marriage would negatively affect us and how we raised our families. We just have to stay prayerful." For many of the women, focusing their attention on their marriages became a way to combat the ambiguity embedded in their decisions to leave or change their relationships with their careers. Like Frances, the women talked about what "God" wanted them to do and used the Bible to figure out and know if they were doing the right thing.

I met Monica and Richelle through the Mom's After God's Heart support group. Monica said God chose her husband for her. "He was not my choice," she said, a bit tongue-in-cheek. "I thought I would have a nice romantic, affectionate husband, but I guess God had some other things he needed me to learn." When they met, Will was studying to be a minister, and the two would talk for hours about their understanding of different passages of the Bible. "We became friends, and then it just made sense for us to get married." Monica still contends that she had a lot to learn. "I never thought I would have a blended family, and the way Will and I were raised is so different it shows up in our parenting." Monica said of the support group, "I really had to rely on that group for how to be a wife to my husband who had a really rough childhood and how to be a parent to his daughters from his previous relationship." Monica often felt that she was not only married to her husband but also to his daughters' mother. "I guess that is what they mean by blended family, but I really did not know what I was getting myself into; mostly because we are coming at parenting from such different vantage points." "I'm just prayerful," she concluded. "That's all I can do."

Richelle had similar sentiments. "I had to rely on the Word for a model since my parents didn't provide one." As a founding and active member in Moms After God's Heart, Richelle knew it was a change in heart that kept her married. Richelle and Jeffrey met in college, and Richelle knew as soon as they married that she no longer wanted to pursue a career in medicine.

I was initially on the career track because I wanted to be able to take care of myself and my kids, just like my mother. But I knew that was not her desire for herself. She did not want to be a single mom taking care of her kids by herself. When I met Jeffrey, I knew I did not have to worry about that anymore. It was difficult letting that go initially, but I came into it through Bible study and understanding my role. It's [biblical role] not always easy to accept, nor easily done. Sometimes it can be really challenging. You know what the Bible says, but it can be challenging to do it sometimes. You don't have to always agree with what it says. A lot was hard for us to swallow. You don't have to like it, but it's what you are called to do. The Word is the Word. It might not be what others expect or what I want to do but it's what's best for my family.

For many onlookers the reliance on "God" and the "Bible" seems like a recipe for disaster, an approach that leads one to fundamentalist rhetoric that makes people, and women in particular, pawns in a type of patriarchal religiosity. More than a century ago Karl Marx referred to religion as the opiate of the people. While the popular phrase has been interpreted in myriad ways and joined together with his beliefs on capitalism and bureaucracy, we can infer that he means religion is designed to keep people unaware of their true condition; this constant state of illusion allows the state and the "owners" to be in control. For the Black community, however, a dependence on the Bible and "the Word" has often meant the difference between communal survival and self-destruction. A world void of the "illusion" is a world that two centuries ago offered no hope to African Americans. Dependence on "God's Word" has made both present and past African Americans and Black women in particular desire to live to see another day for themselves and their families. According to Evelyn Brooks Higginbotham's influential work on Black women's role in the Black Baptist church, Black women have historically used the Bible to provide a model for not only how to survive various racialized and gendered oppressions but also how to resist and defeat them (Frederick 2003; Higginbotham [1993] 2006). Higginbotham writes of the Black Baptist Women's Movement, "Mrs. G.D. Oldham of Tennessee asserted: 'The home is the first institution God established on earth. Not the church, or the state, but the home'" (Higginbotham [1993] 2006, 130). Higginbotham continued,

Although Oldham acknowledged that exceptional women would seek work outside the home and indicated her hope that they not be excluded from careers in government and the natural sciences, she firmly believed that most women would confine their activities to domestic duties. She exhorted women to be the ministers, not the slaves of their homes. . . . For feminist theologians such as [Mary] Cook and [Virginia] Broughton, the image of woman as loyal, comforting spouse transcended the husband-wife relationship to embrace that of Jesus and woman. (Higginbotham [1993] 2006, 130–131)

The Black church has been a space where both individuals could commune with and grow closer to God and the Black community as a whole could seek safe spaces to set aside an agenda for its holistic good. For each of these women, and for Black women in particular, the church has and continues to provide guidance for making it through this realm to the next. It has spurred spiritual growth as well as familial, communal, and political action, and it has been a noble weapon for what has ailed the Black community across time and space. But the church is not without its flaws, even as it regards women. Nevertheless the Black church continues to be a necessary mainstay in the lives of Black women (Frederick 2003).

Only four of the families in this study were members of the Moms After God's Heart support group, but all were engaged in a religious life that they found important to their roles as wives and mothers. Like Monica, Sheri believes God brought Clarence and her together, a belief she revealed when I asked about how they met. She told me she thought her husband was a playboy: "My girl-friend introduced us, but I wasn't interested because he had all of these 'little sisters.' They were supposedly friends, but I did not like that. But he made me laugh, and he is still making me laugh. He was nice and smart. He told me that he was going to marry me. I thought he was crazy. After six or seven months I could picture myself with him." The two were sophomores at the same college. They dated through college, went their separate ways to attend graduate school and start their careers, and both ended up back in Atlanta, where they married shortly thereafter. "God knows he brought two imperfect people together, and we made a covenant relationship with God not with man. When you look at it that way it [marriage] is a lot easier."

Each woman talked about her prayer life, her ministries, and what she saw as her commitment to God, to be a good wife and mother. Many also saw church attendance and prayer life as ways to de-stress. "I sing in the choir. That's how I get away," said Cory. "That's how I keep my energy up, and it's how I keep going and keep it all balanced." Cory's husband is a part-time pastor of a church that they started together a few years ago. She said, "My prayer life is very important for my family. When things are getting to be a bit too much, I know I need to go into prayer."

Each woman talked about how challenging it is to maintain the marriage, to keep it healthy and stable. They are managing high-pressure careers or the changes in them, their children and all of their needs, their households, and their husbands. Contrary to media images of family life, religious doctrine, and even models provided by mothers and grandmothers that suggest people, primarily women, can manage all the intricacies of family life by themselves, many women are seeking or employing assistance. Even assistance is a challenge when you are made to feel you should be able to do everything by yourself.

Having to Do It All: Strategizing the Second Shift

Studies by scholars interested in the household division of labor have long held that men and women participate in household labor at different rates, are differentially responsible for household labor, and have different perceptions of who is doing what when and how often (Bianchi et al. 2000; Coltrane 2000; Hochschild 1989; Schneider and Waite 2005). All the studies, regardless of the survey measure used or the social class location of the respondents, find that historically women do more than men or at the minimum contribute the most labor to the household. Some studies suggest that in the last twenty years there has been more participation by men than in the past, but women are still responsible for more and do more. Similar to finances, this is a point of contention in marriages with few opportunities for recourse; women either continue to do all or most of the household labor, or they do the parts that require the highest frequency (e.g., cooking daily vs. mowing the lawn weekly).

When I asked the Black professional women in this study if there had been a change in their household responsibilities after they had children, almost 75 percent of the women interviewed said their responsibilities had increased. Only one woman said she did less now that they had children than she did before and reasoned that this was because her husband knew she was not the domestic type when they married and now they outsource almost everything. For almost all, however, they had either the same amount of work or more, and it didn't matter if they were stay-at-home moms or employed full-time and making the greatest contribution to the family's income.

Despite the mismatch, almost half of the women said they were pleased with the allocation of responsibilities. They all had complaints, but, for the most part, each woman excused the imbalance as a function of the role as wife and mother. Kya said, "I do it all. I feel like I should do more. That is the biggest thing. I know if I ask for help he'll help. But it's my desire to have things done the way I want them done. I also don't want to have to ask for help." Keayba said she felt like they had just fallen into roles that were difficult to break. "I think he would do more, but I don't really let him." Gail got so frustrated that her husband was not "helping" with baths and sleep rituals when he got home from work that it became a source of confrontation. Not until they went to counseling did she realize that he wasn't "helping" because she wouldn't "let" him. Gail said, "The therapist said I had to stop thinking of it as something that was my responsibility that he could help with, but rather it should be something he just does according to the way he wants to do it, not with me telling him how it should be done." Often the women's own internalization of proper gender roles led to the imbalance. According to the women in this study, none of the men, when asked, refused to do anything requested, but, for most of the women, the asking itself was a source of conflict, As Gail stated, part of the problem was that both spouses thought of the husband's roles as one of household "helper."

Most scholars who have surveyed men and women about their household responsibilities have asked about a difference between care and emotional work. Instead of considering that issue, my survey asked the women about their perception of the most common and most contested household responsibilities. Having listened to women talk about their responsibilities during their formal and informal support groups and observing them complete tasks during my observations, I had a pretty good idea of what household members were actually doing on a regular basis. Most did not have children old enough to have "chores" so most of the work was left to either parents or paid help. I gave each woman a worksheet to fill in and gave her five alternative answers regarding each task: (a) her primary responsibility, (b) her husband's responsibility, (c) shared pretty equitably, (d) assigned to the children, or (e) outsourced. There should be no surprise that most husbands either cut the grass and hedges and cleaned the gutters or had them outsourced; the same holds for washing the car and taking out the trash, as these are traditionally male tasks. Of the tasks that are traditionally female, only one husband was in complete control of planning and preparing meals. Three wives believed they shared planning and preparing meals equally. Similarly, two husbands took primary responsibility for food shopping. Although 22 percent of the wives believed they were equally responsible for food shopping, for only one traditionally female task, getting children bathed and dressed, did both husband and wife reach some parity.

According to the women's perceptions, in 35 percent of households husbands were either solely responsible for or shared equally in the responsibility. Approximately 22 percent of tasks that primarily involved household cleaning (bathrooms, dusting, vacuuming, mopping) were more likely to be hired out. Household finances have traditionally been the responsibility of husbands and therefore their primary task. In my survey, four tasks related to household finances: paying the bills, making the budget, organizing and securing investments, and filing the taxes. According to the women, half of the families in this study assign maintenance of household finances primarily to the wives or to both spouses equally. For each of the finance-related categories, approximately twelve families (slightly over half) did not assign the primary responsibility to husbands.

In some respects the reallocation of household finances aligns with literature that has suggested that once women's education levels and careers were parallel with men's their control over household finances would increase and they would have greater decision-making power. All the women in this study feel they have equal decision-making power, but they feel they don't have any more assistance. The women overwhelmingly agreed that they were pleased with the allocation of responsibilities, yet several expressed some problems. Instead of being pleased, it appeared as though they had taken on a quiet resolve. In fact, when I asked what they would change about the household task distribution, most wives responded by mentioning husbands' household activity.

Myra said she wished her husband would take on more household responsibilities: "Maybe do the dishes and clean up after dinner." Kalia concurred. As one of the wives who was responsible for many household and financial tasks, she said, "I would really appreciate it if he did some of the basic household stuff and if he was more involved in the finances." For Kalia, some of the concern had to do with how he would function if something happened to her. "I think it is dangerous," Kalia continued. "Because he is so far removed from how I do things on a daily basis, and he does not want to know. But it makes me the bad guy because I am dictating the budget." Frances, MSH mom of two, was actually frustrated and surprised by how things changed after they had children.

> He wants me to do everything for the children. We were more equitable before the kids. I did not think it would happen. I did not think it would change once we had kids. . . . He takes care of the cars, home repairs, cuts the grass, but not to my standards. I think he should hire someone to do that stuff and help me more. He just barks out orders. It's really frustrating. He doesn't volunteer to do anything. I can do a lot of it, but I would like some help. I don't say anything though. I don't ask him to do anything. I pray for him at the same time that I am trying to get everything done, and maybe he will change.

Some were outsourcing part of the more pressing, regularly scheduled household responsibilities, and some wished they could.

Gia had a housekeeper at one point, but had to let her go when they began paying for three private school tuitions. She said, "We can no longer afford a housekeeper. I'm doing homework, cleaning the house, volunteering at the school. There is not enough time in the day. I am commuting the kids more. To have someone come in and clean would be great. I feel like the house is too big. I'd rather spend time with the kids than clean. I'm spending half of my time on chores. Our parents lived simpler. Homes are too big now. It [cleaning] wastes time." Selena, like Gia, had to stop having someone clean for the family when the real estate they owned took some losses and all extra funds had to be used to keep the properties afloat. While Gia complained about her house being too large, Selena felt her suburban Fulton County home was too far from her and her husband's jobs and wanted them to move a little closer. "I would like to save time on transportation, and have someone prepare our meals. That's definitely a goal."

Interestingly most of the modified stay-at-home moms felt their responsibilities increased once they came home. In contrast many of the full-time-career moms thought things would be easier if they were home or made some modifications with work. In fact, they all felt there weren't enough hours in the day. Sheri was planning to leave her job once she and Clarence earned enough from their real estate firm to replace her income and purchase benefits, which they estimated to be about another two years. Sheri believed Clarence did more to help out than most husbands because his schedule was flexible, but she still felt like sometimes she had to do it all. She said, "I am tired. Now we have someone who comes in to help me, but that's why I want to quit. I want us to have more time together the two of us and us as a family."

During the interviews it became clear that, even though husbands weren't doing much more and still saw themselves as helpers, they did not expect or want their wives to do more. Natalie knew she struggled with keeping the house clean, and that was a point of contention for her and Charles. Natalie felt she just needed some help and wanted Charles to do more around the house, but Charles thought they should just hire someone to come in and do it all. Natalie, like many of the women in this study, felt she should be able to do it all and struggled with hiring help because she felt it diminished her role as wife and mother. Natalie said, "It feels like if I hire that stuff out I am no longer doing part of what I am supposed to do as a wife. Since I work, that means I am already doing something that is supposed to be his role; if I don't clean, what does he need me for besides sex, and we don't get to do much of that either." Natalie was not alone in feeling that if she didn't do it all she was shirking some of her responsibilities.

Keayba said she had to change her perspective on her role as a wife, especially with someone coming in to help her with the housekeeping and paying someone to handle the lawn. Her husband Kareem had to convince her to have someone come in. "I always felt like I should be able to do it because my mother did it by herself. It took Kareem explaining to me that my mom was a school teacher with much more time on her hands so it wasn't fair for me to compare myself to her." As a physician at a teaching hospital, between seeing patients, making rounds with her students, and conducting and writing research, she has very little time for vacuuming floors. "It seems like such a waste of my time. I am vacuuming and thinking, 'I could be working on that paper right now.'" She continued,

"Most of my frustration has to do with my work schedule," she said of her long hours and the days she also has to be on call. "I really want to figure out a change that will have me at home more. Kareem initiated conversations saying that it would not change if I cut back on work, but for me I think I may just want to. I just feel like I am putting too much into work."

One part of the second shift that is rarely discussed is marital intimacy. It is often assumed that married couples with children, especially younger children, do not have time or energy to maintain their romantic connections. I was interested in how these women thought about their after-hours relationships with their husbands and asked each of the participants to share how often they and their husbands go out on dates and where they went or what they did on their most recent date. I was surprised that all but four acknowledged they went on dates rather frequently. Some had standing weekly dates at their favorite restaurants, and others spoke of monthly dates that were designed to be a bit more special (e.g., weekend getaways). In most instances the focus on dating had taken place sometime after the second or third child arrived, when the couple realized they did not have enough time alone.

The couples often found that they could set aside time for a date, but finding time and energy to be intimate was a little more challenging. When asked to rate their sex lives according to enjoyment and frequency on a scale of one to ten with one being the lowest score, most gave somewhere between six and ten for enjoyment. About 80 percent thought sex could be more frequent, rating it between three and five. The most common explanation was being "tired." Kathy's sentiments were shared by most. She said, "We have great sex but not often enough. He is very patient. He understands if I am tired, but I know I should step up, it's not always about me. But at the end of the day, whatever drive I had earlier in the day is gone after I do baths and such." Kathy's understanding of their sex life is to be expected.

Kya discussed going to her gynecologist to complain about her nonexistent sex drive and the problems it was creating in her relationship with her husband. "My doctor said you have what I call the working moms effect; it's where no matter how much you want to be intimate, your busy lifestyle won't allow you to conjure the feelings."[10] Kathy and Kya were the most vocal with how their low libidos affected their sense of their sexual selves. Nevertheless, it was clear that more wives were affected than those who were willing to discuss the issue; they all spoke more in general terms about being overwhelmed than the specific ramifications of busyness on their romantic lives.

Overall, many of the women struggled with what their mothers were able to do and what they felt they are unable to do. They repeatedly demonstrate the ambivalence they feel about their roles as mothers, career women, and wives. Reminders like the one Kareem gave Keayba are key to many of the women's sense of self and accomplishment as they come to realize that their lives as professional women are very different from their mothers, even if their mothers were educated professionals as well. Most of the mothers with advanced degrees were educators, nurses, or librarians. Kia's mother, an attorney, was the only mother who had an advanced professional degree, and she was an entrepreneur who, from Kia's perspective, had found a way to balance her family life with considerable financial success. Sheri's mother has a PhD but used it to advance her career as an educator. Kalia's mother has a master's and completed some doctoral work in engineering but did not finish her PhD and never really worked in her career. As we talked, Keayba remembered that not only did her mother have a lot of time with her three children because she was a teacher but they also lived on the same street as her grandparents, and other family members and close friends were nearby. She said, "Even when my mom wasn't around there was a host of family and friends looking after us." Because their moms often worked in schools, they had the same breaks and holidays as their children. Even those who were not teachers and had typical forty-hour weeks had more flexibility in their schedules. Because many lived near family members, mothers had more familial and community support to help with the responsibilities of childcare.

4

Enculturating the Black Professional Class

Just before high school graduation season, in May 2006, in the midtown area of Atlanta, one teen was killed, one was in the hospital, and three were behind bars after being charged with aggravated assault and armed robbery with a firearm.[1] The teens attacked an African American marine veteran while he was walking down a public street. After trying unsuccessfully to flee their robbery attempt, he was forced to defend himself and ultimately killed one and wounded another of his assailants. The student who was killed was due to graduate with the rest of her class from one of the city's best high schools, and the hospitalized assailant was the son of a local middle school teacher. The community was astonished. Family members of the young woman who was killed described her as a sweet girl who had gotten involved with the wrong crowd. Students and school administrators reported they would not have expected this behavior from these youths, and the general population was in shock. Many people wondered what had gone wrong with these middle-class youths who did not present the common profile of those engaged in this type of activity. Editorials and letters to the editor decried the influence of hip-hop on these youths and its violent, materialistic message that discourages delayed gratification. Family and youth advocates criticized middle-class parents who, in striving for consumer goods, often neglect their children to increase their paychecks.

At the heart of the discomfort—not with the crime but with those who committed it and what their background should say about them—was the Black community's concern that the white community will continue to think "we are all the same"; they will continue to cross the street when they see us approaching or grab their handbags when we pass. That the crime was committed against a Black man in a well-to-do section of Atlanta complicates things even further. Residents of Atlanta are not alone in trying to reconcile and differentiate the images from the realities. Noted sociologist Elijah Anderson discussed these same complexities of race, class, and place in his ethnographic portrayal of the Chestnut Hill section of Philadelphia:

> In the upscale stores here, there is not usually apparent a great concern for security. During the day the plate-glass windows have appealing displays. . . . Once in a while, however, a violent incident does occur in Chestnut Hill. A holdup occurred at the bank in the middle of the day not long ago, ending in a shoot-out on the sidewalk. The perpetrators were Black, and two Black men recently robbed and shot up a tavern on the avenue. Such incidents give the residents here the simplistic yet persistent view that Blacks commit crime and white people do not. That does not mean that the white people here think that the Black people they ordinarily see on the streets are bound to rob them. . . . But the fact that Black people robbed the bank and that Blacks commit a large number of crimes in the area does give a peculiar edge to race relations. . . . Because everybody knows that the simplistic view does exist, even middle class Blacks have to work consciously against that stereotype. . . . Both groups [Blacks and whites] know the reality that crime is likely to be perpetuated by young Black males. The distinction of wealth—and the fact that Black people are generally disenfranchised and white people are not—operate in the back of the minds of people here. . . . Most Blacks in Chestnut Hill are middle class or even wealthy, although others come into the neighborhood as dayworkers. Yet many are disturbed by the inability of some whites to make distinctions—particularly between people who are out to commit crime and those who are not. (Anderson 2000, 17)

The families I interviewed faced this same conundrum, the persistent need to demonstrate middle-class respectability, particularly as they thought about how to raise their children. In this chapter, I discuss the strategies these professional women employed to enculturate their upper-middle-class Black children. Each group of women, MFC, MSH, and AFC, spoke at length about the careful thought they put into family decisions: where to live, where to send their children to school, and with what types of friends and communities to associate. They repeatedly discuss the importance of preparing their children for the "real" white world, while simultaneously grounding them in the history and culture of the African American community. By modifying their relationship with work, Black career moms believe they are ensuring their children's success by being available to prepare and enculturate them for a future that continues to be marred by raced, gendered, and classed oppression.

When asked about the perceived effects of race on their decisions about career and family, the women in the study spoke at length about the remnants of overt racism and the impact of covert racism. These women were particularly aware of the media's portrayal of stereotypes within the Black community and how those stereotypes, although enduring, are more insidious in a contemporary popular culture that sensationalizes a hypersexualized and violent ghetto culture and tags it Black. Kalia said, "I am always mindful about the way I carry myself. About not feeding into a stereotype and trying to improve the stereotype. [At work] I try to focus on girls who are my mirror to show them they could be me in ten years. It does not have to be the stereotypical image." Similarly, Jill said, "Race definitely affects my decisions. I am probably more cautious because we are criticized more often. I try to teach the children to be critical thinkers because we are being watched more carefully."

Housing became a key way professional Black families attempted to avert the effects of racism. Similar to Cory's mom, who insisted that her children go to HBCUs so they would not have to deal with the effects of being one of a few Blacks in a PWCU, most women in this study believed living in a predominantly Black, upper-middle-class neighborhood would similarly protect, instill confidence, and enculturate their children. Housing is one key through which Black professionals articulate a neo-politics of respectability.

Where They Live: Choosing Black Spaces

Two large brick walls on either side of the drive emblazoned in gold trim, gold lighting, and gold lettering announce the name of the subdivision. As I pass the signage and turn into the subdivision I am immediately greeted by what appears to be a "smaller" home with a parking lot, a pool, and a playground to the right; this is the clubhouse. I continue down the stretch of road, where massive brick homes sit on either side with neatly edged yards and trimmed hedges. "Keep straight, through the stop sign. Turn right at the first street on your right. We are in the cul-de-sac to the left," I recalled Sheri's directions to her house for the interview. I could hear the distinct sound of sprinklers gently spraying water to and fro through underground irrigation systems, the faint laughter of children playing and balls bouncing, and birds chirping in the trees. It was a beautiful early summer day in one of Atlanta's high-end suburbs. As I pulled up to the house, which filled half of the cul-de-sac, I parked in the driveway leading to the three-car garage. I could see Sheri's five-year-old son through the ornate lead glass door as he seemed to be expecting my arrival. I walked up the path sprinkled with bikes and scooters and waited as Larry ran to the back of the house to get his mother. I could see the deep colors of the great room through the front door and was excited about seeing the rest of the interior. Sheri came to the door and gave me a warm hug and smile. "Come on in," she said. "Excuse the mess." I could not see a mess. The house was immaculate, warm and inviting with all of the right variations of mahogany and auburn with gold accents. "Would you like a cup of tea?" Sheri asked after she had sent her curious son and older daughter to their rooms and sat down to feed her six-month-old daughter. I accepted and continued to look around her home as she busied herself in the kitchen. The windows in the back of the house gave a panoramic view of the "backyard," which was much more than a yard. Since the foundation of the house sat on a slight hill, the views included an expanse of beautiful blue skies rising above the treetops. "Wow! Is all of that your land?" I exclaimed to Sheri. "Yes," she replied. "Remember I told you my family was here?" I remembered the conversation in which she informed me that her family had just returned to their homes from their family reunion, but I assumed it was a small affair since it was at her house. I was wrong. Her backyard could easily have held close to two hundred people with room to move about, socialize, and play. We sat down to talk over the won-derful aroma of spiced tea. Sheri answered my opening question about how she chose this particular neighborhood:

> We already lived in Southwest because we liked living in Black neighbor-hoods where the kids could see images of themselves. We were looking to move into a bigger house, but we weren't sure if we could afford it. We wanted to stay in Southwest to be close to my parents and church. We had two kids in private school, and Shani [her daughter] is special needs so we had to pay for additional special services and tutors that the school did not provide. Clarence [her husband] was still working for the school system [he was an assistant principal], but he had started doing real estate on the side [buying and then renting or flipping homes]. We were seeing all of these subdivisions going up in Southwest and South Fulton, and we started driving around and just looking, and I guess hoping and praying. This subdivision was just going up, and we were one of the first families to take a look at it. They only wanted 325 [$325,000] for it [the house] which was a steal because now the homes in this subdivision are going for close to 5 [$500,000]. Since we got in early we had our choice of lots, and once we sold our other house we knew we could afford this one.

Like many of the women I interviewed who lived in southwest Atlanta or South Fulton County, Sheri's prospect of living in a community full of profes-sional Black families was a huge selling point. Sheri reflected this common sentiment,

> We love that we are surrounded by Black professional families. There's a couple on the next street over where the husband is an attorney with the District Attorney's Office and the wife is a physician at Emory Crawford

Long. Our kids get to play together. They don't go to the same school, but they play outside together, and our sons are in the same baseball league. We get together sometimes, and the whole community meets up at the pool or at meetings at the community clubhouse. A couple of families even started a community spaghetti dinner. It is really awesome.

Sheri described a community to which upper-middle-class white America is quite accustomed—the luxury of neighborhood amenities, private clubs, and upper-middle-class networks of contacts and supports. For Black America this is a relatively new phenomenon. Upper-class access was usually dependent on whether the predominantly white neighborhood would allow entry to Blacks. For the poor and working class, depending on networks, contacts, and supports has been a historic mainstay of the Black community, but now that optional dependence comes with perks and prestige few have previously experienced.

Atlanta has boasted a strong Black elite for several generations; however, an increase in northeastern and West Coast migrants in the 1990s created an influx in the Black professional population and brought new housing construction and new retail outlets to the Southwest and south Fulton areas of the city that had been predominantly and historically Black. As a native Atlantan, I understand the geography, but often when I drove visiting friends around the city of Atlanta, they were astonished at the neighborhoods and homes where African Americans live. Indeed, tour companies who specialize in providing their customers with an understanding of the city's African American history most often include the King Memorial, the Atlanta University Center, and Atlanta's southwest corridor as must-see attractions.

Many of the women in this study came to Atlanta for college or graduate school and decided to stay. Some ended up in Atlanta as the result of career relocations. Charlotte, who grew up in a rural town in Georgia but graduated from a northern HBCU, said she had college friends who were from Atlanta, and she had always heard about southwest Atlanta; she knew if she ever got to Atlanta that was where she wanted to live. "I heard good things, and I wanted to live close to downtown without heavy traffic. Being able to live around Black professionals made it ideal." Cara and her husband, Anthony, both Atlanta natives, moved back to Atlanta from Chicago.

We wanted to be in an all-Black neighborhood with positive, progressive individuals. There is a lot of history in this neighborhood and a lot of shakers and movers. We lived in an all-white neighborhood in Chicago. It is a great feeling knowing you can live in an all-Black nice area. I thought all cities had that, having grown up in Atlanta, but that is so far from the truth. It is healthy for kids to grow up here. The new suburbs of

Chicago do not blend races. They are predominantly white. There's nothing wrong with it, but for us, that's not what we wanted.

Keayba, a transplant from Michigan, echoed these sentiments. "We wanted a predominantly Black neighborhood. We liked the house and the general area with other African American families, like-minded, similar in terms of career types with resources. And also close enough to things we enjoy doing." In addition to being a great place to live for the Black professional elite, the mothers in this study emphasized that their neighborhood choice was important to their children's and their family's well-being, apparently with just cause because scholars have found that Black middle-class children are at greater risk of downward mobility than their white counterparts (Sharkey 2009). Black parents view preparing their children for race-related challenges they may encounter as paramount in their duties as parents (Feagin and Sykes 1994; Tatum [1987] 2000; Tatum 1999). Residential location has a tremendous impact on not only children's raced identities but also their classed identities (Harris 2013; Lacy 2007; Lareau [2003] 2011; Pattillo-McCoy 1999).

Both members of the couples who participated in this study decided together, in most instances, where they would live and what home they would make their primary residence, but the wives/mothers put the most effort into thinking about how their children would navigate racialized spaces. Not only were they concerned with race as it pertained to Black/white relations, but they were also interested in class-based racial relations as well. In other words, the potential for downward mobility may rise when middle-class children live in poor Black communities (Anderson 2000; Pattillo-McCoy 1999), and race-related education may be harder to perform in primarily white communities (Harris 2013; Lacy 2007; Tatum [1987] 2000).

When I asked Gia what brought her to Atlanta, she said they relocated because of her husband's job. Her family now lives in southwest Atlanta, but she told me when they first moved to the Atlanta area they lived outside the city. According to Gia, the young family was encouraged by their real estate agent to live within the metropolitan area of Atlanta but to look for a house outside the city limits. The couple was directed toward Alpharetta,[2] a northern suburb of the city with a growing population, increasing diversity (Alpharetta had been a notoriously white city until the 1990s), great schools, beautiful homes, and well-known shopping venues. When I asked Gia about why her family decided to move out of Alpharetta to southwest Atlanta, she replied, "We were tired of feeling like we did not belong. We wanted the kids to grow up around people who looked like them but also who acted like us [Black professionals]. We love Atlanta, but it can still be racist especially outside the city." Gia expressed a sentiment common among many women in this study.

Atlanta boasts amicable racial relationships, a by-product of the city's approach to the racial unrest during the civil rights movement. When other major southern cities were enduring violent and public civil unrest, Atlanta was developing a public/private partnership between the city's Black and white elite that paved the way for Maynard Jackson to be elected the first Black mayor of a major city in 1974 (Stone 1989). Mayor Jackson's election, coupled with the growth in industry Atlanta experienced as businesses looked for places they could open in the South, paved the way for the growth in the Black professional class (Pomerantz 1997). Atlanta developed a reputation as a model for racial harmony, especially in the South. The image appeared true as long as Blacks lived in one area and whites in another (Bayor 1996; Brown-Nagin 2011; Bullard and Johnson 2000; Sjoquist 2000). Gia continued,

> I will never forget. When we first moved here and we were driving around [in Alpharetta], we got a little turned around and were holding up traffic a bit, yes, I'll admit it [she laughed]. Anyway, this white guy rolls down his window and says "Get out of the way, 'n—r." I grew up in Michigan so I am used to a bit of that, but I did not expect it. It is much more blatant here, their disdain for Black people, and we did not want the kids to grow up around that.

In Black upper-middle-class communities most of the families were trying to re-create the neighborhoods of their youth. They explained that the benefits to their children were insurmountable.

When talking to the women it became clear that many grew up in tight-knit communities surrounded by family and friends, and re-creating some of that connectedness for their children was very important to them and informed some of their choices. Because Gia did not decide to become a stay-at-home mom until her youngest child was a few months old, all of her children experienced day-care, and all three went to a home-care provided in her neighborhood. Gia reported, "I was skeptical of home care at first because I was raised by my grandmother who was always at home. But Ms. Brenda was in my subdivision and had her whole basement dedicated to taking care of kids. Most of the children lived in the neighborhood, and I knew the parents, and it ended up feeling like home . . . like how I was raised." In the expected African American cultural ethos that believed younger women had children and older women raised them, Gia's mother left her child to her mother, who raised Gia while surrounded by family and family friends. As the history of Black family life demonstrates, socializing and sheltering children has rarely been the sole responsibility of the parents of origin. Often to whom the children belong or what household is responsible for their care is not "a particularly meaningful question" (Stack

[1974] 1997, 90). This communal focus on children is the way most of these women were raised. Even for those raised in two-parent households, family members and family friends were always around and a constant source of care. It seemed that these women experienced similar things, despite the different geographic locations of their childhoods.

Marilyn, who spent many of her formative years in rural Georgia, talked about spending time with her uncles whom she saw as extensions of her father. Kalia, born in Washington, DC, talked about being raised by a community of "Aunties." Keayba, raised in the Midwest, spoke of "MaDear" who lived across the street and several aunts and uncles who lived in the same neighborhood. Natalie's mother is from rural south Georgia, and she remembers the tight-knit network that characterized the community of her youth: "My mom has six siblings, and they have multiple children, and I have a stepfamily that is very big, and everyone lives in Georgia within an hour's drive. My great-grandmother was still living when I was a child, and so we were around my grandmother's extended family, and they were all involved in my life. We saw each other regularly, and all of the children spent a lot of time together. We got together for church and holidays, and visiting was expected all of the time." Similarly, Jill talked about being with her extended family on her father's side every weekend when she was growing up and visiting her mother's side for every holiday. And Sheri, who grew up in Atlanta, said she had family in North Carolina, and she and her siblings spent just about every summer with them. "My grandmother would make bologna sandwiches and send us to Vacation Bible School," she reminisced. Memories like these make these women and their husbands very adamant about making sure their children grow up with similar experiences. "It really is part of the reason why I convinced Clarence to let me host my family's reunion here," said Sheri. "I wanted the kids to have that feeling that I had when I was growing up of being connected to something larger than myself and larger than my immediate surroundings. I think it is really important, especially for Black children."

Myra most exemplified the desire for the family and community "feel" she grew up with to be a part of her children's daily experience. Neither Myra nor her husband lives near family, but they both grew up in families where fictive kin and extended family were very important to their development, so they chose their neighborhood for precisely that reason. Myra, a small woman with a big personality, described her 1970s upbringing. It reminded me of movies such as Matty Rich's *The Inkwell* and Spike Lee's *Crooklyn*:

R. What motivated you to choose this neighborhood?

M. This neighborhood reminded me of my neighborhood in New Orleans when I was growing up.

R. Did you grow up with a lot of family nearby?

M.   Yes! [with enthusiasm]. There was family and like friends of the family. Like my parents' friends that they grew up with lived near us and they had kids and so all of us were growing up together. Girl, we rolled in this big posse of kids ranging in age from like eight to sixteen, and we were all family, real cousins or fake cousins. We all thought we were related so we couldn't even date each other . . . even if we weren't.

R.   Why did this neighborhood remind you of home?

M.   We wanted this neighborhood because it is full of Black professionals with young families, and we figured we would all know each other and our kids would grow up together. A lot of us knew each other before we moved here or had known each other through other things, or met pretty quickly. Like one of my neighbors is in New Century Moms [one of the support groups] with me, and our kids take swimming lessons together.

R.   That is really cool. Where do they take lessons?

M.   Right here in the community pool. We just have a private coach come and give lessons just for the kids in our neighborhood.

R.   Wow! That's really cool and convenient.

M.   Yeah! In this community we look out for each other! I really like that. It's what I wanted.

And Myra is not the only one who seems to be searching for a sense of community or actively building community. When I asked the women about their social networks and supports, they all acknowledged leaning heavily on family and friends and a few select formal organizations.

It Takes a Village:
The Importance of Black Women's Support Structures

As discussed in chapter 3, these professional Black women relied on their church attendance and their relationship with God to help them navigate their roles, particularly as wives. All (but one) of the women in this study were active members of a church. Although they belonged to various denominations, all considered themselves Christian. They were all members of predominantly and historically Black congregations, and two worshipped at churches where their husbands were the pastors. I heard the importance they placed on spirituality or a relationship with God when they discussed their reliance on prayer, faith, or biblical scriptures for insight and direction. I also saw how important the social networks formed at church have been to offset some complications of childcare. In addition, the church communities offer the caveat of social support to the women, not only for developing ideas of marriage and motherhood, but also for promoting active participation in communal welfare, especially as it pertains to raising their children.

Cory and Brian, transplants to Atlanta in the 1990s, created a "village" through their church membership that outlived allegiance to that church. Before Cory and Brian started their own church in the early 2000s, they had been members of one of the older churches in southwest Atlanta for about ten years. With a congregation of a couple thousand members, it had at one time been considered one of the largest churches in the city, but the influx of megachurches, both new and old, have recently changed the definition of a "large" church. Cory and her husband were very involved in the church. Brian, an associate minister to the senior pastor, was well liked and respected for his clear and concise sermons that linked the scriptures to everyday struggles. While Cory did not hold any formal role in the church, almost everyone knew her. Like most of the women, she was in the women's ministry, and her children could be seen on Wednesdays in children's Bible Study and on Sunday in Sunday school and in the children's choir. Through close friendships with several of the women in the women's ministry Cory and Brian began to socialize outside church with these families; these professional parents were close in age, and their children were close in age. Similar to Myra's description of the New Orleans neighborhood in which she grew up, these friendships blurred the line between family and not family. Kids called their parents' friends "Aunt" and "Uncle" and referred to their playmates as family.

This network of family was not only present on Sunday at church, but for many of the families—especially transplants like Cory and Brian—it was also in operation every holiday, for many vacations, and even for some of the children when they got to school. "We have Thanksgiving breakfast together, we have New Year's brunch together, and we have Kwanzaa together . . . every year." Three of the core families in the network of friends (about ten couples, each with one to four children) host a holiday gathering as a pot-luck. According to Cory, the host family makes the primary meal, and everyone else brings sides, desserts, paper products, and drinks. "It all started with Thanksgiving":

A lot of us were from out of town. The break was too short to travel home. We knew some people did have family in Atlanta and would want to have dinner with their family, so Nia decided to do breakfast. Nia and her kids prepare pancakes, her husband fries a turkey. The rest of us bring toppings and all the other stuff, paper goods, fruit, Champagne for Mimosas! It's great. We all sit around eating, and once we're done and it's all settled everyone plays flag football in her backyard. The kids and the adults . . . it is truly great. One time Brian gave Nia's little boy the ball, picked him up and ran with him for a touchdown because no one could reach his flags. It was the cutest thing.

By the time Cory finished telling me the story I couldn't help but laugh. I could just imagine all the fun they were having, and, given the typically mild weather in Atlanta for Thanksgiving, it's the perfect picture of families in the fall. According to Cory, the families in their network have a similar set-up for Kwanzaa and New Year's Day. These annual activities have become so popular that families prepare their schedules around them. And their family members, who live out of town, arrange their schedules to be in Atlanta to attend these events. Cory used her parents as an example. "My parents usually come for Christmas. They used to leave before New Year's. Now they stay for our Kwanzaa dinner and our New Year's brunch." She continues, "Some families have even moved away from Atlanta, but if they find themselves back for Thanksgiving, Kwanzaa, or New Year's, they make sure they come by. . . . We're still family."

Cory and Brian's story, while the most extensive, was not the only one where families had formed bonds with other families and created their own "extended family village." Keayba has a network of friends from her church that she sees once a week. "We all go out to brunch every Sunday after church with the kids. It gives us a chance to get caught up and just be together like family. I love having the kids grow up like this."

Creating Family Support Networks

Understanding that most of these families are not natives of Atlanta, one of the pointed questions I posed to each woman was which individual(s) they listed on forms for their children in case of emergency. This is usually a role reserved for the parents, sisters, or brothers of the mother or father so that the children are being taken care of by family members, consanguineal or companionate. For families whose closest kin are either not present or unreliable due to age or illness, close friendships take the place of blood.

When Jill was negotiating the care of two small children and an ailing mother and grandmother, a family friend intervened. "I met Rosa through a casual friend, and I think she realized I was having a hard time and she just adopted me into her family. I remember just after those first few weeks when you stay inside with your new baby, Rosa called and said, 'bring the baby over and you and Paul go out for the evening.' It was just what we needed, but we would never have asked. Now I refer to her as my godmother, and she is my kids' godmother. I really do not know what I would do without her." Rosa, the woman Jill refers to as godmother, is approximately Jill's mother's age. "She treats us all as if she were my mother and the kid's grandmother. She babysits for us, we spend holidays together, and she is truly like my mother." When Jill was taking care of her mother who had dementia and her grandmother who was in the final stages of heart disease, she said, "Rosa kept me from going under. There were times when I did not think I was going to make it, and she was there for me even though she had her own family to worry about." According to Jill there really is no distinction now. "I am her daughter, and, even though I still have my mother, Rosa is my mother. She is who I call when something is on my mind, and I don't even have to tell her. She knows. I am so blessed. . . . My family is so blessed to have her."

Rosa entered Jill's life as a surrogate mother of sorts. Other women in the study depended on women their own age or slightly older for support. Gia talked about her long-time friends, the Johnsons. Ciara Johnson, Gia's best friend, was the person she relied on in case of an emergency. "She is who I talk to about everything. We talk about the kids, our marriages, work, everything." Gia's and Ciara's families also get together regularly. Gia explained, "The Johnsons are definitely friends that are extended family. We do things together, we spend a lot of time together, and we trade-off on Sunday dinners. We are two different families, but we spend time together like we are one, and it's great."

Even families with extended family ties to Atlanta got together with other unrelated families primarily to support their child-rearing and marriages. Linda said she relied on one particular couple a lot. "Our husbands have known each other since high school. They are both from Philadelphia, and we all got married around the same time and became good friends. They have a second home in Florida, and we all go there for vacations. It's really cool, and it's fun and really helpful to be able to share so much in common with raising the kids and you know . . . marriage stuff." Selena also talked about friends she and her husband got together with regularly. "Our group is kind of formal because we have a name, and we get together kind of regularly. We were also started with the goal of supporting marriage and children so it's for men and women. Really it's for families." Selena explained,

> We meet once a month and for birthdays and special occasions. It's like Mocha Moms, but our goal is to support marriage and children as best as we can. It's comic relief and stress relief. The woman who started it and named it struggled with breast cancer, and it was her way of pulling all of her friends together as she was going through treatments and fighting to get better. She's a survivor now, but when she was sick we all pitched in to help her and just kept it going once she was doing better. We do outings together, and we try to do a trip once per week. We have different connections. There is one core person, and we are all affiliated with her. She has the party house. All the men know each other, too, and that makes it a lot of fun. We really just try to support each other's marriage and family goals.

Similarly to Selena and Linda, Cara has family in the Atlanta area. She and her husband are one of the few couples where both husband and wife are from Atlanta. While Cara has enlisted the support of her family and close friends for helping with her children, she says most of her support comes from being a member of New Century Moms, a support group that focuses on the needs of African American professional mothers as they balance careers (previous and current) and families. This group is similar to the nationally recognized Mocha Moms (a support group for stay-at-home moms of color), and, although it was initially founded for career moms, it now includes the needs of stay-at-home moms, too. The mothers who are members periodically join together for meetings, mom's night out, play-dates, and networking opportunities. While the organization has no charter and is not yet nationally recognized, Cara and other participating mothers say they do not know what they would do without it. Cara, a member since her daughter was born, sees it as the friend she needed when she was negotiating being "at home" and starting her own business. "It was great to be around like-minded women. These were women who were trying to do things we have not seen before." She continued, "I had not seen a stay-at-home mom/entrepreneur before, and I look for women to be in empowering situations. This [New Century Moms] gives me a support group for that."

In addition to stay-at-home mom support groups and the informal support they found in "just like family" friendships, most women in this study were also members of two of the oldest historically Black sororities and found much support there.[3] Both of these sororities are service organizations; unlike predominantly white sororities that focus on college-age women, these two historically Black sororities as well as the other members of the National Pan-Hellenic Council see their charge as mobilizing college-age and adult members of the Black community for public service throughout their lives.[4] Their membership and active participation is seen as "a lifetime commitment" (Giddings [1988] 2009). Each of the fifteen women has varying levels of activity within their sororities. Only five were active either on the national level (simply paying dues and voting in national elections but not affiliated locally) or on the graduate chapter level. Of those, only three went to their monthly sorority meetings and participated in committee activities. The majority believes it is difficult to maintain a commitment to the sorority with such busy lives, particularly as mothers, wives, and career women, but most plan to return once children are out of the house. Nancy said, "I only have time for one activity so it was Delta or church. I figured I need church," she said with a laugh. "I can come back to Delta once the kids are older." Although many of the women were not actively engaged in the formal structure of their sororities, they continued to rely on the friendships they had developed through their college membership, before marriage and children. Many also used their lifetime membership to connect to other sorority "sisters," locate support systems, get referrals, and network for jobs, schools, and other resources.

Marilyn said she had not been "active" for a number of years, but she and some of her "sisters" made a point of getting away together once a year. She said, "They are some of my closest friends. We all live in different cities now and don't get to talk all of the time. But they are who I turn to when I really need help, and when we get together it is a real opportunity for us to just 'be'; not worry about anything but supporting each other." Keayba is one of the few women active in her sorority. She attributes her commitment to her mother and father who were always active in their respective organizations throughout Keayba's childhood. Not only does Keayba stay involved because of her own commitment, but it is also a way for her to spend time with her mother, sister, and sister-in-law, each of whom is a member of her sorority. "It is something we all get to do together and have in common. We go to meetings together. We go to regional and national conventions together. It's just really fun to have that."

All of the women engaged in some sort of "village" creation, despite their at-home status. They found these "villages" to be very important to their personal sanity as well as the development of their families. For many of the women in the study, these "villages" imparted a lot of value about their raced- and classed-based identities that they wanted to transmit to their children.

Most of the families lived in southwest Atlanta or south Fulton County. Only nine lived outside the area, scattered throughout four metropolitan counties (Cobb, DeKalb, Douglas, and Clayton), and five of these families resided in majority white communities—four in Cobb County and one in Dekalb County. When I asked Frances if and how she stayed connected to her community even though her commute was almost an hour, she said, "I grew up in southwest Atlanta, so even though we live in Duluth, we drive back to southwest so I can make sure my kids grow up in the Black community." For each of the women, regardless of whether they lived in the southwest Atlanta/south Fulton County geographic boundaries, the region remained a considerably important part of their lives. They commuted into the area to attend church and visit with family and friends, and some came daily to drop their children off at school. Indeed, a lot of thought went into children's schooling, with the focus on not only academic rigor and college preparedness but also investments in Black cultural heritage.

School Choice: Strategizing Raced and Classed Identities

Several scholars have written about middle-class Blacks' access to premier schools and neighborhoods. In *Black Picket Fences* sociologist Mary Patillo-McCoy discussed the fact that the college-educated parents she interviewed in a subsection of Chicago still had to deal with mediocre schools that served the poor, working class, and middle class. In Karyn Lacy's *Blue Chip Black*, some African Americans living in Prince George's County, Maryland, and Fairfax County, Virginia, chose these locations according to their views on their own and their children's best chances at navigating the "real" world. While residential location was an important factor in developing race and class identity for the subjects in these studies, choice of school—at the lower, upper, and collegiate level—was equally important. Middle-class and upper-middle-class families had to consider how their children would be perceived in Black and white social and educational locations.

We know what happens when the combination of racial and economic disadvantage converge upon a neighborhood or school district (see Fordham 1996; Pattillo-McCoy 1999; Wilson 2009). Even when a subdivision is middle-class or upper-middle-class Black, it is rarely in a school district by itself or completely among other subdivisions with the same demographics. With the mix comes a school setting where the school's overall poor performance, low teacher expectations, and less challenging instruction limits the abilities of all students but particularly those of the middle class, who should presumably be buffered from these weaknesses. As suggested, purchasing (through private schools) or finagling (through magnet schools or the No Child Left Behind Act)[5] a "better" education is only beneficial in the school setting if youth are not still intrigued by outside forces that beckon them to mimic the performance of "ghetto" culture as authentically Black in defiance of what their parents teach them (Jackson 2001).

Most children in this study were younger than school age at the time of the study (six and under). Nevertheless, schools' perceptions in relationship to families of color and schools' performance in their neighborhoods were primary considerations for all the families as they studied early childhood education and encouraged cultural education and pride as main focuses. Most of the women were zoned for southwest Atlanta schools and south Fulton schools. A few were zoned for west Cobb, and one family was zoned for south Dekalb. Of the families who participated in the study with school-age children, eleven sent their children to the Monroe School,[6] three enrolled their children in public schools outside their neighborhood schools, and one enrolled their children in another private school. For the remaining eight families, their oldest child had not reached school age, but this did not diminish parental concern about where to educate their children. All of the parents wanted to make sure their children received the best education possible. This, like residential choice, often meant they wanted their children not only in high-performing schools but in schools where they would be educated by African American professionals and with the children of professional African Americans.

Myra, who is the main caregiver for her not-yet-school-age children, said she saw herself doing private school for their elementary years and then public high school because the neighborhood elementary school was not meeting the needs of the residents. She said, "I know some parents who have been trying to work with the school, but the principal doesn't seem to want parent involvement." Kathy and Monica, who are also primary caregivers for children who are not yet school-age, had similar sentiments. Monica said with a bit of disdain, "I don't like public schools. My family taught public schools. What I know and what I hear, I know I don't like it. My oldest is not meant for public school. Private school is a better education, and it's without me being on top of it all the time, which I know public school would require."

Echoing some of Monica's and Myra's sentiments, Kathy said, "The public schools are missing some things. They are deficient in some things. He [her son] has a head start being at home. I do not want him to be held back or to not reach his potential because of issues at school." And Keayba, who grew up in public schools but has some reservations about how they have changed, said, "We are in the process of comparing. I would like for them to go to public school, but I am concerned about the things I've seen in regard to public school—the focus on test scores, problems with discipline, and overcrowding." Most have some trepidation about public school due to poor academic conditions.

While academic performance is a major concern for all of the families, most seemed to feel that providing students with an academic environment that was conducive to learning, celebrated the child's strengths, and kept discipline issues at bay were wonderful foundations for whatever academic rigor they may need past elementary school. Protecting their children from racial incidents with whites and cultural incidents with other Blacks is a large part of their concern and focus. Myra said, "I am really concerned about school, and I factor [race] in when I look at schools. The places we go I make sure there is no rebel flag. I know that there are certain places where we are not accepted. I am conscious of that." Linda said, "I expose my kids to Black history, but I do not teach prejudice." Kia, Selena, and Jill concurred when they said they wanted their children to be proud of their heritage. "Maintaining their self-esteem is of the utmost importance." To that end families found the Monroe School curriculum to be exactly what they were looking for in early childhood and grade school education. Children were learning about their cultural heritage, developing self-confidence, and getting a strong education, and the school prided itself on being affordable for working families. Kia and Trevor enrolled their three children in the Monroe School. Trevor said, "It is excellent. It reinforces our ideas of producing a positive self-image. We went to predominantly white schools when we were kids. But we want them to go to school where our ideas are reinforced."

For the three families who chose public schools, they were schools that their children were not zoned for, and it took considerable effort to get them enrolled. When Karen's family moved from New Orleans after Hurricane Katrina, they were living in West Cobb County. The school they were zoned for was okay but had a good deal of residential turnover because much of the population was seasonal Latino migrant workers. While Karen assured me she had no problem with the composition of the school's demographics, she was concerned because she believed her children, who were already coming into a new situation, needed greater stability. Believing her family was not financially able to pay for private school tuition as she and her husband had taken pay cuts upon moving to Atlanta, a friend told her she could apply for the lottery at another school to try to get "permission" to enroll her kids in a different zone. Karen soon learned that it was not as simple as going down to the board of education to apply for a number. She learned from the same friend that the lottery really meant first come/first serve. Each school in the district had a certain number of out-of-district spaces depending on how many spaces were left once the students zoned for the school were enrolled. This meant that when the out-of-district sign-up date was released, you had to get to the district office early enough to get assigned a space at the school of choice. Many people literally "camped out" for these spaces. Karen and a friend camped out, like fans camping out at the box office to get tickets to their favorite concert as soon as the box office opened. "I didn't know what else to do," Karen said,

> Steve and I weighed our options. We knew this was one of the best schools in the city, and we knew if we were there early we were likely to get a spot. The guys decided to take the late shift for safety. They didn't want us outside overnight at the district office. Steve and Darren [her friend's husband] got there at about eleven [that night], and they still weren't the first in line. They had a tent, chairs, blankets, and snacks. My friend Tiffani and I got there at about six and took over our place in line from Steve and Darren so they could get ready for work. The office didn't open until 8 A.M. so we were still waiting for a while before it opened, but we made it. The office opened. We were first and second for Walton. Thank God, the people in front of us wanted Smith. And we got our kids in. It was such a relief. . . . We heard from another parent that Walton was full by nine.

When I asked Karen how her friend Tiffani knew what to do, she said Tiffani had heard from parents who had gone through the same process the year before. No one told you at the district office. If you showed up at eight when the office opened, or even at six like Tiffani and Karen but without someone in line already holding your space, you were likely to have to go to your neighborhood school and try again the next year. "That would have been devastating," Karen said. "I mean I am sure they [her kids] would have been fine. But I would have felt like a failure . . . you can't get that year back."

Karen and Steve were not the only parents to go to such lengths to ensure their children got into "good" schools. Natalie and Charles sent their three children to private school through kindergarten and then did a mix of public, independent, and magnet schools. According to Natalie, "They all went to private school for the first years. It had more to do with controlling the environment and giving them a leg up on the competition." Selena and John initially had their children enrolled in private school. When their middle child was ready to go to first grade, they moved him and their oldest daughter to a highly sought-after public elementary school outside their home's school district. Selena anticipates sending her kids to private school again for middle school. Cory's daughter, like Karen's, was out of zone, but they were using the address of a family member and hoping no one would wonder why she never rode the bus and neighbors never saw her outside playing. Once national news outlets started reporting on women facing federal criminal charges for "falsifying" records, Cory got a little nervous and started looking for alternatives.[7] "We are going to have Kesah apply for the magnet program at Rivington next year when she goes to high school. We don't want her to have to lie about where she lives, and we want her to feel free to invite friends over after school and on weekends."

Private schools seem to be a great alternative, particularly when they can address all of a parent's needs, but they can also be quite costly. Denise and her husband pay $22,000 per year for each of their two elementary age daughters to attend an area private school. Denise says it is well worth it because the public schools in her area are "academically deplorable." Kalia has chosen a charter school as a viable option for her kindergarten son because it has "public school diversity and private school standards without the cost." Sheri and Clarence had both of their school-age children enrolled in the Monroe School, until their daughter's speech therapy needs became too much for the school to handle. "By sending her to the neighborhood school we are able to get free speech therapy. They will come to her school, and we do not have to deal with the logistics of the therapist at Monroe and then seek additional therapy outside of school for what Monroe is unable to do."

Gia has her two youngest children at the Monroe School, but she commutes with a carpool for her oldest to go to a magnet middle school on the north side of town. She said she worried for more than a year about where her son would go to middle school. She was concerned about the environment of her neighborhood school where delinquent behaviors instead of academic success were celebrated. She opted to send her son to a school almost an hour's commute on the other side of town because it was a math and science magnet school where her son could excel in the subjects he liked and receive encouragement from parents, teachers, and peers. Gia explained,

> I would love to do public school in my neighborhood, but Georgia is number forty-nine on test scores and the schools are overcrowded. A new middle school in our area opened overcrowded. How do you open overcrowded? Aren't you supposed to do projections that include anticipated neighborhood growth? You can tell by stuff like that that Georgia is still segregated. A new school in Alpharetta would not be overcrowded when it opened. Parents take control and run their schools. The school in our area dropped science lab. My son loves science. He goes to school so he can do science so I cannot send him to a school that does not have science lab. We love this area but the trade-off is the schools.

Gia is referring to the trade-off in neighborhood versus school excellence, a complaint most of the women discussed. Gia and her family moved to southwest Atlanta from Alpharetta so that her son could see African American professionals on a regular basis and have visual role models of African American success, but Gia said she was forced to juxtapose this agenda with combating the youth culture that threatens to undo all her efforts toward preparation for his future. Gia said she travels almost an hour one way for her son's magnet science school because "what their friends think is so important to these kids, and I need to make sure that what his friends say lines up with what we are telling him." Gia also struggled with what she saw as the reality of raising an African American boy into a man. "He needs to be prepared for a lot of things his white counterparts will not have to think about. He has to excel at school, but he also has to know how to cope in a world that will always see him as Black no matter how successful he is." Gia felt she had prepared her oldest son for these challenges by first sending him to the Monroe School to develop his knowledge of self and sense of Black pride, but she had to find something else for him when it was time for middle school because Monroe stops at fifth grade.

Gia and many other study participants who had children enrolled at the Monroe School believed Monroe to be one of the premier schools in the area. Located about ten miles from the Atlanta airport on the southeast side of the city, 48 percent of the families in this study had at least one child enrolled in that school. They chose it for its academic standards and its attention to the self-esteem of African American children. Linda said, "We sent them to Monroe because we wanted them to have a strong foundation. In these times our kids have to get a jump. We wanted to get our children exposed earlier. Be on point. We will look for public schools, but we wanted the early education to set the foundation for public school."

Kia, who attended majority white schools through her formative years, agreed that Monroe's focus on Black history and pride were paramount for her and her family. Additionally, having a preschool program (ages two to five) and a grade school program (grades kindergarten to fifth), many parents liked the fact that Monroe could see their children through to middle school. Gia's two grade school sons had attended since preschool, and Gia was looking forward to enrolling her daughter as she was quickly approaching two.

Some of the women I interviewed were friends of Gia. I met others while following Gia to various sporting events and programs for her children. Over and over again, regardless of their children's age or how far they had to commute, these women explained to me that it was highly important that their children get a foundation in a predominantly Black school that stressed Black history, Black culture, high self-esteem, and high expectations. "They get a good dose of education, high expectations, and love," said Marilyn, mother of three, with two enrolled at the school. And according to Cory, who is zoned for her neighborhood's predominantly white county school, her children "would be able to deal with the real world once they were older and secure in what they could do as Black people rather than what they could not do."

None of the families chose the school for its good education alone, but all were adamant about its focus on African American cultural values that held in high esteem education and respect for oneself and one's culture. With tuition less than $8,000 per year, Monroe was also $10,000 less than its closest majority white competitor.[8] "They do a really good job with the children," said Linda. "I know Melissa is going to be taught, disciplined, and loved when I drop her off every day." Not only does the school take care of its children, but it also plans its offerings with the children's mostly professional parents in mind. The after-school program, for instance, offers dance classes, music lessons, and homework help. Monroe also organizes team sports and asks parents to volunteer as coaches. And with an active parent-teacher association (PTA), the school, a privately funded corporation rather than a 501(c)(3), organizes its own fundraisers and family fun outings to raise funds for its operations and curricular and instructional needs.

At one of these school-sponsored events that I attended with Kya we talked about her decision to leave her job. She had been working as an administrator in one of the county school systems and, after having her son, decided not to return to her position. In between the scenes of the children's play, Kya and I talked about her decision to leave her job and enroll Sean, her son, in the Monroe School. "It was a bit of a struggle having Sean at the Monroe School on only one salary [her husband worked full time as a marketing director], but I am able to be more attentive, to volunteer at the school, and to just be a more present part of his life. I know this is a great opportunity for both of us." She continued, "I get to be the mother I want to be, and he gets to have the childhood I think will set him up for life."

Kya and her husband Timothy were taking pictures as the children in Sean's kindergarten class commemorated some of the people involved in the civil rights movement. Sean was dressed as Ralph David Abernathy, the Atlanta native and friend of Dr. King who rarely gets acknowledged in the national record. Other children, whose parents were barely born during the civil rights movement, came parading onstage dressed as Fannie Lou Hamer, Thurgood Marshall, and Daisy Bates. During a break between scenes, Kya and I resumed our conversation. She leaned over and told me how difficult it was to be in the public school system, to simply educate kids: "It seemed like all of the forces were against them, and we were just trying to give them life vests knowing the vest might keep them from drowning but could never get them to safety. I could not have that for Sean, and I could not risk Sean being in that kind of space because I was too busy to pay attention to him or give him what he needs." Kya anticipated enrolling her daughter at the Monroe School once she is two or three and having Ms. Bridgette pick them both up after school.

Like Kya, all of the families were consciously concerned about their children's racial or cultural identity and chose to place them in environments where they felt their children would be shielded from the varied effects of race-based inequalities. Whether choosing a predominantly Black school, a predominantly Black neighborhood, or a Black church, parents focused on developing their children's sense of self in what they felt was a protective environment marked by not only racial and cultural immersion but also classed identity. While they did not explicitly identify this as a reason to change their relationship with their careers, it became clear as I got to know them and their families that "being available" was a strategic mothering principle rooted in both economic and cultural considerations.

Cultivating Black Middle-Class Children

Sociologist Annette Lareau, who interviewed the families of fifth-grade children, suggests a strategy of "concerted cultivation": parents engage in an intense focus on preparing children with the skills they will need to be successful in mainstream American life. She argues that parents' dual focus on keeping children involved in extracurricular activities and learning to have conversations with adults teaches children how to negotiate for what they need, question authority (in presumably respectful ways), and expect relationships with adults that are more egalitarian than authoritative. For Lareau, these practices, while not limited to upper-middle-class families, are most often rooted there and, by extension, delivered by a host of coaches, tutors, activity directors, and so on. In contrast, the process of "natural growth" is practiced most among those in the lower social classes wherein children do just that, grow naturally. In this pattern parents have neither the time nor the resources to keep their children involved in activities outside those offered by their schools, and children spend more time with relatives and in free play in their neighborhoods than they do in organized activities. Likewise, according to Lareau, these families often do not have a good relationship with the authoritative bureaucracy of the schools their children attend, in large part because they have had to engage with these bureaucratic figures in various agencies to obtain social resources. Their children, in turn, do not learn to negotiate these spaces; instead, the children learn to distrust them and in some instances be antagonistic toward them. Lareau reiterates her belief that both parenting practices are valuable, but, given the social class markers that are valued in our society, she says that children raised with concerted cultivation are likely to acquire the cultural capital useful to navigating professional spaces.

Lareau's study mingles with Karen Hansen's *Not-So-Nuclear Families.* Hansen skillfully identifies the various ways in which network-organized childcare is rarely completely reliant on nuclear family supports and differentially incorporates others based on the class position of the family, the geographical and spatial location of the family, and the availability of reliable kin or fictive kin (2005). By looking across class, Hansen expands Carol Stack's focus on the networks of the poor and working class and disrupts the dichotomous perspective asserted by Lareau, which pits the poor and working class against the upper middle class for reaching the American ideal of success. Hansen's explanation of how kin and fictive kin networks sustain families across class is a much-needed addition to the literature. Hansen also produces a noteworthy and important analysis of male participation in these familial networks. We still, however, have very little insight on professional Black women and their families because Hansen's study features only white families.[9] When I attempt to situate Black professional women's caregiving networks within Hansen's study, I find that as Black professional women leave the safety and familiarity of the poor and working-class network model, family focused and family reliant,[10] they wrestle with what to do when they enter the professional middle class and are trying to maintain the shared matrifocal culture, the foundation of Black family and community survival.[11]

Lareau includes race and class in her explanation of the importance of cultural capital in the lives of Black children ([2003] 2011). Lareau presents the very compelling case that Alexander Williams (a Black boy) is more similar to Garrett Tallinger (a white boy) because they both come from similar class backgrounds and both sets of parents practice concerted cultivation. For Lareau, although Alexander may experience some social differences because of his race, his class and particularly his parents' emphasis on developing his cultural capital so he may compete in the predominant social system make him more like Garrett than a Black boy being raised poor or working class like Harold, the Black boy being raised in the housing projects and guided by "natural growth."

Lareau's analysis is particularly compelling as it relates to the families in this study. All but three of these families, even when their children were not yet school-age, had their children engaged in organized music, sports, or arts lessons; two of those three focused their energy and time on church activities or informal play groups. Only one family did not focus on their children's calendar of extracurricular events, but in our conversations the family indicated that they were expecting to begin such engagement in the near future. All of these families, as Lareau suggested, saw this as a way to give their children an advantage in an increasingly competitive world.

Gia, who complained that her husband wanted the children involved in so many things but expected her to take them to all the activities, was frustrated with herself for not enrolling her youngest child in as many activities as a toddler and preschooler as her two older children:

> I feel guilty because I have not put Alese in anything yet, but it is so hard because I am running around with the other two, and I do less for Andre than I did for Arthur at his age. Andre has not had piano yet. I wonder if they are missing out or if I want it too badly for them. I have to be the Hannah [referring to the biblical character]. I am constantly asking myself am I a bad mother, am I supposed to be more hands-off, but it seems like they need so much just to get a chance.

When I asked Gia what her children were involved in she gave me her weekly schedule, "Tae kwon do for Arthur 7:30 to 8:45 Monday and Wednesday; soccer practice for Andre on Monday 6:00 to 7:15; games for Andre and Arthur on Saturday and Sunday during the fall; basketball for Andre and Arthur during the winter; swimming for all at the YMCA on Saturdays; church activities during the week and on Sunday; Alese gymnastics Tuesday and Thursday." Of course, the level of activity for each family depended on not only the number of children but also the availability of moms to act as chauffeurs. Gia continued,

> Since we had the kids and I have been home, my responsibilities have increased. We do not have a housekeeper anymore. I have to do housework, manage homework, volunteer at school, and there is not enough time in the day. I am commuting the kids in and out of Atlanta. Before I

was home when I was still working, Ben would take them to school, and I would pick them up. Ben would get home to take them to their activities. Homework was still on me, but I just had Arthur, and then it was easier. It was simple. Now there are more children. Andre is older, and now he's in more activities. We went from one child to three, and Andre and Alese are only eighteen months apart. The boys were in choir, piano, and t-ball, at five years old. Now that Arthur is older, Ben tries to take him more places and do things with him so he can talk to him one on one. But he travels a lot in the spring, and then it all falls on me again.

While Lareau's study amplifies the ways in which white families and Black families are equally concerned about their children's access to competitive opportunities, its view that concerted cultivation equalizes the chances of the Black and white middle class and natural growth equally disadvantages those of the Black and white working and lower classes is an incomplete analysis. Pattillo-McCoy's *Black Picket Fences* tells us that race does matter, even across class:

> For those families who cannot afford the rising costs of private school (or choose not to make the financial sacrifice), or who are not chosen from the long waiting lists for the magnet schools and do not have influential friends, the area high schools [referring to Groveland in Patillo-McCoy's study]—with their lower graduation rates and less rigorous curriculum—are their only option. Under a system of class-based affirmative action that disregards the racial disadvantages that middle-class African Americans face, these students would be expected to compete for college admission or jobs with middle-class white students who have not been disadvantaged by the composition of their neighborhoods. (Pattillo-McCoy 1999, 217)

Pattillo-McCoy sees the disadvantage as rooted in the neighborhoods and the less than adequate schools in these neighborhoods and argues that a class-based response inadequately addresses the needs of African American students. Similarly, the families discussed in *Raising the Race* point to assumptions made about African Americans who perform their Blackness in ways labeled "ghetto" or lower-class (Jackson 2001). These assumptions negatively affect the entire Black community as middle- and upper-middle-class Blacks attempt to distance themselves from these articulations of "authentic" Blackness (Lacy 2007).

Strategic cultivation is the term I develop to better conceptualize the plans these families find themselves trying to implement for their children. They must combine the benefits of strategic assimilation and concerted cultivation. With strategic cultivation Black middle-class families, particularly the upper-middle-class, have to perform class markers that offer two signals: one to Black Americans that they are authentically Black, and one to white Americans that they are not like "those" Black people ("ghetto," "ratchet," or outside mainstream class markers) (Lacy 2007). In addition, through concerted cultivation, children must be taught the practices that will ensure social class reproduction as represented in particular cultural capital cues (Lareau [2003] 2011). For Black children this behavior is often viewed as "acting white" and comes with a host of issues related to internalized racism (Tyson 2011). The Black career moms in this study strategize and navigate this fine line of demarcation between the two behaviors; the moms both prepare and protect their children, in myriad ways.

Gail and I sat in the carpool line waiting for her to pick-up two of her children.[12] Her two oldest school-age children are enrolled in her neighborhood school. The school is 99 percent African American or Black, and 74 percent of the students are from disadvantaged homes.[13] According to No Child Left Behind (NCLB), the school met with Adequately Yearly Progress (AYP) measures in 2011. In 2009, the school was part of a standardized teaching scandal that resulted in the dismissal of two teachers and questions about the then-principal's knowledge and involvement.[14] "I am not too worried about it," Gail said as she relayed the story. Her children had not yet started school when these events transpired. "I feel like they have everything under control now. The teachers are good. They are willing to work with parents and the principal is really open to innovation by the teachers." As we sat in the carpool line waiting for the students to be dismissed, Gail stated she was more concerned about the impact the class differences in the school would have on her kids.

As one of the 25 percent of parents whose children are not from disadvantaged homes, Gail says she can see the influence of some of the poorer families on her own children and their values. "Look at this woman right here," she said of one of the women who got out of the car to retrieve her child who looked to be in the pre-kindergarten class. The woman had her hair covered, but it was clear the scarf was attempting to cover rollers. The woman was also wearing pants that looked like pajamas and furry slippers. "It is 2:30 in the afternoon," Gail said. "Why is she coming to pick up her child from school in her rollers and pajamas?" As we tried to find some explanation none made sense. If she worked the late shift at her job she would just be getting home and could have waited to put her pajamas and rollers in until after she picked up her child. If she worked a split shift, she would be getting ready to go to work and could have gotten dressed before coming to get her child. From Gail's perspective, this woman just didn't care how she left her house, and for Gail, having been raised by a single mother with five children, "My momma taught me not to leave the house in rollers. You just don't come out of the house like that." Gail assured me she did not mean to be judgmental or disparage the woman's choices, but she was concerned with the example she may be setting for her own daughter and for those around her. Gail's statements are rooted in respectability politics. "If my kids see enough of that foolishness, they start to think that is the way they are supposed to be . . . to be cool . . . to be accepted. They don't see how hard I work, they don't understand why it matters." Shortly after the woman leaves, we pull up to get Gail's children; her five-year-old daughter comes bouncing out of the school. "Look at her . . ." says Gail smiling and shaking her head. "She's already working on being a hoochie mama." Gail's daughter has a visible bounce in her step and looks like she is in perpetual ready-to-dance mode. She clearly has a lot of confidence and a lot of spunk. "She is just like me," said Gail. "So I know I have to watch her. We have to keep all of that gangsta in check."

Gail was not the only mother concerned about strategic cultivation and the influence of "authentically Black culture." Selena shared Gail's concern about the influences of hip-hop culture in particular that shows up on television and occasionally in their neighborhoods and school hallways. Selena said, "Imani, my oldest, likes to be cool. She's not really a follower, but if the cool kids are acting like hoodlums, she'll be the leader of the hoodlums. She needs to be in a strong, structured, small, strict environment. She needs a structured Christian environment so we will probably send her to Southwest Christian Academy [a local predominantly Black Christian school in Southwest Atlanta]."

But paying for private schools, extracurricular activities, and cultural experiences and opportunities places a time and money burden on the already precarious position in which these upper-middle-class professionals find themselves. They pay for a professional neighborhood in gated and manicured subdivisions; they pay for private school or supplements to public school education; many choose to be at-home moms or part-time professionals so they can give their families more direct attention; and they create and maintain extensive relationships with like-minded families to provide an additional layer of support and protection so their children do not fall victim to the fast money, glamorous life they think is the "real" representation of Black wealth. This fear is so pervasive that when First Lady Michelle Obama, in a show of respect for the talents of Beyoncé Knowles, revealed that she would love to trade places with the world-renowned pop star there was a tremendous backlash from many members of the Black elite media. The critique aimed at the First Lady disparaged her for having accomplished so much—a Princeton University and Harvard Law School graduate, attorney, corporate executive, wife, mother, and first African American First Lady—but willing to give the impression to the millions of little girls and young women who look up to her that she would forgo all of that to be a "bootylicious" pop star.[15]

All of the women in this study expressed concern over the images their children are exposed to and agreed that so much falls to the parents to make sure the children are not influenced by detrimental factors. Charlotte said of her son, "He's an African American boy. . . . There are so many things he can get caught up in in our society, and that has to do with our parenting." Richelle, who grew up in a single-parent, poor household that was very ambitious and stressed education, said she and her friends are confused by the way that youth respond to rules and discipline today. She said, "There have to be differences in the way we raise our kids. . . . Little white boys out playing pranks are just being boys. Black boys do it, and they're in jail. We can't raise kids thinking they can be out in the world doing whatever. Ethnic groups are different, and, of course, you're going to do things according to that." Gia summed up the sentiments of most of the mothers:

> I am an African American mother raising African American boys, and I absolutely have to stay on top of them because our society has stereotyped them. I have to be careful about where they go to school . . . who their friends are. I don't teach racism, but I do teach Arthur that he won't always be considered smart even though he is. I tell him don't get it twisted, stay close to your roots. . . . And to my daughter I have to teach, don't let anyone think you are loose.

This is the part of the concerted cultivation theory that Lareau's analysis ignores. This very real work of the Black professional class does not get discussed, and what is even more alarming about Lareau's omission is that the enculturation of middle-class Blackness is not new; it's just showing up in new ways. The Black "uplift" movement and the "politics of respectability" marked the beginning of the Black middle-class attempt at disavowing images of the Black community that were not deemed "respectable." Black women in particular were charged with making sure the presentation of Black womanhood, motherhood, and career were representative of strong moral character and proper decorum. The earliest forms of Black respectability can be seen in the political, social, and cultural movements of the late nineteenth and early twentieth centuries. Founded by free-born Black women whose families had been free and educated, the Black women's club movement along with historically Black sororities and Black women's participation in the NAACP created a forum for the movement that took the motto "lifting as we climb." These women married Black men who were becoming some of the foremost leaders of the Black community and saw themselves as forming a model for correct behavior. In addition, they "sought to take advantage of their social status and wealth to fight for the rights of their race and their sex."[16] The movement, however, was criticized by the Black community as being elitist, a persistent moniker thrust upon those of the upper-middle class who are viewed as policing, discriminating against, or disparaging those who do not conform to the ideology of respectable Blackness. Yet without a clear alternative to the stereotypes, they persist undeterred and unabated.

Correspondingly, it became clear over the course of the study that few of the women were in constant contact with anyone with fewer educational or financial resources than their own families. Part of this can be ascribed to geography. Like the white families that live in gated communities and manicured subdivisions to the north of Atlanta, these women live primarily on the south and west sides of the city in similar subdivisions, often built by the same builders. These subdivisions have been noted for their ability to maintain class boundaries (Blakely and Snyder 1997; Low 2004). Since most were not from Atlanta, they did not have a connection to the older, not yet gentrified neighborhoods of the inner city and the first ring or inner ring suburbs (Pattillo-McCoy 1999; Weise 2004). Thus, their connections to the poor and working class come in the form of occasional family gatherings and financial contributions to less fortunate family members, church or community organizations, or to paid childcare givers and household helpers in the form of lawn maintenance and housekeeping. Their "villages," although Black, are stratified and isolated by class. For many, this is a point of pride. To be in a position where Blacks can garner the same housing stock, retail industry, and services as upper-middle-class whites is something to celebrate. For many the long, difficult struggle toward parity had been reached, and they could be a shining example to America as a whole and the Black community of lesser means in particular. Such distinctions could, however, create a class divide that the Black community historically has not been allowed to have because the divide between the Black haves and have-nots has in the past been nominal at best.

With few models for how to combine marriage, career, and family as part of the Black upper-middle class, these families combine a hodgepodge of strategies that are rarely mentioned and never analyzed in social science research. In addition, it remains unclear if and how these families relate to the larger Black community or if communities of support form across class. The majority of the families in this study saw a significant movement in social class mobility from their family of origin to their companionate family, which makes this last point particularly critical to filling in a more complete picture of the choices of professional Black women when it comes to career and family. This prompts a conversation about the literature that suggests a perceived disconnect between the Black middle class, the Black poor and working class, and the Black upper-middle class.

5

Black Career Women, the Black Community, and the Neo-Politics of Respectability

"What do you mean by middle class?" was the response Cory gave me when I began my interviews with her. I was still refining my interview questions. I knew I wanted to investigate how Black career women saw their own class position, and accordingly one of my first questions during that initial interview, at her $350,000 home with a two-car garage and two children in private school, was "Do you consider yourself middle class?" I answered her query by relaying the definitions as understood by sociologists looking at socioeconomic status and anthropologists looking at culture, political economy, and power. Cory was intrigued by this because she did not see herself as middle class. "My neighbor is middle class," she eventually responded, referring to her white American neighbor. "She can stay at home with no problem and is seriously thinking about it. If I stayed home, it would change our lifestyle too much." Cory lives in a relatively new swim-tennis community in Cobb County. Homes range in price from $300,000 to $600,000 on less than a quarter acre lots. She and her husband have planned for retirement, her parents have established a college fund for her children, and her latest "big-ticket" purchase was an upgrade to a luxury SUV. Cory knows she is well-off. She knows she does not have to struggle for necessities. She does not, however, consider herself middle class. "Working class," Cory said. "Whenever you have to get up and go to work everyday and you need that paycheck, you're not middle class." Indeed, her answer is mired in a long-standing theoretical debate about how we define the middle class in mainstream US society and how it has been understood within the Black community. The construction of Black middle-class identity is further mired in the question of women's individual class positions, a relatively recent area of inquiry in mainstream analysis (Crompton 1989; Davis and Robinson 1998; Sorensen 1994), and almost nonexistent among scholars of African American family, class, or gender (some discussion in Landry 2000; Mack 1999).

In this chapter, I focus on the apparent growing class divide within the Black community and study the experience of these divides among professional Black women and their families. If they do perceive a growing divide, I explore its effect and their response. Using their own discussions about their housing decisions, their responses to stereotypical images, and their purposeful connections to the Black community, I explore how these Black professional women feel about their relationship to the larger Black community and how they reconcile their often ambiguous position within the African American status and class structure and the mainstream white class structure. Recognizing the collective strength embedded in a neo-politics of respectability that focuses on sustaining marriage and family, I suggest these women take up the early twentieth-century charge that sought to protect and raise the race in the eyes of whites and Blacks, and for twenty-first-century women this strategy is particularly important with respect to Black youth.

The families featured in this study continue to maintain vestiges of the historically communal structure of Black social networks. Nevertheless their membership in "the Black community" becomes precarious as the wage gap between the middle class and lower class widens and as ideological and cultural differences thicken. For the women in this study, their professional status and ability to make decisions about their career and family, although in some instances constrained, placed them in a privileged location that can separate them from their poor, working-class, and even middle-class counterparts. In most instances they are faced with reconciling a connection to the Black community, which has historically supported them emotionally and financially, while simultaneously withdrawing from many parts of the culture that are deemed "Black." As a result, a difference emerges in not only socioeconomic location but also cultural behaviors linked to class performance and designated as authentic Black identity.

African Americans now have a multitude of ways, independent of respectability politics, to represent and understand the performance of race and class, both interracially and intraracially. Recent shifts in the class structure including greater wealth differentials, as well as the influx of Black immigrants from various countries in Africa and the Caribbean in recent years, have begun to challenge what is meant by "the Black community." Additionally, with the global influence of hip-hop and its representation of Black urban youth culture, respectability is no longer the goal for many and has been challenged, particularly in media images, as the only successful representation of Blackness. Unlike the politics of respectability, which was most concerned with how whites viewed the Black community, the new era of the neo-politics of respectability, in its construction of racial identity, has to be concerned with not only "how whites view Blacks or determine Black life chances vis-à-vis the outside white world; [but it also has to be] used to make sense of racial affinities, politics, and interests within the Black community" (Jackson 2001, 190).

Several theories have been used to explain social class and status among African Americans and how that structure operates within what we call the Black community (Jackson 2001; Lacy 2007; Landry 1988; Massey and Denton 1993; Pattillo-McCoy 1999; Weise 2004; Wilson 1987). As we consider social class formation within the Black community, it is important to note that African Americans have not always had what we now refer to as "the Black community." The Black community is a social construct that was developed in response to the racism that ensued following the abolition of slavery and the rise of Jim Crow laws. The respectability era, developed in response to white supremacy at the turn of the twentieth century, was influential in creating the boundaries of the Black community and establishing its mission. By connecting African Americans from all walks of life to particular representations of Blackness at the height of the white supremacist era, members of the Black elite demonstrated their commitment to responding to collective Black needs. The uplift movement and the Black women's club movement helped to establish an expectation that the Black community would not only represent itself well through individual accomplishments but would also accept group responsibility for less fortunate members of the community, precisely because, in the end, all Black people were viewed without distinction. From the respectability era to the civil rights era, the notions of Black uplift and respectability were the most effective measures for ensuring Black people's survival, particularly in the South. Likewise the grassroots organizing of the civil rights movement did much to rearticulate the collectivity of the Black community. Furthermore, because the movement was primarily led by Black ministers and Black civil rights organizations and was largely fought by high school and college students, much of its success was built on notions of middle-class respectability.

The events following the passage of the Civil Rights Act of 1964 called many of the efforts of the activist civil rights leaders into question. Two factors began to put pressure on respectability politics. First, the Civil Rights Act was successful in helping the Black working class, middle class, and professional class access jobs and housing outside the Black community, but the legislation did little to help those trapped within urban and rural wastelands, thereby creating what we now call "the underclass" (Wilson 1987). Likewise the combined effects of deindustrialization, the recession, and high inflation of the late 1970s pushed inner city neighborhoods and their residents into a cycle of joblessness, low-performing schools, drug selling, drug abuse, and crime. Second, the more vocal and militant leaders who spoke on behalf of the diversity of the Black experience placed more pressure on respectability politics, as even those who were able to achieve higher education and more secure employment remained trapped just outside the inner city in "rings" meant to buffer suburban whites and urban Blacks (Pattillo-McCoy 1999).

Not in My Backyard:
Negotiating Race(d) and Class(ed) Behaviors

Policy analysts and conservative social scientists assumed that the first bene-factors of the civil rights legislation of the 1960s had escaped segregation and enjoyed the first advantages of newly opened suburban neighborhoods, thus moving our society toward the goal of integration. We know that this was not then and is not now the case. For example, Prince Georges County, a suburb of Washington, DC, featured in Lacy's study on middle-class Black identity, gives the appearance of an integrated community. A more careful look reveals the fact that the county's population is indeed approximately 50 percent Black and 50 percent white, but each group has its own distinctly separate enclaves; the only depictions of integration are in the form of predominantly white neighbor-hoods with a few Black families (Lacy 2007). One rarely finds a situation in which African Americans comprise the majority or even 50 percent of the population because studies have shown that when a neighborhood reaches a tipping point of about 20 percent Black, white flight sets in and white families begin to relo-cate. As whites withdraw, housing values decline, the tax base disappears, and, as a result, tax hikes are necessary to maintain the same level of public service (Conley 1999). Correspondingly, as housing values decline, the "like-minded" neighbors of professional middle-class Blacks begin to change. Lower housing values make housing more affordable to those who previously could not afford to live in the community, and often more accessible housing means lower com-mitment, whether financial or psychological, to home maintenance and com-munity appearance (Feagin and Sikes 1994; Lacy 2007; Pattillo-McCoy 1999).

The circumstances in Atlanta are slightly different. The Cascade corridor was initially built for whites in the pre–civil rights movement era. As tensions flared in other parts of the South over the rights of African Americans to equal housing, employment, and public accommodations, Atlanta decided to mini-mize public scrutiny and took careful, calculated steps to alleviate pushback. Already having established a long-standing history with the city's Black elite (including the King family and the Jackson/Dodd family), Atlanta "allowed" Afri-can Americans to move into some of the city's "nicer" white neighborhoods, a strategy that proved effective to prevent widespread civil unrest. The Cascade corridor on the west side of the city, where the Atlanta University Center and several prominent Atlanta neighborhoods had long histories of Black middle-class residents, was ripe (although still contested) for greater expansion of the Black middle class (A. Barnes 1989; Bayor 1996).

Most of the women in this study lived in the Black suburban enclaves that are in or extend from the Cascade corridor. They intentionally sought these spaces as ideal for the needs of their families and particularly their children (see chapter 4). It became clear as I continued to talk with the women that, as scholars have suggested, Black middle-class families who worked to provide their children with additional opportunities for advancement found that they and their children were never far from the "ghetto," both spatially and psychologically (Pattillo-McCoy 1995). As a result Black middle-class families exist in a constant state of ambivalence as they try to make sense of the fact that they continue the same struggles previous generations fought for equal access and opportunity. Some scholars suggest Black upper-middle-class families are trying to imitate whites in a way that is less than satisfying for all participants; to others, they are trapped in a system that neither allows them "easy" passage into the middle class nor sees them as such.[1]

Selena articulated her displeasure with the changes she has seen in her neighborhood, where homes cost upward of $300,000. She and her husband bought early, and they have since seen the rising cost of homes in the subdivision. When she chose the neighborhood, she expected a quiet enclave with like-minded neighbors. After witnessing people with multiple cars in their driveways when they already have a three-car-garage and seeing people leave their Christmas lights up for the entire year, Selena fears that her neighborhood expectations do not match the reality. "I wanted to be in a neighborhood with people like us, African American professionals," she said. "I wanted to be with upwardly mobile Black people. What I was looking for and what I have are two different things. There is no way to avoid the 'ghetto.' I thought I was in a more sterile environment, but it's not that at all. . . . It is a fairly new subdivision. Real estate investors got in early, and I think when they couldn't sell for what they wanted they started renting." Selena anticipated that her Black neighborhood would have fewer aspects of stereotypical Black neighborhoods, most of which she sees as working class or lower middle class. Now Selena fears the entry of people with less money and less cultural capital will have a negative effect on her family and her property values.

Denise, whose home was in the $250,000 range, felt the same way when her community pool was often overrun by young boys who did not live in the subdivision but jumped the locked wrought-iron fence when no homeowners were around. "I would get there with the kids and find all of these boys I didn't know at the pool. I'm Jamaican so I know how to handle it.[2] I'm not afraid of them or anything. It's just that these kids have this bravado about them and this entitlement like it's theirs . . . but we worked for it and then they want to come in and tear it up. It's really frustrating." As a self-trained interior decorator, Denise put a lot of effort into decorating her two-story, five-bedroom home. Hers was the center lot on a quiet cul-de-sac and often won the yard-of-the-month award. Denise continued, "I wouldn't mind letting people have access to it, but there should be some type of system for that. I realize there is no community pool in the area where families can just pay a membership. Maybe that's something we can look into. But as it stands, they're using it, they're trespassing, and there's no way to hold them accountable if they tear something up."

Gail, whose home was just under $200,000, had a similar issue. Instead of dealing with children she did not know, Gail had to call her local police department to handle her next door neighbor's son. According to Gail, while his mother was at work he had friends over and sat on the front steps smoking marijuana. "They are not going to bring my property values down!" she exclaimed. Gail said the neighborhood kids weren't the only problem. "It doesn't help that the subdivision's community basketball court, pool, and swing set are at the front of the subdivision where anyone driving by can see them and think they can access them. . . . I don't know whose bright idea that was." Realizing they had to take control of the neighborhood themselves, Gail and her husband set up a neighborhood watch program with some other like-minded residents and added a code to the community pool gate, and the property owners association was considering installing a coded gate at the subdivision's entrance. In addition to these measures, Gail said the property owners association has already installed speed bumps and posted a five-mile-per-hour sign at the front of the subdivision because, according to Gail, "people would come flying through the straight-away when you first come in and it was really dangerous for the kids."

Gail and her neighbors have just cause to be worried. The Section 8 Rental Voucher Program, which increases affordable housing choices for very low income households by allowing families to choose privately owned rental housing, offers a telling example of the way race and class get conflated and then permuted. Since Atlanta began experiencing a downturn in the housing market,[3] Section 8 tenants have been renting homes in half-million-dollar subdivisions because the owners are unable to sell and need a guaranteed source of income to maintain the mortgage payments or risk foreclosure.[4] Natalie, whose family lived on the eastern side of the city, told me about houses in several upscale, gated subdivisions being rented to Section 8 tenants who, because they had no stake in the community, did not follow the property owner association rules. Because Natalie lived not in a gated community or a subdivision but on a residential street free of the new "McMansions" that most Section 8 tenants wanted, she didn't feel her neighborhood was in jeopardy. "I hope not," she said. "That's part of the reason we moved out here instead of southwest. We wanted to make sure we retained our property values." Natalie and her husband grew up in south Fulton County, one of the few couples who were both native

Atlantans. Natalie and her husband paid about $375,000 for their colonial-style five-bedroom home and expected its value to increase.

For homeowners dealing with the impact of Section 8 renters, some property owner associations were beginning to implement rules to limit the percentage of homes that could be private rental or Section 8. Although the associations had little jurisdiction over how owners handled their properties, the regulations were intended as deterrents to neglect and warnings to renters; that is, the associations sought to convey the message that renters were welcome only if they followed the rules. Denise explained that the typical limit on rentals was about 20 percent, the same presumed tipping point when Black movement into white communities triggers flight and a similar example of protecting class interests.

Choosing White Suburban Spaces

Frances, Cory, and Kathy, who lived in predominantly white communities, did not face the concerns of those who lived in the Black suburban enclaves, at least not in the same way. Kathy, however, who paid $215,000 for her home in West Cobb County, noted a change in the demographics in her neighborhood as more Black families moved in and white families moved out:

> It bothers me that we are still dealing with white flight in the twenty-first century. When we moved in there were only five Black families in our community of thirty-five homes. There was still new construction, and about twenty homes were still under construction so we expected the community to end up being about 70/30 white, give or take a few. It's leaning more towards 60/40 Black at this point. Some people have moved. I don't know if it's really because more Blacks are moving in. But that's what it feels like. They weren't families we knew or hung out with so I don't know if they had friends in the community or if they moved for work or whatever. I really don't know.

I asked Kathy if she thought the change in demographics changed the neighborhood or if she was worried about changes in the neighborhood. She continued,

> No. I actually love it. I grew up in a Black neighborhood, but it was a poor neighborhood. We don't mind it being majority Black at all. We love our neighbors. We haven't had any problems on either side. I think the only thing is since Ronald and I moved out here from Midtown, which is much more diverse, and we really liked it, we were looking for that in our neighborhood. We didn't want to be the only ones either way, the only Blacks in a white neighborhood or a neighborhood of only Blacks. But

now that we're here it really is great. I love that we can make a dinner party and it be mostly our neighbors and a few friends. Our kids are growing up together, and there are a few other women who are stay-at-home moms and we do Mocha Moms together.

Most of the women, like Kathy, were living in new subdivisions, some of which were still under construction when they moved in so they didn't know the demographics until the proverbial "dust had settled." These subdivisions often had recreational amenities that older neighborhoods lacked. These amenities, obviously a draw for nonresidents as well as for residents who were placing their homes on the rental market, typically generated more problems for the neighborhoods than those encountered in communities without these amenities. Likewise, gated communities gave the appearance of being less accessible to nonresidents than those that were open. Of course, as Natalie suggested, homes in older, more established neighborhoods had comparably fewer problems with nonresidents, and homes at higher price points had fewer difficulties than those that were lower. For instance, when I talked with Kia and Cara, who both lived in much more expensive subdivisions with homes valued between $300,000 and $500,000, respectively, they were not experiencing the same problems that Selena, Denise, and Gail faced. Nevertheless, for families that purposefully chose higher price-point neighborhoods full of professionals and their families, the presence of families who do not fit that description could create a threat not only to their property values but also to the values they were attempting to teach their children. As Mary Pattillo-McCoy stated, the "Black belt" has always expanded and is typically marked by a shift in neighborhood demographics, schools, and retail establishments (1999).

Gail, Selena, and Denise each expressed some discomfort with the elitist and, in some respects, racist tone of their descriptions about perceived income changes in their neighborhoods. When I pushed them to elaborate, they contended, however, that their interest in maintaining their communities does not detract from their allegiance to and responsibility toward the rest of the African American community, a sentiment that further illuminates the complex position these upper-middle-class families inhabit.

Choosing Black Poor and Working-Class Spaces

Families that did not live in new, gated, swim-tennis Black or white suburban enclaves did not have to worry about losing property values. Nancy's and Linda's families purposefully bought homes in historic neighborhoods that were being gentrified by young professionals. Both said they wanted to be close to the Black community and the city, and they clearly recognized that they were moving into areas with high crime statistics, a mix of residents from poor to middle class, and various communal values. Both Nancy and Linda moved into their homes before they had children; now as mothers with children they expressed growing concerns over safety, schooling, and the drawbacks of living in gentrifying neighborhoods.

Nancy's home is in one of Atlanta's oldest neighborhoods, featuring large Victorian homes with wrap-around porches and intricate architectural detail. She and her husband moved into their neighborhood to purchase one of these Victorian homes that had been neglected for years. "It was ridiculous how inexpensive these homes were and how little they needed to be brought back to their original beauty and character." Since Aaron was growing a real estate development firm he wanted a home that both demonstrated his skills as a developer and afforded him easy access to the downtown area, the hub of his business. Not only was the couple able to purchase and restore their home, but they also renovated a small office building within walking distance from their home. Nancy said, "We knew we didn't want one of those really expensive cookie cutter homes out in the suburbs. They're really nice, but we wanted to be in the city. Aaron grew up in the city so it was really important to him. And I wanted to be near my patients. I wanted to live in the neighborhood where my patients lived."

Nancy and Aaron have been able to make a home and become a part of the community, but it has been at a cost. As Pattillo-McCoy discusses in her Chicago-based ethnography of intrarace gentrification, Nancy and Aaron operate as "brokers" within the community, advocating for the "little" people with less power and fewer resources (2007). Many residents appreciate their focus and concern, but the class politics remain a thorny issue:

> We were broken into twice in our first couple of years, but we installed a security system and haven't had any problems since then. We also know now that when we go on vacations and stuff we need to get a house sitter because people can tell when we're gone. Sometimes when I come home late, especially if I have the kids with me, if there's someone kind of hanging around outside I'll drive around the block or call Aaron to come to the door. I don't really like that I feel uncomfortable like that. I wonder if I would feel that way in a white neighborhood, but I'd rather be wrong and safe.

Nancy also said she didn't like that the kids, as they got older, wouldn't have a yard to play in. "That's part of city living too, and Aaron grew up like that, but I didn't. I grew up outside!" she said with laughter. Nancy grew up in rural Texas. "We were always outside. My grandmother had a garden, and I would be out there with her and just really running around outside all the time. I want my kids to have at least some of that." Nancy is fortunate because they can walk to a nearby park, but she says it's not the same. "The park is great for when I want to take them outside, but it's not the same as being able to send them outside. I'll never be able to do that because even once they're older and can go by themselves; it's still a city park." For now Nancy said they are committed to staying in the area. "It just makes the most sense for what Aaron is trying to do but I already told him, when the kids get ready to go to middle school we might have to figure out something else."

Linda concurred with Nancy's sentiments. She and her husband don't live very far from Nancy, but they bought a newly constructed home in another gentrifying neighborhood. Unlike Nancy's neighborhood, which was historically white but went through a racial transition with white flight during the 1960s and 1970s and is now being redeveloped by a mix of Blacks and whites, Linda's neighborhood has historically been Black. Linda said, "It cracks me up when I hear people talk about all of the different neighborhoods that are at different stages of redevelopment. If it's being redeveloped by white folks it's a new 'in-town' neighborhood. If it's being redeveloped by Black folks it's still an inner-city neighborhood. When did inner city and in-town become code for Black and white?" Linda's assessment was correct and reinforced the perception that there is no class differential in Black neighborhoods (Pattillo-McCoy 1999).[5] On one occasion when I visited Linda's home, situated in the middle of a city block where very few people have driveways or garages, most of the street was full of cars. Two cars were double-parked, and a group of young men, dressed in A-shirts (white undershirts colloquially known as "wife-beaters"), was standing around the cars and talking to the drivers. A look up the block in the other direction found middle-aged women sitting out on their front steps ("the stoop") with scarves ("doo-rags") on their heads.

Issues of respectability were played out on a daily basis in Linda's neighborhood, where the exterior and the interior of the homes often varied drastically. The couple paid $325,000 for their home in a neighborhood where most of the homes were purchased in the 1940s through 1960s for $2,000 to $10,000 ($20,000 to $45,000 in today's dollars).[6] With a floor plan similar to a northeastern row house, the entryway opened into a large combination living room, dining room, and kitchen painted in rich browns, with dark hardwood floors, beige furniture, and brightly colored throw pillows and rugs. Although their home was new construction, it was clear they had not skimped on attention to detail. Each room had crown molding, and the dining room walls had chair rails. In the rear to the right was the entrance to the basement, which led to the two-car garage, part of the reason they had decided to build their home themselves, and a screened porch overlooked their small fenced-in backyard.

The people residing in Linda's home likewise differed from her neighbors. Linda, an orthodontist, and her husband, a sales manager with an insurance firm, are married with two children. According to Linda, this is not the average neighborhood profile. Even though most residents are homeowners, their homes are multigenerational. According to Linda, most of the homes are owned by the grandparents' generation, usually the first owners back in the 1940s when the community was home to many prosperous African Americans. Their children and grandchildren still own the homes, but the community hasn't been as prosperous since the effects of urban decline in the 1960s and 1970s. There are many single middle-aged women with teens or grown children; many do not go to college. Linda described the complications of such diversity:

> We didn't mind it at first. It felt like a real neighborhood, a real community. Not like the suburbs that are so dead. We wanted to be a part of a community. Now it's a bit more challenging. Since we had the kids we have to be concerned with the images they see on one hand. But on the other hand, I like that they are being taught that they can live with Black people who have less money than them. We grew up with people like our neighbors, in communities like this. Our dads didn't go to college at all, and neither one of our moms graduated. So what about finishing college and getting degrees makes us unable to live with them . . . with us really? We just realized we had to get over ourselves and whatever perception we thought people might have of us living here on either side. Whether it was the community thinking we were rich so we didn't belong or our friends' thinking the neighborhood was poor so we didn't belong. We hope we bring just as much value to the community as the other members of the community give to us.

Linda's and Nancy's experiences as "pioneers" in their gentrifying neighborhoods add details to the discussion about intraracial class warfare in Black communities as the Black middle class not only moves in but also attempts to provide some "value" to the community (Pattillo 2007). Unlike white gentrifiers in Black poor and working-class communities, who typically isolate themselves from the Black residents by systematically changing it instead of immersing themselves into the existing culture, Black gentrifiers actually want to become a part of the culture, but they want to restore its former glory. Accordingly, Blacks of all incomes can agree that they do not want their neighborhood overridden with crime, robberies, and so on, and they want access to middle-class amenities and services. They can also agree that the middle class is in a better position to broker those amenities and services with the powers that be. The class divide then becomes one over respectability: residents have conflict over late-night loud music during the week, street barbeques, young men in wife-beaters double-parked on the street, or middle-aged ladies in doo-rags sitting out on their stoops.

As strategic mothering suggests, the life course of the mother and her children plays a large part in these issues. We can appreciate some of the ambivalence expressed by Nancy and Linda, and both foresee more conflict as their children get older. Nancy expects to have to make different decisions once her children are ready to go to middle school as she is not sure she wants her children to go to their zoned schools, given their failing marks. Linda is concerned about school as well, but she acknowledges even more concern with the images her children see of Black people in her community. Having already learned the rules of respectability, Nancy and Linda anticipate some apprehension about how to "teach" those rules as their children get older and their neighborhoods offer few examples.

Representing the Race: *The Real Housewives of Atlanta*

Black career women presented here were interested in neither policing nor chastising those less fortunate in the Black community, and they did not act out of an elite sense of privilege. They continued to be interested in the ethos in which the Black community is seen as interconnected: the success of one is representative of the success of the whole. They repeatedly referenced a growing economic and spatial wedge between the Black elite and the Black poor and working class, which, as scholars have predicted, could begin to disrupt the "communal" nature of the "Black community" (Dyson 2005; Pattillo 2007). Without the now defunct "uplift movement" and the close proximity enforced by racial segregation, class positionality often polarizes the Black haves and have-nots. Familiar notions of respectability previously gave most ambitious Blacks, regardless of class, common ground. That common ground, however, is increasingly challenged as multiple representations of the race vie for public attention and youth consumer potential.

The women discussed rarely seeing themselves reflected in images of the Black community and felt they were often penalized for this apparent void. In fact, they felt a sense of ambiguity and intermittent ambivalence, particularly as applied to their "integration" into the mainstream American context and their ability to enculturate their children with Black middle-class values. They felt they had to resist media and popular culture representations of Blackness in general and Black womanhood in particular.

The new images of upper-class Black women frustrated most of the women in this study, and the fact that many of these images were discussed as if they were real was especially frustrating (Harris and Goldman 2014). "The Real

Housewives" franchise, a series of reality TV hits, was a primary culprit. Because the show *The Real Housewives of Atlanta* focused on upper-income "wives" in Atlanta, many professional Black women were deeply concerned that this was their most prevalent national image. Kya said, "It's different when it's a drama or a movie. Most of the time people understand that the cast is acting. When you say 'reality TV' and people are using their real addresses, their real names, and their real family dynamics, it's no longer a stereotype, it's the way things are." When I asked what they thought the show conveyed about Black women, the women in the study agreed that the show just reinforced already pervasive stereotypes of Black people. Marilyn summed it up: "We're angry, we're gold-diggers, we're petty and full of drama, and we still can't stay married." Marilyn was referencing the fact that even though the show is called *The Real Housewives,* throughout most of the seasons of the show the majority of the "wives" weren't married. Gia said, "It makes us look like ghetto chicks with money. We're still welfare moms. We just don't draw checks from the government." When I talked with Natalie she revealed a disdain for what she called "the housewives genre."[7] Making no distinction between the *Housewives of Atlanta* and any of the others, Natalie said, "I do not watch any of that mess. . . . It is a bunch of foolishness."

Many of the women expressed such frustration because they knew, based on how they were raised, that married Black women of financial means are supposed to present themselves in a particular way. They are supposed to be representatives for the rest of the race. Unlike many of the women in this study who articulated an attempt to maintain a cultural divide that resonates with the "respectability" of the Black community through their residential choices, the women of *The Real Housewives of Atlanta* blurred the line of respectability in numerous ways.

Of course, there have always been members of the Black elite who did not achieve their financial success through higher education and professional occupations. Respectability, however, has historically been a class performance for which one strove, especially if one was not an original member of the "talented tenth." Many of these women, both in this study and on the show, were descendants of families who were not members of the Black elite. New and particularly problematic, yet interesting, is the fact that the women of *The Real Housewives of Atlanta* who did not comply with the politics of respectability were given a platform in both Black America and white America. These housewives had not gone to college, and they made their money either through lucrative marriages or some form of entertainment and self-promotion. The women of this study did not consider the program a problem on its own, but it became a problem because the housewives presented one of very few images of upper-middle-class Black women on television. Gail explained, "It's like when hip-hop was getting big and calling us bitches and hos. And the videos were portraying us as all about sex, really showing us like we were hos. That image traveled to other places, and all of a sudden that's how all Black women are, and there's proof. At least with the videos we could still say it was fake; calling it reality makes it that much harder." From Gail's perspective the discussion is not just about images of Black womanhood, but she objects to the presentations as authentically Black and then authentically Black womanhood.

We know that race is a social construction, but the way social inequalities have been mapped onto phenotypic differences makes it a lived reality even though it is a biological fallacy. Because Black people have been forced to develop their own cultural models for the purposes of their group survival, an understanding of Black racial authenticity has been developed to describe the characteristics of the Black community. On the positive end of those characteristics is a view that all Black people are related and should collectively look out for one another, most often through various iterations of family life and group memberships, including the church and fraternal organizations. On the negative end of those characteristics are the stereotypical assumptions that range from serious issues including pervasive welfare, rampant crime, and absentee fathers to the more lighthearted assumptions such as "all Black people can dance" and "all Black women can braid hair."

People who operate outside those characteristics or who have no knowledge of their existence are considered inauthentic or "acting white." Phenotypic features that have historically been deemed "Black," through the one-drop rule,[8] often dictate where one grows up, and the social actions one makes become key to defining racial identity (Jackson 2001, 228). When one grows up with the phenotypic features but outside the social location (stereotypically poor or working class), and without recognizable social actions (requisite "communal" knowledge), one can be critiqued as inauthentic. The Black elite and upper middle class are often targets of such critiques (Harris 2013). Both the Black elite and the Black poor and working class use these variations in social location and social action to criticize and "police" one another into each groups' acceptable images of Blackness. John Jackson, author of *Harlemworld: Doing Race and Class in Contemporary Black America*, clarified these distinctions:

> The Black poor can use class-inflected behaviors to manipulate and critique the Black middle class; Blacks higher up the class ladder use class(ed) and racialized actions to critique lower-class race-mates and to make sense of race in their own lives. Racial performances can be read through gender to create divergent Black male and Black female behavioral mandates. But even these mandates can be questioned when people go against the grain. One can challenge other Blacks for their lack of achievement by linking race to high performance in a battle against

institutionalized and internalized racism. In such a context, academic achievement can be a testament to Black racial identity and not a compromising of it. . . . Just as the same type of striding gate, for instance, can be taken as lower- or middle-class, the same intellectual achievement can be racialized as "white" or "Black" depending on the context and the purposes of the label. In this sense, it is important to stress that race(d) and class(ed) behaviors are mutable, allowing people to dispute the racial and class-based implications of their social actions all the time. (2001, 190).

Many of the Black professional women in this study choose to live in self-segregated communities, and they all choose to be a part of the Black community. In this performance of social location they are celebrated as models of race(d) and gender(ed) progress. They are not, however, exempt from the racial discourse around "acting white," particularly in regard to their children, who often have to interact with both poor Blacks and middle-class whites. Employing strategic mothering, these professional women focus on the health and survival of their families as intact units that will buffer their children from the performances of Blackness that may endanger them both literally and figuratively. They simultaneously use the neo-politics of respectability to provide alternative ideas of authentic Black identity for members of the poor and lower class Black community.

"Feeling the Need to Contribute": Black Career Women and Communal Responsibility

As these women think about what it means to articulate their race and class position, they seek to develop their own creative expression for defining themselves as mothers, wives, and career women. They recognize the privilege and responsibility they have as successful Black women but realize the limitations to what they can do. Moreover, without clear models, they experience fractious images of themselves from their workplace, the society at large, and, often most painfully, their friends and family.

Denise, the lawyer who works in community affairs in the district attorney's office, said she always has to consider how she presents herself to the public. "I always have to put a positive out to society for my job but also just as a Black woman, and it is a burden. I am educated so I have to put my best foot on the street, and the children have to be the best of us." Like much of the Black professional class, Denise believes a lot of the negative images that get through to the kids stem from hip-hop music and the images that entertainers sell to young people. She said, "We owe our children enough not to listen to the music. We cannot show them the Imus thing." Denise is referring to the radio personality Don Imus, a white man, who in 2007, when the Rutgers University women's basketball team was competing for the NCAA women's basketball championship, referred to the players on the team as "nappy-headed hos." Denise continued, "Imus, like a lot of other white people, believe it is okay to say these things because we say it in our own communities. It's the way we portray ourselves, so why shouldn't people think it's okay to refer to us that way." Many people had a problem with his statements, not because he called Black women "nappy-headed hos," but because he called Black women who were in college, playing basketball for a Division I team, with a Black woman head coach, "nappy-headed hos." Denise continued, "If those, who are supposed to be the best of us, can be disparaged in this way, we [the Black community] are doing something wrong. This is why we have to be careful of what we portray. It's because we always risk being lumped into one."

Kalia, whose nonprofit organization specializes in youth services, agreed with the observation that white people get most of their understanding of Black people from the media, which creates huge problems when trying to disseminate human services. Kalia said, "I work with African American families. I struggle with that environment that is not always understanding of African American families. The volunteers are mostly Caucasian. Staff and volunteers have to be prepared to work with African American families and understand family history. They have to understand that these families are hard-working and that they are building on our ancestors. They have to know the history."

The women in the study articulated the desire to use their careers, their time, and their money to benefit the Black community. They discussed things they learned from their parents, their social organizations, or their college experiences, things that taught them the importance of giving back to the Black community. Keayba's parents, both educators who raised their children within a tight-knit extended family structure, were often called upon to assist family members through rough spots. "I know that is where I get my desire to be of assistance to my community from," Keayba said. "It is so important to me to be in a position to help . . . especially the Black community." All of the women discussed a general responsibility to help and a particular responsibility in the Black community.

Gail and Selena are both active members of community service organizations, and their households contribute significantly to the financial resources of family members who require economic assistance. As the oldest child of five, Gail was often called upon to help with family members' needs. She was explaining that she was helping to pay for a family member's education; then she added, "I don't get to see my mother unless I go there or pay for her to fly down here." Others discussed stepping in for family members who needed other kinds of help. Myra helped her cousin enroll in a college in Atlanta after Hurricane Katrina temporarily closed her college in New Orleans. Karen talked about close friends who had taken in her family during their hurricane displacement, and that assistance put her family in a position to be able to help others. Jill's cousin put her son in a private high school to keep him from getting caught up with the wrong crowd in his local public school. When her cousin lost her job and couldn't pay his last year's tuition, Jill paid it. When I asked Jill if she expected her cousin to pay her back, she said, "No. I didn't tell her it was a gift just in case she does find a way to pay me back. But I don't lend money to family. It destroys family. If I can't give it to them freely, I don't do it. If she pays me back, I'll just find another way to invest it in someone else who needs it." In their business, Nancy and Aaron often employed family, especially college kids who were looking for internships. "We can usually pay them a few dollars, and they get a look at what it's like to be an entrepreneur."

Many of the women had families of origin who, like them, were doing well financially. In those cases they tried to offer help to others. Charlotte is very active in her church and works with the women's ministry and the children's ministry. Marilyn is the manager of her church bookstore, a completely voluntary, unpaid position. Richelle described her work with young mothers at church to teach them mothering skills: "You don't have to be an at-home mom with a husband who is supporting your family to be a good mother." She draws on some of the matrifocal cultural models of her childhood in her lessons: "Your focus is on your children, and you do whatever you have to do to make life right for them. That's what my mom did, and that's what helped me get to college and graduate and be able to be in a position to choose to be an at-home mom."

In addition to wanting to make a difference themselves, many of the moms did community work that involved their children. With their church Marilyn and her husband Jonathan took their children to do homeless ministry once a month; the ministry made brownbag lunches and then passed them out to people in areas with a high concentration of homeless people. Marilyn said, "They learn to be kind to everyone and not to judge people by what they do or don't have." The family also participates in some of the "Feed the Hungry" programs that take place throughout the year. "They have so much. We give them so much. It's great to see them serving others. And it's wonderful to see the effect it has on them." Like Marilyn, many of the women felt it was important to make sure their children had a connection to the Black community—not only to establish their place among family members through reunions and family trips, but also to understand their identity as Black children and upper-middle-class Black children with access to opportunities. Monica, whose children aren't old enough to do community service yet but are members of the children's choir at her church, said, "The question becomes, what will they do when they grow up?

What connections will they have? I don't want their connection to be just that they are Black [referring to their skin color]. I want their connection to be to their history and to the promise that our people hold within them. That's the great part about being Black. If you look from where we have come, you can see that there is nothing but promise."

Negotiating Race and Class Privilege: "Jack and Jill"

As I probed the women about their participation in their social and communal organizations one of the moms told me she had been invited to membership in "Jack and Jill." The organization had only been mentioned a couple of times with other women in the study, and only as it pertained to organizations in which the women held membership. In most cases, when it was brought up, the women said they had been members as children but were not planning to enroll their own children and cited the lack of need. Others thought they would never get an invitation based on their families' lack of social capital. Like the sororities most of the women were members of, Jack and Jill was started as a private, closed membership organization for the Black, college-educated middle class. It differs from the sororities because applications for membership are not open to all college-educated women; membership is by invitation only, and an invitation is based solely on position in the social, cultural, and educational Black elite. For instance, Kya was in college when she found out about Jack and Jill, and she realized why she had not been introduced to it earlier when she learned more details from some of the girls she went to college with who were members. "My family was so far outside that world I had never even heard of it," she said with a laugh. Her college friends who were members were the children of doctors, lawyers, and business executives in the northern suburbs of big cities. "They were from New York, DC, Philadelphia, and Chicago," she said. "I was from the South. My mom was a high school teacher, and my father died when I was little. If Jack and Jill did exist in my community, they never would have picked me."

Just after the hey-day of the "uplift movement," a group of Philadelphia's African American mothers wanted to create an organization to provide social, cultural, and educational opportunities for children between the ages of two and nineteen; to that end, they founded Jack and Jill in 1938.[9] Historically, invitations were sent only to those mothers (and fathers) who "best" represent the professional upper-middle class through their marital status, their level of education, their professions, and their neighborhoods; this selective process has generated conversation about the extent to which the organization represents only the most privileged and elite members of the African American community. Because the civil rights movement expanded Black American access to upper-middle-class professions, some have critiqued the organization for continuing to focus its membership criteria on the very small social and economic elite of the pre–civil rights era. They were doctors and lawyers just like the professionals of today, but they were also the children of doctors and lawyers. The women in this study, as highly educated professionals married to professionals, would be prime candidates for membership. For some, however, the class standing of their family of origin would complicate their applications to Jack and Jill; the organization, viewed as a "gatekeeper" for the political, cultural, and economic Black elite, makes it difficult for mothers to gain admittance simply because of their or their husband's financial status.

The mother being recruited into Jack and Jill contemplated whether she would join the organization, and, because of its complicated history in the Black community, she was not completely sure she wanted to accept the invitation.[10] Many in the Atlanta area believe the organization, founded primarily for the cultural education of Black children who were growing up in predominantly white schools and spaces, is not necessary in Atlanta, a city that has a large and thriving population of upper-middle-class and elite Blacks. African Americans are fully represented in the government and the business community, as well as in educational leadership. This mom, who lives and works and educates her children in a predominantly Black environment, does not see this organization as necessary for her children. "If I join, I think it will be for the other mothers and children who have bought into an ideology of assimilating their African American children into the American mainstream at the expense of their cultural heritage." She said these mothers seeking membership live primarily on the north side of town in semi-integrated neighborhoods: "Instead of falling into that trap that does not value the African American cultural experience, I want to use my membership in Jack and Jill as a way to deepen the membership's original purpose." She critiqued an outing to a white bank where a white bank manager taught the children about the banking industry. "Why not visit Capitol City Bank? Or visit Atlanta Life Insurance Company?"[11] This mother felt that the organization had lost sight of its goal and mission, and she wanted to refocus the group on the social, cultural, and educational opportunities that could strengthen the children's commitment to the Black community rather than teaching them to assimilate into the white mainstream (see Harris 2013; Tatum [1987] 2000). "That's the only thing that bothers me. It's like they are caught in the idea that middle class is white and poor is Black. We, as Black professionals, should be long past that idea at this point. It demonstrates such deep-seated internal racism."

Negotiating Race and Class Privilege: Hiring Help

As the contradictions over the relevance of Jack and Jill reflect, upper-middle-class families walk a thin line, a "buffer zone" of sorts, similar to the inner city housing "rings" Mary Pattillo-McCoy analyzed in *Black Picket Fences* (1999). In this ambiguous space Black career women have to navigate a deep-seated belief that they are in many ways like the Black poor and working-class masses, and yet they are responsible to and for them. In addition, Black career women must deal with the fact that they do feel a bit of fear and distrust toward the poor and working class and figure out how they, as Black professionals, are going to respond to that feeling. My question regarding domestic help brought some of these issues to the fore, an apparent site of intraracial class conflict.

Marilyn lives in one of the older upper-middle-class neighborhoods on the southwest side of town. When she and her husband first saw the house, they liked the land but didn't like the floor plan. They decided to do some extensive remodeling and turn the house into their dream home. The house sits on a lake in a heavily wooded neighborhood and gets very little traffic. Marilyn and Jonathan, both busy professionals with three children, decided to hire a house-keeper even though Marilyn only works part-time. From Marilyn's perspective it allowed her an opportunity to spend the time she had at home doing stuff with the kids, not cleaning the house. The housekeeper, Anna, was an African American woman in her late forties who had been referred by a friend. According to Marilyn everything was going fine until one day she realized her engagement ring, which she remembered leaving on her dresser, was missing. She retraced her steps, asked her husband, asked her kids, and tore the house upside down. But the ring wasn't there. After being tormented by her inability to find the ring, she realized that it went missing the day Anna came to clean. She had already had to speak with Anna a couple of times for bringing people Marilyn and Jonathan did not know to the house with her while she was cleaning. She would tell Marilyn this person had given her a ride and would wait in the car, but Marilyn always felt uncomfortable making the person wait in the car so she would ask them in and offer some water, "just to be pleasant," she said with a bit of sarcasm. Marilyn remembered that she'd had to leave Anna at the house by herself while she took the children to story time at the library, but she did not want to accuse her of stealing her ring. It didn't make sense. "Why would she jeopardize her job to steal my ring?" Marilyn asked. "I paid her more consistently than she was going to get for the ring, and I had referred her to other people. She had to be making pretty good money." Marilyn talked it over with her friend and her husband and decided to just ask her about it.

> Jonathan was with me when I spoke to her and we basically said did you take it? And she said no. But there was no other explanation. I tried to tell her I just wanted it back because it was my wedding ring, you know, plead with her emotions, but she said no. There was nothing we could do. We couldn't prove she had it or that she stole it. We fired her and told all of our friends I referred to Anna what happened. . . . I felt

really bad because you always feel like people are doing housekeeping because they need the money, and it can be really good money if they are good. Anna was good, and I hated that it came to that. I think that guy she brought over had something to do with it, which is why I didn't want her bringing people. We had a relationship with her . . . that guy just saw our stuff and figured we wouldn't miss anything, but we worked hard for all of this so we know what it is, where it is, and how much it cost and for my wedding ring. It wasn't really about the cost, it wasn't a "rock" or anything . . . but it was my wedding ring!

A lot of Marilyn's conflict came out of a connection to Anna as another African American woman trying to better her situation. Outsourcing domestic help is already difficult for many African American women. First, the ability to hire personal assistance is outside what most consider the African American norm. Second, a history of being the help rather than employing the help is a large part of the collective memory of the African American experience. While none of the women in this study had mothers who were employed as domestics, these professional women can think back to the not-too-distant past and name female family members who were. This explained some of Marilyn's discomfort with the situation with Anna.

Marilyn made sense of her role as the employer of an African American woman domestic through seeing herself as "helping" someone who needed work, and, given her skills, Marilyn could refer her to others, which allowed Anna presumably to make more money than she could when pawning an engagement ring. Marilyn's analysis of "helping" was not unusual, and sometimes domestic "helpers" felt the same way. A casual conversation with an African American graduate student revealed her relationship with a woman she now considered her mentor. She said she met the African American professor when she was interning in her office, and the woman asked her if she would clean her house. The student said she was not offended because it was something she had done before and mentioned to the professor in passing. Interesting, however, was the student's acknowledgment that through this relationship as the professor's housekeeper she developed a mentoring relationship with the professor because the student looked up to the professor and used their time together to question her about her profession and to develop her own plan for graduate school. In this case, the power dynamic had changed from one of employer/ employee to mentor/mentee, and the student was paid for it.

This was not the only way African American women avoided what they found to be awkward power relationships. Some of the women in this study employed in-home caregivers and admitted that they had to balance their roles as granddaughters or nieces of former domestics and nannies against their current roles as employers. To do this, many adopted their childcare givers into their families by calling their childcare givers "Aunt" or "just like a mother." For example, Ms. Bridgette had taken care of Kya's children since they were born, and Kya's daughter Laura called Ms. Bridgette "Mommy" until she was old enough to realize the difference.

For most of the families paying someone to do their childcare, housekeeping, and gardening elicited a bit of discomfort, especially when they had to negotiate pay or confront the employees about something missing or broken, but most difficult for many was dealing with the feeling that, as strong Black women, they could not "do it all" like their mothers had before them. Many said they were not willing to hire help until someone else had convinced them or they knew friends who were doing it. "My mother did it all," said Keayba. As a result, Keayba felt very apprehensive about hiring someone to clean her home after the birth of her first child. "I didn't want to do it," Keayba recalled. "Kareem had to convince me to let someone help. I was out of town for a conference, and when I got back the house was clean. After that it became a line-item in our budget, but I still wasn't completely comfortable." Others expressed feeling awkward having people clean for them. "I just didn't grow up with it," said Kathy. "My mom did all of the cleaning and cooking. We lived in the city so there wasn't that much outside stuff to do. Then when we were old enough, we did the cleaning, the cooking, and the outside stuff. Paying someone to do it was completely foreign. Now I don't know what I would do without it." Kia stated that she often "cleaned" before the housekeeper arrived. "I just feel uncomfortable if I do not pick up something."

For most, hiring help is a luxury that can be given or taken away depending on the household expenses. Denise said she would love to hire help. "I could hire a nanny," she said. "I can't change his [her husband's] schedule. His job allows us to do what we do so just getting some help would be nice . . . maybe a housekeeper would be good. But we pay over 30k in tuition so I don't want to press the issue. Is it worth the argument?" Linda said she would pay someone to come in and cook every day. "That is the biggest thing after work." And for Karen, calling upon the forces of Oprah was her answer to the change in household duties since she and her attorney husband and three children relocated.

> It's been the biggest difference in our roles since we got here because our jobs changed. He did much more in New Orleans because he had his own practice, and I worked full time. Once we moved here we decided he would get a full-time position, and I would work on a contract basis. Until two months ago he did nothing. We've been renegotiating. He's been more open to reallocating the household responsibilities with some arm-twisting, but he says he's had an epiphany. If I could, I would have a maid

at least once to get everything organized, and then I would maintain. Just
to get organized. I need Oprah!

For African American women domestic labor was not a choice during slavery, and it was the only choice in the Jim Crow South and during northern discrimination; therefore, an African American woman in a position to purchase
domestic services encounters much uncertainty. Black women are conflicted
over issues of race and class. When I talked with her about her decisions, Cara
asked, "If they [white women] can be at home, why can't we?" This query points
to another conversation with Cara, who suggests that other identity formula-
tions may be materializing. When people learned she worked from home, her
children attended preschool, and she employed a housekeeper:

> They say "What do you do all day?" But I say why shouldn't I have a house-
> keeper or someone to help out around the house? White women have
> been doing it for years. . . . White women have an option. We have to
> work. I never thought about it, but if Black wives wanted to stay home
> most husbands would say, no you have to work. There is a different men-
> tality. When you've always had to work hard to attain it [wealth/status],
> it has a different feeling. We can have the same as Caucasians, but it still
> seems harder for us. When you don't have to struggle it's easy to sit back
> and wait for someone to give you something.

Cara's statement was clearly defensive. She wanted what she perceived as the
purview of middle-class white women: freedom, flexibility, and leisure, especially as markers of her class status. Cara, however, understood that most
Black women did not have that opportunity, and even if they did they were less
inclined to take it. As granddaughters and nieces of domestic workers, nannies,
or washerwomen, they find hiring women to do similar tasks synonymous with
hiring their own kin. They are well aware of the history of the exploitation of
Black women's labor and understand that women who provide productive labor
for one household are typically unable to afford household services for their
own (Brown 2011; Romero [1992] 2002).

The ambiguity in these women's race(d), class(ed), and gender(ed) position
is best articulated when the connection to their past race(d) and gender(ed)
social location as Black women, who are descendants of Black women domestics, most clearly contrasts to their present class(ed) location from which they
can hire Black and women of color domestics. From the women's perspective,
there is something perverse about doing it and something perverse about not
doing it. As Cara suggests, Black women have to be concerned about what they
are saying about themselves when they presume they cannot hire help. If help

would be beneficial to them, then perhaps hiring white women domestics is the answer—as a type of historical quid pro quo. Should their interactions, as in Marilyn's case, be steeped in uncertainties about employee trust and power differentials?

This contested site tells us a lot about the Black community as a whole: it is complicated and includes several communities. The ongoing debate about which group represents the community is part of the stuff that holds the community together. Common understanding at its core allows the community to be all-encompassing and accepting, even when some members are chastised. So many Black citizens balk when the community problems are aired publicly because these issues are seen in response to the white mainstream community, which, on the surface, appears to function without fracture. As long as members are identifying as Black but negotiating and debating what it means to be Black from within, the importance of the community remains intact as various groups redefine it for their own purposes. As Mignon Moore's study of lesbian Black families reveals, understanding the Black community means recognizing that membership does not require "sameness or having one voice, but [is] about having a commonality, a perceived link that connects it members regardless of other differences that might also exist" (Moore 2011, 214).

Unlike Moore's study participants, the heterosexual, married, career women featured here are in a socially privileged position. They fit into and often work to maintain the Black status quo through their enactment, acknowledgment, and enforcement of the politics of respectability. Regardless of their frustration with some members' personification of stereotypical images and others' disconnect from Black neighborhoods, schools, and businesses, these women remain committed to the whole Black community through neighborhood and church affiliation, social organizations, financial support, and social services. Nevertheless, Black career women, engaging in the neo-politics of respectability that privileges married, nuclear families, face communal conflict because, as a minority group, their community role is increasingly ambiguous.

Conclusion

Strategic Mothering, Black Families, and the Consequences of Neoliberalism

In the same way that Black women have always worked, there have always been some Black women who were in a position, or created a way, to stay at home. Since slavery, Black women have looked for ways to sustain and maintain their families; they particularly sought to ensure the survival and success of their children. This has historically meant gathering and rallying all members of the Black community to help raise children.

Correspondingly, the women in *Raising the Race* articulated decisions that focused their attention on their marriages, their children, and their communities precisely because of their racial identity. These decisions make the politics of respectability a potent way to consider contemporary Black women's decisions. For these women the promise of "respectability" provides protection for themselves and their family members, namely their children, from the stereotypical images that remain a mainstay of the American imagination. In this way, the neo-politics of respectability is not an elitist notion, and they do not see themselves as individual representatives of the race because they are not activists on a national, local, or community platform (Ferguson 2002; Gaines 1996). Instead, these women work quietly within their communities, for their churches, and at their workplaces to provide "real" perspectives on Black women and Black families that are contrary and contradictory to mainstream stereotypes and images. Most are engaged in public service through church and/or sorority. Some of the women, notably Kalia, Keayba, Kya, Jill, and Natalie, made service their profession. A couple, like Gail and Nancy, were purposefully engaging in relationships with poor and working-class women. Their desire to change the way popular culture, academia, and media outlets depict African Americans likens them to the respectable elite of the early twentieth century. They want to counter the myths and the stereotypes about Black women, Black families, and Black youth through their maintenance of stable Black families.

Although I believe this position is problematic as it insists upon hetero-normativity, Christianity, and Victorian gender mores, I see these women as attempting to develop communal salvation in response to the continued and devastating effects of racism, classism, and sexism in the Black community. Nevertheless, they do not realize that this cultural model, the neo-politics of respectability, is designed to offer some reprieve from the racist ideologies perpetuated against them, but this cultural model is also complicit in that very process (Collins [1990] 2000). As a result of a horrible trick played on Black women who devised a political campaign to be considered "ladies," elite Black women, particularly in the public arena, now must conform to ideologies of being a proper wife, mother, and daughter and feel that they are punished in the public's eye if they do not. According to previous Black feminist scholarship, one has only to look to the ways Anita Hill, Condoleezza Rice, and Michelle Obama have been criticized when they have stepped outside the construction of what Lisa B. Thompson calls the "Black lady." By aligning themselves with the image of the "Black lady," a successor to the mammy, Black career women inadvertently single themselves out as caretakers and mothers of the race, and they constrain all other Black women to the image of the jezebel. In each case, Black women as a whole are seen as some iteration of hypersexual-ized, domineering, and undesirable.[1]

Like most contemporary women, the Black career women in *Raising the Race* were too engaged in the day-to-day activities of their lives to consider the larger meaning and implications of their marriages to their high school sweethearts or college beaus or the structural reasons why they are "choosing" to modify their relationships with their careers. In an essay reflecting on Black feminism, bell hooks (1999) wrote, "Often individual Black women are so worried that they will be regarded through the lens of racist/sexist stereotypes that portray us as dominating, vicious, and all-powerful, that they refuse to make any coura-geous or non-conforming act. They may be more conservative in standpoint and behavior, more upholding of the status quo, than their non-Black and female counterparts."

Few women in this study realized that the things that kept marriage from being attainable and sustainable in previous generations were less about the failings of Black men and women and more about the social and economic inequalities that had long affected the rate and quality of marriage in the Black community. They, similar to other mothers, saw their negotiation of the career and family balance as an individual or family issue. Black mothers felt compelled to address a Black communal problem because they form part of the commu-nity. From these women's perspectives, their decisions had nothing to do with the mainstream conversation around work and family conflict or the feminist engagement with women's and mothers' rights. In fact, as hooks suggests, the perspectives of these Black career women were quite conservative when they discussed their household and community roles.

"Patriarchy Will Not Heal Our Wounds"

When I asked about the role of feminism in their lives and if they saw themselves as feminist, sixteen of the twenty-three women did not see themselves as feminist. Most of the women stated they believe in women's rights but only to a small degree (Winkle-Wagner 2008). Karen stated, "I believe men and women have certain roles. I am a little bit more old-fashioned. Women should have rights, but they should not be fighting in a war. I don't personally want to take the trash out. I will if I have to, but I don't want to." And Natalie astonishingly admitted she did not think a woman should be president.

> I think feminist ideology is valuable because it says men and women are valuable. What it turned into does not support who we are and has led to women ending up on the brunt end trying to do everything and children and men suffer. Women should not be subservient, but there are certain things we're designed to do. I do not think a woman should be president . . . I don't know why. I've put a lot of energy into accepting the headship principle. I think it would be inappropriate.

When I pushed her to elaborate a bit more she said, "I guess I see feminism as a political movement to ensure that women have the rights they should and shouldn't have opportunities denied solely based on being female. But I do not think feminism is how it is practiced. Other movements get lumped under feminism that I don't agree with." Natalie said she didn't agree with abortion and she didn't agree with homosexuality. "I don't have anything against the people who do it. I just think it's not what God ordained." Many of the women agreed with Natalie on this point, as does much of the Black community (Cohen 1999; Frederick 2003; Moore 2011).

For other women the issue was the way feminism was likened to white women's concerns and not Black women's issues. In *Ain't I a Woman* (1981), bell hooks suggested that Black women's concerns and realities have long been left out of white women's pursuit of equality; therefore, Black women have found little reason to join or support their causes. Charlotte stated, "As African Americans we have broader issues to deal with. The struggles of my people have been greater than just my gender. I think things should be fair and equitable and we should not be denied based on our gender but I don't see myself as a feminist." When I asked her to define feminism, she said, "A strong women's advocate and someone who fights for women's rights because they think women have been wronged and denied privileges and opportunities." She continued, "I believe in teaching girls to believe in themselves not because of their gender but to teach them self-confidence so they are strong in themselves; for Black girls that is about being strong as girls and particularly as Black girls." Charlotte articulates most acutely the difference in the ways Black girls and women have been and continue to be raised to address their differential experiences in the American context, and with just cause (Hurtado 1996). In most instances they are portrayed as "sapphire, welfare queen, baby mama, or unmarriageable," and it's a refreshing change to feature a new image suggesting that alongside the image of the strong Black woman you can have a nurturing maternal side for your own children, not just white children. Black mothers seek to be able to care for their children, not just to teach them how to cope and survive. Indeed, as Tami Winfrey Harris stated, "many Black women, including feminist ones . . . are delighted to see an African American woman [referring to Michelle Obama as Mom-in-Chief] publicly celebrated in ways that we are commonly not."[2]

Even those who did embrace some aspects of feminism were cautious. Cara said, "I think I am womanist," referring to Alice Walker's (1983), differentiation between Black women's feminism and white women's feminism. Denise, one of few who identified as feminist, said she reads *Pink* magazine, an Atlanta-based magazine for corporate women, and said we all should be feminist, "But not in the Nazi feminist way. We should all stand up for equal pay, etc., but I realize we are different from men, and we should embrace that. I think we have to be careful not to lobby or legislate ourselves out of being feminine; making laws so equal that being a woman is no different from being a man at work."

In the articulations of all of the women there is a clear disconnect between the desire for equal access and opportunity for Black women and the Black community as a whole and what is understood as feminism—Black, white, or otherwise.[3] Paula Giddings challenged this notion in her ground-breaking history, *When and Where I Enter: The Impact of Black Women on Race and Sex in America*:

> It is the historical concerns of Black women which are at the core of the Black and women's movements. When she is at her lowest ebb, the racial struggle flounders. When she is compelled to articulate her needs and become active in their behalf, the Black movement advances. . . . The fundamental goals of White feminists have been historically defined through the Black movement. . . . So the relationship between race and sex, one linked by the Black woman, means that her role is of the utmost importance. History suggests that it is only when her convictions are firm in this regard can a society—one born in the depths of racism and sexism—be transformed. (1984, 348)

Concurring but adding a class analysis, Patricia Hill Collins states, middle-class Black women have several decisions to make: Will they join in solidarity with their working-class and poor sisters, or will they become the "mammies" of the corporate structure who know their place and maintain the class structure (Collins [1990] 2000, 67)? Will they challenge patriarchy even within the Black familial model, or will they embrace it in an attempt to gain the male protections so many have not had due to absentee fathers? A Black feminist standpoint asks how our cultural models will change to ensure our collective survival. If professional Black women are concerned about representations of Black womanhood and Black culture and if that concern is rooted in the racist ways our community continues to be stereotyped out of opportunities, what will be the response? What theme will endure?

The legacy of the "politics of respectability," although modified, has endured and is particular to professional Black women's standpoint. According to recent news pundits and bloggers, by focusing on the health of their marriages and rejecting the model of the "strong Black woman," Black career women are potentially committing a revolutionary act that is similar in its construction and goals to the last century's politics of respectability.[4] But what is the cost?

Privatizing Black Strategic Mothering

As I talk with women about the study, I am struck by the fact that all the women with whom I talk, white or Black, of Latina or Asian descent, believe the model of communal support that has long been a hallmark of Black families is most important for sustaining all families. Since the 1970s when white women began going into the workforce in larger numbers, until now, when 70 percent of women in the workforce are mothers (Williams 2001), multiple studies have suggested that the increase in white mothers in the workforce coincided with an increase in crime and juvenile delinquency and a decrease in school performance (Aizer 2004; Hoffman and Vander Ven 2007). Scholars have since found that these trends had nothing to do with mothers' entry but everything to do with the fact that no corporate or government supports were put in place to offset mothers' need to focus on work (Vander Ven 2003). Mothers and their families were expected to negotiate these shifts on their own (Gerson 1986; Hochschild 1989).

Alongside women's massive entry into the paid workforce, the nation faced tremendous deindustrialization and a large-scale restructuring of the political economy marked by neoliberalism. According to anthropologist Carol Greenhouse (2011), neoliberalism has restructured the most prominent public relationships that constitute belonging, including work and self-identity. People are encouraged to settle their needs through consumer-based individualism.

Additionally, neoliberalism is marked by ambivalence precisely because it complicates and fragments the fields of personal and collective choice in managing the everyday (Greenhouse 2011, 5). In other words, there is a decline in both public sector supports and their value (Craven and Davis 2013). For most professional women, the personal "choice" to be at home is connected to the idea that women themselves need to be able to care for their families. This framework grounds the dominant nuclear model and helped to create the consumer-based individualism marking suburbanization in the 1960s and 1970s (Coontz 1992).

The effect of this model on Black women has reflected the decline in government support and set up the dilemma facing these professional Black women because their cultural model has historically privileged collective decisions and actions rather than individual ideas or personal choice. While the women's feelings of being responsible to and for the Black community have continued, the route of response to that responsibility has shifted, particularly for Black career women. Although Black families are increasingly away from their extended family and family of origin, many of the families in this study try to replicate the communal structure they remember from their childhoods. They lovingly and longingly recall the way they grew up with close-knit families. Yet trying to create such environments for their own children and maintain meaningful alternatives requires work. In the attempts to manage their family lives these mothers find themselves having to pull back in some areas and be more insular in others.

Many have noted the importance of communal supports through the African proverb, "it takes a village to raise a child." First Lady and Secretary of State Hillary Rodham Clinton popularized the idea in the United States with her similarly titled book *It Takes a Village* (1996). Nevertheless, the United States continues to struggle with garnering support for or developing programming that will truly assist people, families, and communities. The Black community, traditionally leaning on its own institutionalized support structures, has recognized the fact that private institutions and public services were not designed for them; instead, the Black church, historically Black colleges and universities and community schools, and Black sororities and fraternities are steeped in communal support and connected to the uplift movement and the politics of respectability (Gaines 1996; Higginbotham [1993] 2006). As the proximity to and significance of these institutions wane, however, the Black family and Black women in particular are left to fend for themselves.

Changing Work-Family Policies Can Provide Additional Strategies

While it is important that Black women create "safe spaces" of communal and "just-like kin" support for themselves whenever they can, not everyone has access to people on whom they can rely to fulfill their needs. In this case and contrary to the neoliberal model, the government must step in and seek ways to repli-cate responses to these needs while maintaining public interest and connection. According to a review of recent literature by Stephanie Moller, Joya Misra, and Eiko Strader (2013), some policies have been implemented globally that could assist families in the United States. They suggest "work-family policies target the pressures families face in balancing care and employment. Leave policies (i.e., maternity, paternity and parental leave) support caretaking while allowing par-ents to stay connected to employment, and state-subsidized childcare programs support parents' employment and children's education." According to several studies and reports, as Moller, Misra, and Strader assert, "With the exception of the United States (Fass 2009; Walsh 2011), most economically advanced coun-tries offer some form of federal paid maternity and/or family leave, though the specifics of policies vary across countries" (Moller, Misra, and Strader 2013, 139).

The United States continues to mandate unpaid parental leave through the Family and Medical Leave Act (FMLA). The decisions to provide paid parental leave and the employees to whom this benefit is extended continue to be left to the employer's discretion. Under this rubric, parental leave policies in the United States typically benefit professional women, leave working-class women to support themselves, and demonize poor women for utilizing the minimal bene-fits offered (Albelda 2001). According to a Pew Research Center Report, the United States ranks last when compared to thirty-seven other nations in the amount of paid time and protected time off that is available to employed new mothers in each country.[5]

As the United States continues to consider the degree to which it will pro-vide familial supports, the extent of support should not require increased sur-veillance, as it typically does for people of color and the poor (Roberts 1997). Rather, the government should seek to model programs in other areas of the world where social supports and funds are offered to help families take care of themselves and then in turn take care of others. Janet Walsh, deputy women's rights director at Human Rights Watch and author of the report "Failing Its Fam-ilies: Lack of Paid Leave and Work-Family Supports in the US," stated, "We can't afford not to guarantee paid family leave under law—especially in these tough economic times. The US is actually missing out by failing to ensure that all work-ers have access to paid family leave. Countries that have these programs show productivity gains, reduced turnover costs, and health care savings."[6] Accord-ing to bell hooks, this is a cause for which all women, especially feminists and especially black women, should be fighting. Almost thirty-five years ago in her seminal text *Ain't I a Woman* (1981), hooks wrote:

> To me feminism is not simply a struggle to end male chauvinism or a
> movement to ensure that women will have equal rights with me; it is a

commitment to eradicating the ideology of domination that permeated Western culture on various levels—sex, race, and class, to name a few—and a commitment to reorganizing U.S. society so that the self-development of people can take precedence over imperialism, economic expansion, and material desires (1989, 194).

The key seems to be making sure everyone understands feminism the way hooks does.

US Development of People Should Start at Home

US neoliberal policies have negatively impacted all mothers and their families. Black families have historically been able to rely on friends and family, and they still do. As they move up the corporate and social class mobility ladder, often accompanied by relocation, it becomes increasingly hard to maintain communal ties. At the same time, the overworked schedules of upwardly mobile parents and children have serious effects on child-rearing strategies (Schor 1992). On the other end of the class structure, the systematic destruction of the public school system, the shrinking economy, the higher costs of postsecondary education, and the withdrawal of social safety nets leave Black women in communities where social structures that in the past ensured a modicum of survival are breaking down and in many instances failing.

In the case of both childcare and public education, our current system reifies the distance between the haves and the have-nots: families with means are able to pay for private schools, and families without means are relegated to floundering in schools that don't meet their needs. Additionally, working-class families must rely on family and communal support for help with their children's educational needs, while upper-income families can often pay for necessary supports and tutors. Creating and maintaining structures that create class divides divest in our nation's primary resource, the American people and children in particular; this dichotomy creates a caste system where only those with financial and cultural capital are allowed to succeed. With the recent recurring challenges to affirmative action and women's right to choose abortion, and the repeal of the Voting Rights Act, we are turning back our political clock in some scary ways that have yet to be fully articulated and explored at any cohesive systematic level. Indeed, as womanist scholar Layli Phillips suggests, "in the absence of changed minds and changed practices, dismantled social institutions will only re-form in newly oppressive ways" (Phillips 2006, xl).

The Realities of Constrained Choice:
Dismantling the Master's House

The constraints of race, class, and gender continue to permeate the daily lives and decisions of Black women regardless of their education, marital status, or socioeconomic background. To continue to talk about Black career women's ability to choose in the context of marriage and motherhood is not to rekindle feminism or identify revolutionary ways in which some professional Black women are exercising their right to choose. Defining Black women's ability to choose between systems that are not designed for their benefit upholds the patriarchal, white supremacist order that leaves middle-class and upper-middle-class women of all racial and ethnic groups in isolated gated communities with small children or climbing corporate ladders with rungs missing, or both. Likewise, poor and working-class women who cannot attain these forms of privilege are forced to try to attain and or dismantle these models in ways that are potentially harmful to themselves and their children. We can look to the growing rates of incarceration for Black girls and women to confirm that the system is not working on either end of the social order (Crenshaw 2012).

Yet, as always and as the women in *Raising the Race* demonstrate, Black women's position and response remains instructive. Race is not supposed to matter any longer, especially for upper-middle-class elites. This study reveals, however, that overt racism, while it still exists, has been mostly replaced by covert racism, with which the women in this study negotiate and contend every day. In thinking about the impact of their race as mitigated by their class these women choose whether to invest in their marriages, whether to be at-home-moms or part-time employees, where to move, who to engage to care for their children, and where to send their children to school. It also affects the context in which they interact with their families of origin, their in-laws, their extended family and friends, and their church and communal organizations. Thus, when African American professional women are left out of the scholarship on work and family conflict and when college-educated Black women are stereotypically dismissed for having difficulties getting married, we miss much of the complexity in shaping national conversations about strengthening the middle class, reforming education, and building equity in marriage and family policy.

Many have articulated, studied, and fought for strategies that would affect changes for women and their families; unfortunately few alterations have had the express purpose of benefitting Black women. I agree with bell hooks when she states that "patriarchy will not heal our wounds," and this is at the center of many of the constraints on black women and children's lives. But I acknowledge the fact that Black women have wounds, and with little to no assistance we have been coming up with strategies to help alleviate them for centuries. I also acknowledge the fact that I, as a social scientist trained in research methods with an insider/outsider perspective, can see the ways in which my study participants have embraced a patriarchal system, which is persistently detrimental to them, in an effort to protect themselves and their children. I further understand that from their perspective few viable alternatives exist, and the risks are too great if those alternatives fail. With that in mind, I have developed my own thoughts on how we may be able to move forward and assist private families through public supports. I understand because of our imperialist, white supremacist, capitalist patriarchy, my suggestions do not stand a chance if they are designated for only Black women. I therefore frame them to be more universal in their construction; nevertheless, I would be remiss if I did not say I hope that if/when they are implemented, instead of a trickle-down or boats-rising approach we use Anna Julia Cooper's century-old awareness that when and where Black women enter, the whole race (read: human) enters with her. I have focused my investigation on Black women, but I am sure others have read this ethnography and found that it speaks to portions of their reality. It should be clear, then, that all of our fates are tied together. As the social justice adage attributed to Aboriginal activists working in Queensland in the 1970s states, "If you have come to help me, you are wasting your time. If you have come because your liberation is bound up with mine, then let us work together."[7]

I have identified four actions public policy makers can implement to assist us:

1. Require companies to provide paid sick leave and paid parental leave for all parents and caregivers. The best companies do this, and it is important for workers. Some states have recently passed laws to allow for paid sick days, but the federal government still does not mandate it in federal employer policies.

2. Provide better subsidies for childcare. People should not have to choose whether it is worth working because most of their paycheck is going to childcare.

3. Truly invest in public education reform, not through the free market but by working with families and communities to design schools that meet the needs of parents and children.

4. Dismantle prejudice, racism, and anti-Blackness through public policy and public education, including educating all young people about the history of people of color in the United States.

Making Feminism Work

As feminist scholars have repeatedly suggested, feminists must do a better job of understanding and relating to the everyday lived experiences of all women (hooks 2000). It is not enough to call out patriarchal, racist, imperialist systems when there are few alternatives and no clear organized action. We must first see people where they are and then educate them on the ways in which these systems operate without demonizing historically useful survival strategies. One thing rang clear throughout each of my interviews and observations: these women wanted to have not only careers but also children and husbands. There should not be anything wrong with that desire. Developing a feminist framework that demonizes marriage, particularly in the Black community, essentially puts us back at square one. Yes, aspects of the way marriage has been set up bind it with patriarchy and capitalism (Hartmann 1979; hooks 2000). For Black women who have not been protected by the state, marriage becomes even more important, especially as Zora Neale Hurston's Nannie reminded us in *Their Eyes Were Watching God*—so many women fall into the perpetuation of patriarchy in an effort to protect their daughters (Hurston [1937] 1990). The work of finding and implementing viable alternatives should start there.

Future scholarship should explore other ways in which various groups and historic institutions within the Black community are redefining the politics of respectability for their own survival purposes. Scholarship should also investigate the ways individuals and groups resist respectability as a strategy. As Mary Pattillo (2007) and Mignon Moore (2011) suggest, part of defining the Black community is recognizing it as a space in which varied identities and voices are heard and debated. Perhaps making more people aware of the diversity of experience will mitigate some of the work these mothers feel they must do to protect their children. For instance, with more academic work on the varied experiences of the Black middle class, we disrupt the idea that all Black people, with a few exceptions, are poor. Future studies should also employ strategic mothering as a theoretical tool to help identify other spaces where structural impediments force women to make decisions that continue to reinforce raced, classed, and gendered power differentials. Some studies on Asian American women have begun this work through the lens of race, class, and nationality (Kang 2014). In creating the necessary tools and building multiple sites of contestation we will be able to remove the onus from individuals and place it on systems. Only with these new tools will we be able to "dismantle the master's house" (Lorde 1984).

Epilogue

Whatever Happened To . . .

Whenever I present the data collected here, the audience inevitably wants to know what has happened to the women and their families. Have they gone back to work? Are the couples still together? What's going on with their kids? These questions arise because everyone is clear that family decisions are not static; they are shaped by their past, their present, what lies up ahead, or just around the bend, and the fluidity is also important in shaping family structure and how they function. Since I both began this research and concluded this study, the change that has taken place on a much larger national scale is part of what makes my description of the happenings compelling. When I was in the midst of interviewing these women, the momentous, historical event that resulted in the election of President Barack Obama had not yet happened; in fact, it was not even on most people's radar, and his election was definitely something that I would have included in these interviews because these women were potentially rethinking their views on race as it pertained to their families. I have had an opportunity to speak with most of the women in the study since completing the work, and they have been influenced in their thinking on the opportunities available for their children, primarily recognizing how important an impact President Obama, First Lady Michelle Obama, and even the Obama daughters, Sasha and Malia, have had on the ways they and their children think about their potential access to just about anything they want. The adage that many of us grew up with, "if you can believe it, you can achieve it," takes on a different meaning now. Nancy confided, "There were just some things you wouldn't even allow yourself to dream before."

Many in the Black community have speculated, however, that President Obama's success in winning his first election was the result of a perfect storm. Much of the country was frustrated with the Republican party and the way President George W. Bush and his advisors left the economy. The country was in the middle of two wars and an economic crisis that threatened to destroy the US economy and much of the global market. The connections between the US economy and other economies became quite clear, and the public saw how much that interdependence hinged on international debt. Simultaneously, the American people were frustrated with the state of affairs in Washington, DC, as it seemed Congress had very little interest in supporting the American people. A seemingly grassroots arm of the Republican Party, the Tea Party, with extreme right-wing conservative politics, was growing up and strengthening the Republican base, and, while Tea Party members seemed like they were concerned with everyday Americans, a closer look at their politics revealed an evangelical religious thrust that threatened many freedoms already fought for and won and that upon closer inspection seemed eerily racist and sexist. Nevertheless, many saw President Obama's move into the White House as a step in the post-race, color-blind society Dr. Martin Luther King promised in his speech.

It has been a rocky road politically and economically for many of the women in this study. Just as I was finishing the interviews, Atlanta was starting to feel the pinch of the decline in the housing market. Because most of the women were living in homes they could afford, and most of those homes were "newer," built since the 1990s, their housing values did not see very much decline. Denise's family was able to sell their home at a profit and move just outside the city limits to a larger home in Douglassville for around the same price. Likewise, Marilyn's family was able to move from the home they had bought when their children were smaller; they sold it at a profit because they bought it before the market went up and bought another home in a nearby, but more exclusive neighborhood. Their new home was purchased from a couple who was facing foreclosure. According to Marilyn, they were able to get the home for $200,000 below what the sellers had bought it for. "It was great for us," Marilyn said. "We had been looking for a long time, but we had a price point and we knew what we wanted. But when we got to the closing and we had to sit across from those sellers who were basically losing everything, it was the saddest thing I think I have experienced." The sellers were a retired couple who had been a part of one of the waves of African American buyers moving to Atlanta from the West Coast. A $500,000 home in Atlanta was worth a couple of million dollars in Los Angeles. The couple had invested a good deal of their retirement in the home, thinking it would serve them well into retirement as their grandchildren got older. The turn in the economy, diminishing most of their savings, coupled with the fact that their children and grandchildren were still on the West Coast, forced them to sell at a significant loss and move back to California. Marilyn said, "I felt so bad for them."

Nancy's family experienced a similar loss, but they were able to rebound without losing everything. When the housing market crashed, Aaron's construction firm effectively went out of business. According to Nancy he wasn't getting any business, was unable to extend credit, and had several properties in various stages of completion. "It was really bad around here then," Nancy reported, thinking back to the housing crisis. She knew of several cases where couples had gotten divorced, one case of suicide, and one case of suspected foul play where a person may have been murdered for the insurance funds. "Aaron was really smart, though," she said. Unlike a lot of the families she knew where husband and wife were both on the mortgages and the credit-lines, Aaron had put their primary residence in her name, but the rest of the properties, credit cards, and the line of credit were in his name. She said, "For a while we were trying to pay for everything, then we realized we had to let the properties go." If you recall from chapter 2, Nancy, a physician, had been keeping up with her medical licensing board exams even though she was not practicing medicine and considered herself the primary care-giver for her children and the book-keeper for her husband's business. For Nancy it was a precaution just in case things took a turn for the worse, and, in this instance, not her husband but the market had "gone crazy." Because Nancy kept up with her medical licensing boards and had been working part-time as a hospitalist, she was able to go "back to work" with relative ease.

> I had been working in Peachtree City, and one of the guys I went to medi-cal school with was trying to start a group where three or four hospitalists worked together and rotated schedules for some of the smaller hospi-tals. I went from an occasional job here and there to working twelve-to-fourteen-hour shifts on a four- to five-day rotation. Aaron took over the kids; we rented our house in the city out and moved to Peachtree City so I could be closer to work. Our lives made a complete 360 in less than two years.

Nancy confided, "I now know what my mom and my grandmother were trying to tell me. They didn't know what might happen. The only experience they had was the notion that men might leave, but the point was the same, we [Black women] are not in a position to be at home and not bringing in any income." While Nancy could see the benefit in her being home with her children while they were young, her youngest was now in kindergarten; looking back she believed they had put themselves in a really bad position. "It is totally different now. I work all of the time. I never see the kids, and I don't like that either, but I had to do that so we could pay everything back and get our credit together." With her physicians partnership Nancy makes close to $500,000 per year, and she says, "That was just a blessing. Things really could have turned out a whole lot differ-ently." Aaron has not been able to pick up the pieces of the business. According to Nancy, he does a little bit of remodeling and contractor work but no really big projects. For the time being, a lot of projects have dried up as people try to recuperate, and it has been rough on Aaron. Now Nancy is looking for ways for the two of them to have a business where they can both work together that can give them both better work hours and an opportunity to spend more time with the kids. "The last few years that I have been working, I have lost the kids. I don't get to spend much time with them. I really miss them, and I really want that back and so now we are looking for ways for both of us to do that responsibly." It's interesting that Nancy sees a more manageable schedule for her and Aaron as finding a way for both of them to work and be with the kids "responsibly." Nancy finds that neither of their work/family scenarios have been the best fit for their family. In the first version she was the primary caregiver while Aaron worked all of the time, but that didn't work because they were dependent on his income and completely exposed to whatever fluctuations he might have in the business. In the second version, she is the primary breadwinner while Aaron is the caregiver, but that model doesn't work either because "she lost the kids" and Aaron lost his self-esteem by losing the business. The ideal scenario is one in which they can each be "responsibly" engaged in both childcare and career.

Several of the moms in the study had changed their relationship with work when I conducted follow-up interviews. With children a little older than they were when I first interviewed her, Marilyn went back to work full-time and finally received the promotions she had been turning down while she was working part-time. The marketing firm where Cory was able to work from home laid her off, but she landed what she calls her dream job working in marketing and recruiting for a local nonprofit organization. Keayba was able to readjust some of her commitments at the medical school and, as a result, works fewer hours and has a couple of days per week when she can work from home. After publishing two books, Charlotte went back to work full-time as a PR director. Karen's family moved back to New Orleans, and Gia's husband took a new job so her family moved to Ohio. Natalie left the private school where she was teaching to be head of curriculum development at a public charter school and sent her oldest daughter off to college. As children grew older, school choices changed, but the sentiments behind them did not. All of the families were seeking the best way to educate their children and provide as many opportunities as possible. Cara and I repeatedly played phone-tag as she was helping her daughter navigate the interview process at one of Atlanta's prestigious private high schools. Marilyn's husband was teaching her oldest to drive, Kia had her fourth child, and Keayba had her third, prompting her to move her parents to Atlanta.

There was also one divorce. Gail, one of the participants who was the first to illuminate for me the discord between mothers and their daughters over the decision to be a stay-at-home mom, went through a separation and divorce after her husband committed adultery less than a year after she had her third child. "It really rocked my world," she said of the devastating affect it had and continues to have on her life. "I wanted a family. He took that from me." I was able to talk with Gail a few times over the course of her separation and subsequent divorce. While the couple has been able to set up an amicable relationship, Gail says "it is for the sake of the children." Not only did Gail face a split in her marriage, but, while she was going through the separation and divorce, her business partner embezzled funds and forced her into a bankruptcy. Luckily, she had set up her management business to be self-sustaining so she did not jeopardize her home or her personal assets, but she essentially had to rebuild her business, retaining an attorney and dissolving the first company so she could begin the business again with a new name:

> The hardest part was going to my clients and basically saying you have to sign all of these documents all over again because that other company does not exist. All of this was going on while I was going through a divorce and trying to explain to my three children, who at the time were all under six, that their father wasn't coming home and actually had another house. He was living with his parents for a while, and then moved in with the girl he cheated with and I was losing it. I was like, "don't let me see her when you pick up the kids and don't let her touch my daughter's hair." I didn't want to have to beat her. . . .

Gail laughed while telling me the story, but I could tell there was some truth in her joke. As well there should be. From Gail's perspective she and Lawrence never had a chance to work everything out. As soon as she found out he was "unhappy" he had already decided to leave. "There wasn't anything I could do. I tried because I love him, and I didn't want to lose my family. But it was like he was already gone even before he left, and I didn't know it." Gail was building a business, running a household, and taking care of three small children, including a baby. His excuse was she was too busy. Nevertheless, despite the fact that Lawrence "acted crazy," Gail does not think she made the wrong decision in focusing on being an at-home mom for as long as she could. "I think it was good for the kids for me to be around, but mostly it gave me a chance to find a career I really wanted to have and make a way for that to work with me being a mom." Since Gail works for herself, she is able to set up her appointments around the kids' schedules. She has also found that now that she and Lawrence have joint custody he actually shares more of the responsibility for their children than he ever did when they were together. "I actually get time off!" Gail exclaimed. But things remain difficult, even with child support. Gail has noticed a drop in her financial security and often finds herself having to make harsh financial decisions even as it concerns her children. "Our way of life has definitely changed because I make significantly less than Lawrence, but I have a lot of support from his parents as well. I think they realize how f—up it was [for him to commit adultery and leave his family], and that helps a lot."

Gail's experience reveals a harsh truth, not necessarily that men will act crazy; this assessment has been pretty well covered, and the fact that unforeseen things happen is a fact of life. The divorce revealed, however, that Gail was not really able to combine career and family until her marriage was dissolved. Their joint custody arrangement gave Gail time to have a balanced life, and she essentially gained a partner.[1] While she no longer has the companionship or the financial security supplied by her marriage, this unforeseen divorce shed light on the fact that many women are attempting to negotiate it all—even when they are married—by themselves. Studies have shown repeatedly that poor women have more social and familial support with their children when they are not married (Ladner [1971] 1995).

We also know from scholarly studies and the census data that not all fathers play an active role in their children's lives following a divorce (Hamer 2001). We also know that very few women are in a position, like Gail, to pick up the pieces of a marriage and a business and keep going, let alone start over. Even in Nancy and Aaron's case, had Nancy not had a way to reenter her very lucrative field, their family would have been devastated. And, as she reported, many were. The need for policies that help families to take care of themselves is paramount. As our society continues to build neoliberal policies that are on the wrong side of history, more families will end up like the couple who lost their retirement home, and fewer will be able to emerge unscathed on the other side of financial and family hardships. For Black families their hardships are particularly alarming because even high-income Blacks have less wealth, on average, than whites. Nevertheless, many American families are continuously affected as changes in the economy make it increasingly difficult for families both to survive, even on two incomes, and to ensure their children's education and future job prospects.

APPENDIX

MODIFIED STAY-AT-HOME MOM (MSH)				
Name	*Age*	*Occupation*	*Child(ren)*	*Family of Origin*
Gia	42	BS computer programmer	3	working class
Nancy	38	MD physician	3	working class
Frances	32	Some college business management	2	core-middle class
Kathy	43	hotel management	1	poor/working class
Gail	39	BA at-home business owner	3	working class
Monica	38	MPA public relations	3	core-middle class
Richelle	33	BS homemaker	3	poor/working class

MODIFIED FULL-TIME CAREER MOM (MFC)

Name	Age	Occupation	Children	Family of Origin
Natalie	36	BS physics teacher	3	poor/working class
Kalia	33	MS nonprofit management	1	upper-middle class
Linda	38	DDS dentist	2	core-middle class
Kia	35	BS engineer	3	upper-middle class
Jill	46	MD surgeon	3	upper-middle class
Selena	40	MBA financial analyst	3	core-working class
Keayba	38	MD practitioner and researcher	2	upper-middle class
Cory	44	MBA marketing executive	3	upper-middle class
Sherri	38	MBA financial Analyst	3	core-middle class

AVAILABLE-FLEXIBLE CAREER MOM (AFC)

Name	Age	Occupation	Children	Family of Origin
Marilyn	38	MPH medical insurance management	3	upper- middle class
Myra	39	MS occupational therapy	2	core-middle class
Cara	38	MA school psychologist	3	core-middle class
Denise	36	JD district attorney's office	2	working class
Kya	34	MA education consultant	2	core-middle class
Charlotte	44	MBA public relations, book author	2	core-middle class
Karen	47	MD physician	3	core-middle class

NOTES

INTRODUCTION

1. I use Black and African American interchangeably throughout the book. I have chosen to do this for two reasons: first, I denote the phenotypic and the cultural uses of the terms as they are related to people of African descent whose history can be traced to the trans-Atlantic slave trade and those people of African descent who are early twentieth-century immigrants who were adopted into the African American context; second, I account for the fact that the women in this study used both terms interchangeably. I am aware of the contention in the use of both terms for more recent African and Caribbean immigrants, but that contention does not extend to the families who participated in this study and therefore is not the focus of the analysis.

2. Strategic mothering is not a new practice. As the analysis demonstrates, Black women have been employing these strategies for centuries. I conceptualize strategic mothering as an overarching term developed to aid in our recognition and analysis of the strategies women have used to mother their children and their communities. Conceptually, strategic mothering challenges our reliance on the myth of the ideal mother as homemaker in a nuclear, male-headed family and renders visible the ways in which Black women in particular and ethnic minority women more generally have historically strategized their mothering practices. I am not alone in my recognition of women's strategic mothering practices. Sociologist Miliann Kang has also developed a conceptual framework for analyzing ethnic minority mothers. She uses "strategic racialized mothering" in her work on Asian American mothers (2014). While I find value in Kang's analysis, I do not use Kang's terminology because it inadvertently places the focus on racialized identities. This focus may be useful for some racial ethnic women, but for others, namely Black women, it reintroduces notions of pathology and deviance. Limiting the analysis to a racialized perspective "ghettoizes" Black women's everyday lived experiences and disallows a theoretically expansive conversation that crosses ethnicity and even race. Instead, I use strategic mothering to highlight the experiences of Black women, who are often hyperattentive to their raced and gendered position. I center Black women's strategic mothering practices and recognize the lessons that can be learned. I am clear, however, that my future research and that of others should investigate the mothering strategies of ethnic minority women, as well as white women in the United States and globally. Therefore, Kang's exploration of the practices Asian American mothers employ is one of the many examples of strategic mothering that can be used to first navigate and then

dismantle the homemaker-mother ideal and the corresponding mythology on self-reliance espoused by the state.

3. Scholars have shown that, just after the abolition of slavery when Black families began to sharecrop on white plantations, many families tried to keep the wives at home to care for the needs of the family while the husband and children old enough to work the fields worked outside the home. In response, white landowners insisted Black women work alongside their men or be charged a penalty while white women were not expected to work the fields or in their homes; in fact, white women often hired help. According to Tera Hunter's seminal text on working conditions for Black women in the post-Reconstruction era, even the poorest white women "employed" Black domestics, often paying them in goods rather than money. Later, when the government began providing subsidies to families who needed economic and housing support (what we now call "welfare" and Section 8), white women were expected to stay at home and care for the needs of the family and use the subsidy to bridge the gap between their husband's income and what their families needed to survive. When the subsidies became available to Black families, Black women were expected to work (Williams 2004). Women's history scholars Gwendolyn Mink and Linda Gordon also highlight the ways in which "welfare" has been "maternalistic" since its inception, provided as a way to help needy women rather than as something to which all citizens should be entitled, such as unemployment benefits (Gordon 1994; Mink 1995). Its association with Black women, through the stereotype of "welfare queen" introduced by President Ronald Reagan, made Aid to Families with Dependent Children (AFDC) an easy candidate for the cutting back once President Bill Clinton was elected and the Republicans controlled the House and the Senate. The result was the Personal Responsibility and Work Opportunity Act, which limits the number of years a woman can get benefits and penalizes poor mothers for wanting to raise their children themselves. See also Gutman 1976; Jones 1985; and Shaw 1996.

4. Companionate marriage refers to marital relationships wherein the union between the individuals takes precedence over any other kinship ties.

5. "Othermother" refers to Black women who have held the family and community together through their virtues of caring. They can be sisters, aunts, grandmothers, cousins, neighbors, or any other woman who steps in and provides assistance in a nonbiological mother role. According to Patricia Hill Collins, othermothers are often considered the backbone of the Black community and attempt to give anything they can to their communities (Collins [1990] 2000). This reference draws on Angela Davis's conceptualization of the place of Black women in the community of slaves and privileges Black women's role in maintaining the Black community and especially the children at all costs. Davis connects this role to the caregiving role of women in West Africa and the ways in which African American women have maintained the tradition (Davis 1971).

6. Fictive kin are individuals who are not related by blood, marriage, or legal adoption but who nevertheless consider each other family members (Sarkissian and Gerstel 2012).

7. Scholars have been critiquing the assertions made by Daniel Patrick Moynihan (1965) that Black families have a female matriarch and this matriarch undermines the success of Black families because she purportedly "emasculates" Black males so they are unable to take their "rightful position" as heads of their households. For example, Paula Giddings provides a chapter-length rebuttal in her book *When and Where I Enter*, situating Moynihan's comments in a fear of white women following suit and

suggesting Moynihan is warning white women that removing their men from the head position will find them in similar company (Giddings 1984).

8. I have intentionally focused on cis-gendered (where the sex and the gender of the person correspond) heterosexual women to isolate a study group that is historically impacted in particular ways by our capitalist and patriarchal system. A growing body of literature adds to our understanding of the humanity, fullness, and complexity of Black women's sexual and relational lives including Audre Lorde's "Man Child: a Black Lesbian Feminist's Response" (1979), Evelynn Hammonds's "Toward a Genealogy of Black Female Sexuality" (1997), and anthologies *Home Girls* (1983) edited by Barbara Smith and *Afrekete* edited by Catherine McKinley and Joyce Delaney (1995). Most recently, Mignon Moore's ethnographic study, *Invisible Families* (2011), sheds important light on Black lesbian women's constructions of family within the Black community.

9. Kevin Gaines, "Racial Uplift Ideology in the Era of the 'the Negro Problem,'" Freedom's Story, TeacherServe. National Humanities Center. http://nationalhumanitiescenter .org/tserve/freedom/1865–1917/essays/racialuplift.htm, accessed December 21, 2014.

10. bell hooks, "Ain't She Still a Woman," *Shambhala Sun*, 2009, http://www.hartford-hwp .com/archives/45a/186.html.

11. Kaplan is not alone in articulating her view that white women's perspectives will in essence "trickle down" to African American women and other minorities. This is a major criticism of second-wave feminism and was heartily attacked with the advent of Black feminism. It is unfortunate that long after the critical debates of the 1970s and 1980s, feminist treatment of women's lived experiences continues to prioritize and centralize white women's experiences over others (see also Gerson 1986; Hattery 2001; Moen 2005; Stone 2007).

12. The number of studies focused on poor or marginally middle-class Black mothers is small compared to studies on white women. A review of the literature, however, reveals the fact that these few studies are expected to be representative of all Black women's experiences. Some seminal titles are *All Our Kin* (Stack [1974] 1997), *Tomorrow's Tomorrow* (Ladner [1971] 1995), *On Our Own Terms* (Mullings 1997), *Stress and Resilience* (Mullings and Wali 2001), *African American Single Mothers* (Dickerson 1995), *Not Our Kind of Girl* (Kaplan 1997), *Compelled to Crime* (Ritchie 1995), *Killing the Black Body* (Roberts 1997), and *Inequalities of Love* (Clarke 2011).

13. Michelle Cottle, "Leaning Out: How Michelle Obama Became a Feminist Nightmare," *Politico*, November 21, 2013, http://www.politico.com/magazine/story/2013/11/leaning -out-michelle-obama100244.html#.U4jjY_lLWSo.

14. Tami Winfrey Harris, "A Black Mom-in-Chief Is Revolutionary: What White Feminists Get Wrong About Michelle Obama," *Clutch Magazine*, September 11, 2012, http://www .clutchmagonline.com/2012/09/a-Black-mom-in-chief-is-revolutionary-what-white -feminist-get-wrong-about-michelle-obama/.

15. Ibid.

16. "Holding a Four-Year College Degree Brings Blacks Close to Economic Parity with Whites," *Journal of Blacks in Higher Education*, http://www.jbhe.com/news_views/47 _four-year_collegedegrees.html, accessed December 14, 2014.

17. Ibid.

18. Current Population Survey, U.S. Department of Labor, U.S. Bureau of Labor Statistics. For 2008 data, see http://www.bls.gov/cps/wlf-table6–2008.pdf, accessed December 14, 2014. For 2012 data, see http://www.bls.gov/cps/wlf-databook-2012.pdf, accessed December 14, 2014.

19. Washington, DC, Raleigh-Durham, NC, and Houston, TX, have also garnered the atten-
    tion of demographers interested in exploring the lifestyles of the professional Black
    middle class. According to *Black Enterprise Magazine* (May 2007), these cities, along
    with Atlanta, are consistently ranked within the top five of the best cities for African
    Americans to "live, work, and play."

20. Spelman College, Morehouse College, Morris Brown College, Clark Atlanta University
    (formerly Clark College and Atlanta University), the Interdenominational Theological
    Center, and the Morehouse School of Medicine. Five of the schools are included in the
    Atlanta University Center Consortium and enroll a combined 10,000-plus students at
    the undergraduate and graduate/professional levels.

21. Self-segregation has become a very common misnomer to explain spaces where
    minorities choose to live, attend school, etc. The assumption is that no one is dis-
    criminating against them but rather they are choosing to be away from those who are
    not like them. These arguments have been used to dismantle groups and services that
    benefit minority groups and/or to make minority groups feel uncomfortable about
    creating spaces for themselves.

22. Carmen DeNavas-Walt and Bernadette D. Proctor, "Income and Poverty in the United
    States: 2013," Current Population Report, U.S. Department of Commerce, U.S. Cen-
    sus Bureau, http://www.census.gov/content/dam/Census/library/publications/2014/
    demo/p60–249.pdf, accessed December 14, 2014.

23. United States Census Bureau, Department of Commerce, American Fact Finder, http://
    factfinder.census.gov/faces/nav/jsf/pages/index.xhtml, accessed December 14, 2014.

24. Black Demographics.com, http://Blackdemographics.com/cities-2/atlanta/, accessed
    December 14, 2014.

25. See "What Percent Are You?" income calculator, *New York Times*, January 14, 2012.
    http://www.nytimes.com/interactive/2012/01/15/business/one-percent-map.html.

26. Five (22 percent) of the participants' mothers completed a PhD or JD, and four (17 per-
    cent) of their fathers completed a PhD or MD.

27. U.S. Census Bureau, Current Population Survey, 2011 Annual Social and Economic Sup-
    plement, http://www.census.gov/hhes/www/cpstables/032011/perinc/new01_001.htm.

28. Although Black graduation rates are significantly higher than they were at the turn of
    the twentieth century, college graduation rates remain significantly lower than that
    of whites, who have a rate of 64 percent for white women and 58 percent for white
    men. Tim Weldon, "Study: Graduation Rate Gap Exists between Black, White Males,"
    http://www.csg.org/pubs/capitolideas/enews/issue6_3.aspx, accessed December 14, 2014.

CHAPTER 1   THE ROLE OF BLACK WOMEN IN
BLACK FAMILY SURVIVAL STRATEGIES

1. There is a difference between female-headed household used by the census and
   female-headed family. Female-headed household suggests a single woman cares for
   the needs of the household. Female-headed family has historically meant there may
   be a senior woman, her children, and one or more of her daughter's child(ren) living
   with her in her household. Resources came into the home through other females,
   brothers, uncles, boyfriends, and other friends and kin (Ladner [1971] 1995; Stack
   [1974] 1997).

2. William Julius Wilson's *The Truly Disadvantaged* (1987) discussed how underemploy-
   ment and unemployment had an extremely detrimental effect on the ability of African
   American men to sustain long-term relationships and marriage. He outlined these

same factors in subsequent treatments including *When Work Disappears: The World of the New Urban Poor* (1998) and *More than Just Race: Being Black and Poor in the Inner City* (2010). Wilson's findings have been foundational for other studies including Kathryn Edin and Maria Kefalas's *Promises I Can Keep: Why Poor Women Put Motherhood Before Marriage* (2005). Wilson's work has been noted for its influence on the Clinton, G. W. Bush, and Obama administrations.

3. The most recent initiative argues that 14 percent of Black boys and 18 percent of Hispanic boys were scoring proficient or above on the fourth grade National Assessment of Educational Progress compared to 42 percent of white boys and 18 percent of Black and Hispanic girls. Since Black and Hispanic girls have similar scores to Black and Hispanic boys, it does not follow that programming would only be for boys (Jarrett and Johnson 2014). Scholars have suggested a continuing devaluation of Black and Hispanic girls.

4. See Hunter 1997, 2010; Mullings 1997; and Shaw 1995.

5. Several Black women writers have written about their relationships with their mothers and the lessons they learned. Most notable are Audre Lorde's *Zami: A New Spelling of My Name* (1982), Alice Walker's *In Search of Our Mother's Gardens* (1983), and Patricia Bell-Scott's *Double-Stitch: Black Women Write About Mothers and Daughters* (1991). There have been few sociological or anthropological studies centering the relationship between Black mothers and daughters and the actual process of enculturation that takes place. Exceptions are Gloria Joseph and Jill Lewis's *Common Differences: Conflicts in Black and White Women's Perspectives* (1981), which contrasts Black and white women's mother-daughter relationships. See also Suzanne Carother's study, "Catching Sense," in which she interviewed Black mothers to ascertain how they teach their daughters about being Black and female (1998).

6. According to Catalyst (March 3, 2014), in the United States in the academic year 2009–2010, women made up 47.2 percent of law school students. In 2011 women were 31.9 percent of all lawyers. Of those practicing law in firms in 2011, 45.4 percent of associates were women, but only 19.5 percent of partners were women. Women were 36.8 percent of MBAs in 2010–2011, but women make up only 3 percent of Fortune 500 executives. http://www.catalyst.org/knowledge/statistical-overview-women -workplace.

7. Sociologist Dawn Dow argues Black women's approaches are in direct opposition to the intensive motherhood model and more in line with traditional motherhood ideologies. In "Black Moms and 'White Motherhood Society': African-American Middle-Class Mothers' Perspectives on Work, Family, and Identity," Dow suggests Black women have an integrated approach to motherhood. (Dow 2011), UC Berkeley: Institute for the Study of Societal Issues. Retrieved from http://escholarship.org/uc/item/6kr3v4pz.

8. Available-flexible career moms may echo Garey's (1999) discussion of women working the night shift in order to remain available to their children during the day.

CHAPTER 2 BLACK PROFESSIONAL WOMEN, CAREERS, AND FAMILY "CHOICE"

1. Most historically Black institutions were founded as secondary schools, teacher training schools, industrial schools, or seminaries. They were later accredited as colleges and universities as their funding and programming changed.

2. United Negro College Fund website http://www.uncf.org/sections/MemberColleges/ SS_AboutHBCUs/about.hbcu.asp, accessed May 30, 2013.

3. I use pseudonyms for each college name to protect the identities of the study participants.

4. The National Achievement Scholarship Program is an academic competition established in 1964 to provide recognition for outstanding Black American high school students. The award is based upon PSAT (Preliminary Scholastic Achievement Test) scores and awarded to those students with the highest national scores.

5. There has been a significant amount of research on family daycare and how providers and families negotiate the boundaries between paid work and emotional work (see Nelson 1990; Uttal 1996, 1997, 2002; Uttal and Tuominen 1999).

6. The dot.com bubble refers to the tremendous growth that internet and technology firms experienced in the 1990s when the worldwide web went public and related industries grew exponentially. The bubble began to break and essentially "burst" in 2000 when several companies' profits started declining as financial markets began to correct for the overspeculation that had taken place in the previous decade.

7. See a 2011 op-ed in the *New York Times* by Karen S. Seibert for more information about work/family conflict for women physicians. "Don't Quit This Day Job," *New York Times,* op-ed page, June 11, 2011. http://www.nytimes.com/2011/06/12/opinion/12sibert.html ?pagewanted=all&_r=0

8. The pitch in multilevel marketing is that you can introduce business "partners" who become "owners" in the business and a small percentage of each "partner's" sales goes to the owner who signed them into the company.

CHAPTER 3   "JUST IN CASE HE ACTS CRAZY"

1. Jamilah Lemieux, "Anti-Abortion Billboard Targeting Blacks Placed in New York's SoHo Neighborhood." http://www.clutchmagonline.com/2011/02/anti-abortion-billboard -targeting-Blacks-placed-in-new-yorks-soho-neighborhood/, accessed April 14, 2013.

2. Corinne Lestch, "Bronx Council Women Annabel Palma Slams Bloomberg Ad Campaign against Teen Pregnancy," *New York Daily News,* March 24, 2013. http://www .nydailynews.com/new-york/bronx/bronx-councilwoman-slams-bloomberg-teen -pregnancy-ads-article-1.1297703, accessed April 14, 2013.

3. United States Census Bureau, Facts for Features, http://www.census.gov/newsroom/ facts-for-features/2013/cb13-ff02.html, accessed January 28, 2013.

4. See "About Essence," http://www.essence.com/about/, accessed July 9, 2014.

5. Dr. Laura Schlessinger is a national radio talk show host who advocates that men and women put all of their focus on what is best for their children. When listeners call with a dilemma about work or family or extended family, her response is usually "Be your children's parents." Listeners often call in and begin their question by saying, "I am my kid's mom."

6. In Kalia's case, job-sharing allows her to work part-time because she shares responsibilities with another employee. In her arrangement she is off on Fridays and gets off from work early two days per week. Her coworker has a similar arrangement but is off on Mondays.

7. The "Mrs." (pronounced em-ar-ess) degree refers to the period in women's higher education where women went to college to meet viable marriage prospects and would often marry and begin families while still in college or just after graduation.

8. According to Joy Bennett Kinnon, "mother wit" is referred to in the dictionary as simply "common sense." In Black history, the word usage began in the seventeenth century. Thus the word was born and distilled in the brutality of slavery and has survived

to enter the new millennium. It was a code word then and now for the knowledge you must have to survive. Kinnon states, "It is, as author Toni Morrison says, 'a knowing so deep' that the lesson has been instilled and distilled to its essence. Collectively these words are a gift—from your own mother, or anyone's mother. They are wise words for life's journey" (1997).

9. Black women and feminist studies have developed a sizable theoretical canon that explains and challenges the Black community's focus on Black men's success often at the expense of Black women. See seminal texts like bell hooks's *Feminist Theory: From Margin to Center* (1984, 2000), Beverly Guy-Sheftall and Johnnetta B. Cole's *Gender Talk: The Struggle for Women's Equality in African American Communities* (2003), Michele Wallace's *Black Macho and the Myth of the Superwoman* (1978), and more recently Melissa Harris Perry's *Sister Citizen: Shame, Stereotypes and Black Women in America* (2011).

10. Sex therapists have long held that women's sex drive is as much a function of mental space as physical chemistry.

CHAPTER 4   ENCULTURATING THE BLACK PROFESSIONAL CLASS

1. Bill Montgomery and Beth Warren, "Cornered by Thugs, Ex-Marine Kills 1, Rejects Hero Label," *Atlanta Journal-Constitution*, May 13, 2006. http://www.freerepublic.com/focus/f-news/1641181/posts.

2. Public schools serving the city of Alpharetta are among the best in the nation. With approximately 89 percent of area high school graduates taking the SAT, as compared to 48 percent nationally, the average SAT score for Alpharetta schools is 1673, which exceeds the national average of 1494. As of 2013, the median sale price of a home in Alpharetta climbed to $331,700. More than 77 percent of Alpharetta residents are employed in professional, managerial, technical, sales, and administrative positions (Atlanta Regional Commission, and the City of Alpharetta Department of Community Development).

3. Alpha Kappa Alpha Sorority, Inc., was founded in 1908, and Delta Sigma Theta Sorority, Inc., was founded in 1913. Both were established at Howard University at the height of the Black women's club movement, and in their early years both shared the efforts of Mary Church Terrell, a trailblazer for Black civil rights and women's rights.

4. Separate from the National Pan-Hellenic Conference, the National Pan-Hellenic Council is composed of the nine historically Black Greek letter sororities and fraternities. The council was formed at Howard University in 1930 as a permanent organization designed to allow for the fraternities and sororities to come together on the collegiate level. Charter members were Omega Psi Phi and Kappa Alpha Psi fraternities, and Alpha Kappa Alpha, Delta Sigma Theta, and Zeta Phi Beta sororities. In 1931, Alpha Phi Alpha and Phi Beta Sigma fraternities joined the council. Sigma Gamma Rho sorority joined in 1937, and Iota Phi Theta fraternity completed the list of member organizations in 1997.

5. NCLB refers to President Georgia W. Bush's No Child Left Behind education reform initiative signed into law in 2002, an attempt to address the achievement gap in U.S. public schools by requiring states to implement statewide accountability systems covering all public schools and students.

6. It is important to note that I did not meet all of the families enrolled at the Monroe School through the school itself. I only met six families through the Monroe School. Interviewing contacts located through the stay-at-home mom support groups and

other snowballing methodology revealed the fact that an additional five of the women who participated in the study had children enrolled at the Monroe School.

7. Cory was referring to the case of Kelley Williams-Bolar, who was accused of falsifying documents and evading out-of-district enrollment fees. (http://colorlines.com/archives/2012/05/kelley_williams_bolar_school_choice.html, accessed June 11, 2013).

8. The Monroe School had one set price of $7,700 for the entire primary school. The tuition for the majority white schools many parents considered comparable was $10,000 for pre-kindergarten, $14,000 for kindergarten, and $18,000 for grades 1 through 6.

9. Connections can be made to Hansen's analysis of the Cranes for understanding the networks of single, working-class women. Patricia Crane, the single mother in the analysis, is able to not only rely on her younger brother for parenting support but also the paraplegic father of her son. Stack documented the involvement of brothers, uncles, and grandfathers in networks of support. According to the data on unmarried, noncohabitating fatherhood participation, coparenting by noncohabitating/noncustodial fathers, is not a common experience for most single mothers (Fagan and Palkovitz 2007; Hamer 2001). Likewise, the other families Hansen includes in her study are the wealthy Aldriches, the professional middle-class Duvall-Brennans, and the middle-class Beckers.

10. Here I am referring to Hansen's description of the Cranes.

11. Hansen discusses how each family network is grounded in an ideology that supports their shared values and culture that makes a sustainable difference, except the Duvall-Brennans (Hansen 2005, 97)[not in Refs, please add].

12. We had this conversation during a follow-up interview conducted in 2012, and Gail has had another child since we finished (in 2007) our initial interview time together.

13. Atlanta Public Schools Website (http://www.atlanta.k12.ga.us/Page/1) accessed June 11, 2013.

14. In 2013, thirty-five educators from the Atlanta Public School system, including the superintendent, Dr. Beverly Hall, were indicted for cheating on standardized tests. The cheating may have dated back to 2001, but according to the indictment, for at least four years, from 2005 to 2009, test answers were altered, fabricated, or falsely certified. Following a five-month trial, ten educators were convicted of racketeering and other lesser crimes related to inflating the test scores of children from struggling schools. Superintendent Hall maintained her innocence but died of breast cancer before facing trial. District administrators, teachers, principals, and testing coordinators were said to have cheated for bonuses, to enhance their careers, or to keep their jobs. Michael Winerip, "Ex-Schools Chief in Atlanta Is Indicted in Testing Scandal," *New York Times*, March 29, 2013, and Ashley Fantz, "Prison time for some Atlanta school educators in cheating scandal," *CNN*, April 15, 2015, http://www.cnn.com/2015/04/14/us/georgia-atlanta-public-schools-cheating-scandal-verdicts/.

15. Keli Goff, "Did Michelle Obama Make a Major Misstep with Beyonce?" *Huffington Post: The Blog*, May 29, 2012, http://www.huffingtonpost.com/keli-goff/michelle-obama-beyonce_b_1554425.html.

16. Evangeline Holland, "Lifting as We Climb: The Women's Club Movement," Edwardian Promende, February 1, 2010. http://edwardianpromenade.com/african-american/lifting-as-we-climb/.

CHAPTER 5   BLACK CAREER WOMEN,

THE BLACK COMMUNITY, AND

THE NEO-POLITICS OF RESPECTABILITY

1. See seminal works by E. Franklin Frazier, *Black Bourgeiosie* (1957), Joe R. Feagin and Melvin P. Sikes, *Living with Racism: The Black Middle-Class Experience*, Mary Pattillo-(McCoy), *Black Picket Fences* (1999) and *Black on the Block* (2007), and Dalton Conley, *Being Black Living in the Red* (1999) for detailed discussions about social and structural constraints on the making of the Black middle class.

2. This was the first time Denise articulated herself as Jamaican in a way that differentiated her from African Americans. Denise identified herself as Jamaican at the beginning of our interviews but called herself African American because she had been raised in the United States and saw herself as a part of the African American community. Here Denise's statement about her Jamaican nationality refers to her ability to respond to threats since Jamaicans are stereotyped as violent. See Elizabeth Thomas-Hope's (1998) research on violence as one of the key factors in Jamaican migration and a *New York Times* article on Jamaican efforts to reduce crime and violence, http://www.nytimes.com/2013/08/18/world/americas/jamaica-fights -to-break-grip-of-violent-past.html?pagewanted=all&_r=0, accessed December 14, 2014.

3. Atlanta's downturn precipitated the housing market crash by a couple of years (2006) because Atlanta's housing market was undervalued and Atlanta did not participate as much in the housing bubble (see report by the National Center for Policy Analysis http://www.ncpa.org/pdfs/st335.pdf, accessed December 14, 2014). Most of the foreclosures that occurred in Atlanta's crash were caused by Atlanta's low housing costs. This led people to buy more house than they could afford. The housing crash caused nationwide buyer insecurity and sharply declining housing values, a trend that extended Atlanta's economic and housing downturn (Sjoquist 2009).

4. With Section 8, the public housing authority (PHA) generally pays the landlord the difference between 30 percent of household income and the PHA-determined payment standard—about 80 to 100 percent of the fair market rent (FMR). The rent must be reasonable. The household may choose a unit with a higher rent than the FMR and pay the landlord the difference or choose a lower-cost unit. http://www.hud.gov/ progdesc/voucher.cfm, accessed July 22, 2014.

5. Atlanta's *INtown* magazine, a monthly circular, says it distributes to neighborhoods inside "the Perimeter" including "Midtown, Virginia Highland, Ansley Park, Druid Hills, Emory, Decatur, Inman Park, Grant Park, and Buckhead and more." http://www.atlantaintownpaper.com/about/ accessed July 22, 2014. None of these neighborhoods or the city of Decatur is historically Black. Indeed, they are all located on the Northeast side of the city and, with the exception of Midtown, which includes the Old Fourth Ward, Edgewood, Kirkwood, and Reynoldstown, are known as historically white neighborhoods. See Rob Gurwitt's article "Atlanta and the Urban Future," http://www.governing.com/topics/politics/Atlanta-and-the-Urban.html, accessed July 22, 2014.

6. See Census of Housing, https://www.census.gov/hhes/www/housing/census/historic/ values.html, accessed July 22, 2014.

7. Natalie is referring to the Bravo Television Network's series of prime time reality shows whose titles begin with "The Real Housewives of . . ." and situate the women in several major United States cities. *The Real Housewives of Atlanta* is the only one of the network's shows that features a predominantly Black cast.

8. The "one-drop rule" was established as law in the 1924 Racial Integrity Act of Virginia. It defined a person as "legally colored" (Black) for classification and legal purposes if the individual had any African ancestry. Prior to this time social acceptance and identification had historically been the key. http://www.encyclopediavirginia.org/racial _integrity_laws_of_the_1920s accessed July 20, 2014.

9. From the Jack and Jill website http://jackandjillinc.org/?page_id=7 accessed October 7, 2012.

10. I don't use her name or any identifiers because she was the only person in the study going through this process.

11. Capitol City Bank, a Black-owned banking center opened in 1994 in Atlanta, now has seven locations. Atlanta Life Financial Group was founded in 1905 by Alonzo F. Herndon as Atlanta Life Insurance, one of the first Black businesses in the country.

CONCLUSION

1. Barbara Omolade (1994) discussed the "mammification" of Black women's work when she acknowledged the fact that Black women in professional and managerial positions continue to experience work where domestic duties and expectations get woven into the requirements of their jobs. Lisa Thompson (2009) draws attention to the "Black lady," an elite, or upper middle-class rendition of the superwoman wherein Black women must render themselves asexual keepers of the Black community. Thompson challenges the desire to read Black women in that light by highlighting literary texts that explore the complexity of Black women's subjectivity. See also Toni Morrison and Wahneema Lubiano in *Race-ing Justice En-gendering Power* (1992); Candice Jenkins, *Private Lives, Proper Relations: Regulating Black Intimacy* (2007); and Melissa Harris-Perry's *Sister Citizen* (2011).

2. Tami Winfrey Harris, "A Black Mom in Chief Is Revolutionary: What White Feminist Get Wrong About Michelle Obama," *Clutch Magazine*, September 11, 2012. http://www .clutchmagonline.com/2012/09/a-Black-mom-in-chief-is-revolutionary-what-white -feminist-get-wrong-about-michelle-obama/, accessed June 15, 2013.

3. Here I refer to the fact that several terms and understandings of feminism are born out of the understanding that feminism as defined by white women never encompassed the needs of Black women or other women of color. And even when Black women defined feminism for themselves, there was enough variation in experience that the definition did not encompass the needs of all Black women.

4. See Harris, "A Black Mom in Chief Is Revolutionary."

5. Gretchen Livingston, "Among 38 Nations, US Is the Outlier When It Comes to Paid Parental Leave," Pew Research Center. http://www.pewresearch.org/fact-tank/2013/ 12/12/among-38-nations-u-s-is-the-holdout-when-it-comes-to-offering-paid-parental -leave/, accessed December 14, 2014.

6. Janet Walsh, "Failing Its Families: Lack of Paid Leave and Work-Family Supports in the US," http://www.hrw.org/news/2011/02/23/us-lack-paid-leave-harms-workers-children, accessed December 14, 2014.

7. This quote has long been attributed to Lilla Watson, an Aboriginal elder, artist, and activist who reportedly made the statement as a challenge to people working toward

social justice. With a collectivist and communal ethic, upon learning that the statement had been attributed to her alone, she reportedly asked that the statement be attributed to Aboriginal activists in Queensland. http://unnecessaryevils.blogspot .com/2008/11/attributing-words.html. accessed 4/18/2015.

EPILOGUE

1. See bell hooks (2000, 78–84) for detailed discussion on the liberating possibilities of heterosexual partnerships as an alternative to marriage.

REFERENCES

Abdullah, Melina. 2012. "Womanist Mothering: Loving and Raising the Revolution." *Western Journal of Black Studies* 36 (1): 57–67.

Abramovitz, Mimi. 1996. *Regulating the Lives of Women: Social Welfare Policy from Colonial Times to the Present.* Boston: South End Press.

———. 2000. *Under Attack, Fighting Back: Women and Welfare in the United States.* New York: Monthly Review Press.

Abu-Lughod, Lila. 1990. "Can There Be a Feminist Ethnography?" *Women and Performance* 5 (1): 7–27.

Aguilar, John. 1981. "Insider Research: An Ethnography of a Debate." In *Anthropologists at Home in North America*, edited by Donald A. Messerschmidt, 15–26. New York: Cambridge University Press.

Aizer, Anna. 2004. "Home Alone: Supervision after School and Child Behavior." *Journal of Public Economics* 88: 1835–1848. doi:10.1016/S0047-2727(03)00022-7.

Albeda, Randy. 2001. "Welfare to Work, Farwell to Families? US Welfare Reform and Work/Family Debates." *Feminist Economics* 7 (1): 119–135

Allen, S. M., and R. A. Kalish. 1984. "Professional Women and Marriage." *Journal of Marriage and the Family* 46 (5): 375–382.

Amott, Teresa, and Julie Matthaei. 1996. *Race, Gender, and Work: A Multi-Cultural Economic History of Women in the United States.* Boston: South End Press.

Anderson, Elijah. 2000. *Code of the Street: Decency, Violence, and the Moral Life of the Inner City.* New York: W. W. Norton.

Andersen, Margaret, and Patricia Hill Collins. 2004. *Race, Class, and Gender: An Anthology.* Belmont, CA: Wadsworth-Thompson.

Assman, Jan, and John Czaplicka. 1995. "Collective Memory and Cultural Identity." *New German Critique* 65 (spring/summer): 125–133. Stable URL: htttp://www.jstor.org/stable/488538.

Atlanta Regional Commission. 2010. "Atlanta Regional Commission County Dash Board." http://www.atlantaregional.com/info-center/arc-region/fulton.

Baker, Lee D. 1998. *From Savage to Negro: Anthropology and the Construction of Race, 1896 to 1954.* Berkeley: University of California Press.

Banfield, Edward C. 1970. *The Unheavenly City: The Nature and Future of Our Urban Crisis.* Boston: Little, Brown.

———. 1974. *Unheavenly City Revisited.* Boston: Little, Brown.

Banks, Ralph Richard. 2011. *Is Marriage for White People? How the African American Marriage Decline Affects Everyone.* New York: Plume/Penguin Group.

Barkhorn, Eleanor. 2013. "Getting Married Later Is Great for College-Educated Women: For Everyone Else, the Results Are Mixed." *The Atlantic,* March. http://www.theatlantic.com/sexes/archive/2013/03/getting-married-later-is-great-for-college-educated-women/274040/, accessed April 18, 2015.

Barnes, Annie S. 1989. "Black Women in the Workplace." *Anthropology of Work Review* 10 (2): 1–12. doi: 10.1525/awr.1989.10.2.4

Barnes, Riché, and Jeneen Daniel. 2008. "Black Women Have Always Worked: Is There a Work Family Conflict among the Black Middle Class?" In *The Changing Landscape of Work and Family in the American Middle Class,* edited by Lara Descartes and Elizabeth Rudd, 189–208. Lanham, MD: Lexington Books

Barrow, Christine. 1986. "Male Images of Women in Barbados." *Social and Economic Studies* 35 (3): 51–64.

——. 1998. *Family in the Caribbean: Themes and Perspectives.* Princeton, NJ: Markus Wiener Publishers.

Bateson, Mary Catherine. 2001. *Composing a Life.* New York: Plume.

Bayor, Ronald H. 1996. *Race and the Shaping of Twentieth-Century Atlanta.* Chapel Hill: University of North Carolina Press.

Beauboeuf-Lafontant, Tamara. 2009. *Behind the Mask of the Strong Black Woman: Voice and the Embodiment of a Costly Performance.* Philadelphia: Temple University Press.

Beauvoir, Simone de. 1989. *The Second Sex.* New York: Vintage Books.

Belkin, Lisa. 2003. "The Opt-Out Revolution." *New York Times Magazine,* October 26.

Bell-Scott, Patricia, and Beverly Guy-Sheftall. 1991. *Double-Stitch: Black Women Write About Mothers and Daughters.* Boston: Beacon Press.

Benjamin, Lois. 2005. *The Black Elite: Still Facing the Color Line in the Twenty-first Century.* 2nd ed. Lanham, MD: Rowman & Littlefield.

Bernard, H. Russell. 2006. *Research Methods in Anthropology: Qualitative and Quantitative Approaches.* 4th ed. Lanham, MD: Rowman & Littlefield.

Berry, Cecilie S., ed. 2004. "Aria of the Matriarch." In *Rise Up Singing: Black Women Writers on Motherhood.* New York: Doubleday.

Besharov, Douglass J., and Andrew West. 2002. "African American Marriage Patterns." In *Beyond the Color Line: New Perspectives on Race and Ethnicity in America,* edited by Abigail Thernstrom and Stephan Thernstrom, 95–113. Stanford, CA: Hoover Institution Press, Stanford University; New York: Manhattan Institute.

Bianchi, Suzanne M., Melissa A. Milkie, Liana C. Sayer, and John P. Robinson. 2000. "Is Anyone Doing the Housework." *Social Forces* 79 (1): 191–228.

Biblarz, Timothy J., Alexander Bucur, and Vern L. Bengston. 1996. "Social Mobility Across Three Generations." *Journal of Marriage and the Family* 58 (1): 188–200.

Billingsley, Andrew. 1994. *Climbing Jacob's Ladder: The Enduring Legacy of African-American Families.* New York: Simon & Schuster.

Blackwood, Evelyn. 2005. "Wedding Bell Blues: Marriage, Missing Men, and Matrifocal Follies." *American Ethnologist* 32 (1): 3–19. Rejoinder to commentary: "The Specter of the Patriarchal Man." *American Ethnologist* 32 (1): 42–45.

Blair-Loy, Mary. 2003. *Competing Devotions: Career and Family among Women Executives.* Cambridge, MA: Harvard University Press.

Blake-Beard, S., M. A. Scully, S. Turnbull, L. Hunt, K. L. Proudford, Jessica L. Porter, Gina LaRoche, and Kelly Fanning. 2006. "The Ties That Bind and Separate Black and White Women." In *Gender, Race and Ethnicity in the Workplace: Issues and Challenges for Today's Organizations,* edited by Margaret Foegen Karsten, 179–204. Westport, CT: Praeger.

Blakely, Edward James, and Mary Gail Snyder. 1997. *Fortress America: Gated Communities in the United States.* Washington, DC: Brookings Institution Press.

Blau, Francine, Lawrence M. Kahn, and Jane Waldfogel. 2002. "The Impact of Welfare Benefits on Single Motherhood and Headship of Young Women: Evidence from the Census." *NBER Working Paper,* National Bureau of Economic Research, Inc. (DOI): 10.3386/w9338.

Blum, Linda M., and Theresa Deussen. 1996. "Negotiating Independent Motherhood: Working-Class African American Women Talk About Marriage and Motherhood." *Gender and Society* 10: 199–211.

Bolles, A. Lynn. 1983. "Kitchens Hit by Priorities: Employed Working-Class Jamaican Women Confront the International Monetary Fund." In *Women, Men, and the International Division of Labor*, edited by June Nash and Maria Patricia Fernandez Kelly, 138–160. Albany: State University of New York Press.

———. 1996. *Sister Jamaica: A Study of Women, Work, and Households in Kingston*. Lanham, MD: University Press of America.

———. 2013. "'Telling the Story Straight': Black Feminist Intellectual Thought in Anthropology." *Transforming Anthropology* 21: 57–71.

———. N.d. "Making It Work in the English-speaking Caribbean: Women as Mothers, Providers, and Leaders." Latin American Studies Association, Working Papers. http://lasa .international.pitt.edu/LASA98/Bolles.pdf, accessed 12/14/2014.

Boswell, Thomas D., and Terry-Ann Jones. 2006. "The Distribution and Socioeconomic Status of West Indians Living in the United States." In *Race, Ethnicity, and Place in a Changing America*, edited by John W. Frazier and Eugene L. Tetty-Fio. Binghamton, NY: Global Academic Publishing, Binghamton University, 2006.

Boushey, Heather. 2005. *Are Women Opting Out? Debunking the Myth*. Briefing paper. Washington, DC: Center for Economic and Policy Research.

Bowser, Benjamin. 2006. *The Black Middle Class: Social Mobility and Vulnerability*. Boulder, CO: Lynne Rienner Publishers.

Bradford, William D. 2003. "The Wealth Dynamics of Entrepreneurship for Black and White Families in the U.S." *Review of Income and Wealth* 49: 89–116.

Branch, Enobong Hannah. 2011. *Opportunity Denied: Limiting Black Women to Devalued Work*. New Brunswick, NJ: Rutgers University Press.

Braxton, Joanne. 1989. *Black Women Writing Autobiography: A Tradition Within a Tradition*. Philadelphia: Temple University Press.

Brewer, Rose M. 1993. "Theorizing Race, Class, and Gender the New Scholarship of Black Feminist Intellectuals and Black Women's Labor." In *Theorizing Black Feminisms: The Visionary Pragmatism of Black Women*, edited by Stanlie James and Abena P. A. Busia. London: Routledge.

Bridges, Judith S., and Claire Etaugh. 1996. "Black and White College Women's Maternal Employment Outcome Expectations and Their Desired Timing of Maternal Employment." *Sex Roles: A Journal of Research* 35: 543–562.

Bridges, Khiara. 2011. *Reproducing Race: An Ethnography of Pregnancy as a Site of Racialization*. Berkeley: University of California Press.

Brodkin, Karen. (Sacks). 1988. *Caring by the Hour: Women, Work, and Organizing at Duke Medical Center*. Urbana: University of Illinois Press.

———. (1998) 2000. *How Jews Became White Folks and What That Says About Race in America*. New Brunswick, NJ: Rutgers University Press.

Brown, Carolyn M. 2007. "Top 10 Cities for African Americans 2007: Our Readers and Editors Select the Best Places in Which to Live, Work, and Play." *Black Enterprise*, May 1.

Brown, Tamara Mose. 2011. *Raising Brooklyn: Nannies, Childcare and Caribbeans Creating Community*. New York: New York University Press.

Brown, Tamara Mose, and Erynn Masi de Casanova. 2009. "Mothers in the Field: How Motherhood Shapes Fieldwork and Researcher-Subject Relations." *Women's Studies Quarterly* 37 (3/4): 42–57.

Brown-Guillory, Elizabeth. (1996) 2010. "Disrupted Motherlines: Mothers and Daughters in a Genderized, Sexualized, Racialized World." In *Women of Color: Mother-Daughter Relationships in 20th Century Literature*, edited by Eizabeth Brown-Guillory, 188–207. Austin: University of Texas Press.

Brown-Nagin, Tomiko. 2011. *Courage to Dissent: Atlanta and the Long History of the Civil Rights Movement.* New York: Oxford University Press.

Bullard, Robert D., Glenn Johnson, and Angel O. Torres, eds. 2000. *Sprawl City: Race, Politics, and Planning in Atlanta.* Washington, DC: Island Press.

Burt-Murray, Angela. 2009 "The Obamas: Portrait of America's New First Family." *Essence Magazine.* March, 90–94.

Byrd, Rudolph, Johnnetta Betsch Cole, and Beverly Guy-Sheftall. 2009. *I Am Your Sister: Collected and Unpublished Writings of Audre Lorde.* Oxford: Oxford University Press.

Carby, Hazel. 1982. "White Women Listen! Black Feminism and the Boundaries of Sisterhood." In *The Empire Strikes Back: Race and Racism in 70s Britain*, edited by Birmingham Centre Collective for Cultural Studies, 212–235. London: Hutchinson.

———. 1987. "Woman's Era: Rethinking Black Feminist Theory." In *Reconstructing Womanhood: The Emergence of the Afro-American Woman Novelist*, 3–19. New York: Oxford University Press.

Carothers, Suzanne. 1998. "Catching Sense: Learning from Our Mothers to Be Black and Female." In *Families in the U.S.: Kinship and Domestic Policies*, edited by Karen V. Hansen and Anita Ilta Garey. Philadelphia: Temple University Press.

Celello, Kristin. 2009. *Making Marriage Work: A History of Marriage and Divorce in the Twentieth-Century United States.* Chapel Hill: University of North Carolina Press.

Chambers, Veronica. 2003. *Having It All? Black Women and Success.* New York: Harlem Moon.

Chan, Selina Ching. 2006. "Love and Jewelry: Patriarchal Control, Conjugal Ties, and Changing Identities." In *Modern Loves: The Anthropology of Romantic Courtship and Companionate Marriage*, edited by Jennifer Hirsch and Holly Wardlaw, 35–50. Ann Arbor: University of Michigan Press.

Chancer, Lynn S., and Beverly Xaviera Watkins. 2006. *Gender, Race, and Class: An Overview* (21st Century Sociology). Malden, MA: Blackwell.

Chodorow, Nancy. 1978. *The Reproduction of Mothering: Psychoanalysis and the Sociology of Gender.* Berkeley: University of California Press.

Christensen, Kathleen. 1988. *Women and Home-Based Work: The Unspoken Contract.* New York: Henry Holt.

Clarke, Averil. 2011. *Inequalities of Love: College-Educated Black Women and the Barriers to Romance and Family.* Ann Arbor: University of Michigan Press.

Cohany, Sharon R., and Emy Sok. 2007. "Trends in Labor Force Participation and Married Mothers and Infants." *Monthly Labor Review* 130 (2): 9–16.

Cohen, Cathy. 1999. *The Boundaries of Blackness: AIDS and the Breakdown of Black Politics.* Chicago: University of Chicago Press.

Cole, Johnnetta B., ed. *All American Women: Lines That Divide, Ties That Bind.* New York: Free Press.

Cole, Johnnetta B., and Beverly Guy-Sheftall. 2003. *Gender Talk: The Struggle for Women's Equality in African American Communities.* New York: Ballantine.

Colen, Shellee. 2001. "With Respect and Feelings: Voices of West Indian Child Care and Domestic Workers in New York City." In *In Our Own Words: Writings from Women's Lives*, edited by Maxine Seller, 110–116. 2nd ed. Boston: McGraw-Hill.

Collier-Thomas, Bettye. 1982. "The Impact of Black Women in Education: An Historical Overview." *Journal of Negro Education* 51 (3): 173–180.

Collins, Patricia Hill. 1986. "Learning from the Outsider Within: The Sociological Significance of Black Feminist Thought." *Social Problems* 33 (6): 14–32.

———. (1990) 2000. *Black Feminist Thought: Knowledge, Consciousness, and the Politics of Empowerment.* New York: Routledge.

———. 1998a. "Intersections of Race, Class, Gender, and Nation: Some Implications for Black Family Studies." *Journal of Comparative Family Studies* 29 (1): 27–36.

———. 1998b. "It's All in the Family: Intersections of Gender, Race, and Nation." *Hypatia, Journal of Feminist Philosophy* 13 (3): 62–82.

———. 2004. *Black Sexual Politics: African Americans, Gender, and the New Racism.* New York: Routledge.

Coltrane, Scott. 2000. "Research on Household Labor: Modeling and Measuring the Social Embeddedness of Routine Family Work." *Journal of Marriage and Family* 62: 1208–1233. doi: 10.1111/j.1741-3737.2000.01208.x.

Combahee River Collective Staff. 1986. *The Combahee River Collective Statement: Black Feminist Organizing in the Seventies and Eighties.* Brooklyn: Kitchen Table/Women of Color Press.

Conley, Dalton. 1999. *Being Black, Living in the Red: Race, Wealth, and Social Policy in America.* Berkeley: University of California Press.

Cooper, Anna Julia. 1892. *A Voice from the South. By a Black Woman of the South.* Xenia, OH: Aldine Printing House.

Coontz, Stephanie. 1992. *The Way We Never Were: American Families and the Nostalgia Trap.* New York: Basic Books.

———. 2006. *A Marriage, a History: How Love Conquered Marriage.* New York: Penguin Books.

Craven, Christa, and Dana-Ain Davis, eds. 2013. *Feminist Activist Ethnography: Counterpoints to Neoliberalism in North America.* Lanham, MD: Lexington Books.

Crenshaw, Kimberlé. 1991. "Mapping the Margins: Intersectionality, Identity Politics, and Violence against Women of Color." *Stanford Law Review* 43: 1241–1299.

———. 2000. "Demarginalizing the Intersection of Race and Sex: A Black Feminist Critique of Antidiscrimination Doctrine, Feminist Theory, and Antiracist Politics." In *The Black Feminist Reader*, edited by Joy James and Tracey Denean Sharpley-Whiting, 208–238. Malden, MA: Blackwell.

———. 2012. "From Private Violence to Mass Incarceration: Thinking Intersectionally About Women, Race, and Social Control." *UCLA Law Review* 59: 1418–1472.

Creswell, J. W. 1998. *Qualitative Inquiry and Research Design: Choosing among the Five Traditions.* Thousand Oaks, CA: Sage Publications.

Crompton, Rosemary. 1989. "Class Theory and Gender." *British Journal of Sociology* 40 (4): 565–587.

Darity, William Jr., David Guilkey, and William Winfrey. 1995. "Ethnicity, Race, and Earnings." *Economic Letters* (47): 401–408.

Davis, Angela Y. 1971. *If They Come in the Morning: Voices of Resistance.* New York: Third World Press.

———. 1972. "Reflections on the Black Woman's Role in the Community of Slaves." *Massachusetts Review* 13 (1/2): 81–100.

———. 1981. *Women, Race, and Class.* New York: Random House.

———. 1999. *Blues Women and Black Feminism: Gertrude "Ma" Rainey, Bessie Smith, and Billie Holiday.* New York: Vintage Press.

Davis, Angela Y., and Cassandra Shaylor. 2001. "Race, Gender, and the Prison Industrial Complex California and Beyond." *Meridians: Feminism, Race, Transnationalism* 2 (1): 1–25.

Davis, Dana-Ain. 2006. *Battered Black Women and Welfare Reform: Between a Rock and a Hard Place.* Albany: State University of New York Press.

———. 2009. "The Politics of Reproduction: The Troubling Case of Nadya Suleman and Assisted Reproductive Technology." *Transforming Anthropology* 17 (2): 105–116.

Davis, Nancy J., and Robert V. Robinson. 1998. "Do Wives Matter? Class Identities of Wives and Husbands in the United States, 1974–1994." *Social Forces* 76 (3): 1063–1086.

Denzin, N. K., and Y. S. Lincoln, eds. 2003. *The Landscape of Qualitative Research: Theories and Issues.* 2nd ed. Thousand Oaks, CA: Sage.

Deutsch, Francine M. 1999. *Halving It All: Equally Shared Parenting Works.* Cambridge, MA: Harvard University Press.

DeVault, Marjorie L. 1991. *Feeding the Family: The Social Organization of Caring as Gendered Work.* Chicago: University of Chicago Press.

Dickerson, Bette J., ed. 1995. *African American Single Mothers: Understanding their Lives and Families.* Thousand Oaks, CA: Sage Publications.

Dill, Bonnie Thornton. 1982. "Survival as a Form of Resistance: Minority Women and the Maintenance of Families." Paper Presented at the Annual Meeting of the American Sociological Association.

———. 1988a. "Dialectics of Black Womanhood." In *Black Women in America: Social Science Perspectives*, edited by Micheline R. Malson, Elisabeth Mudimbe-Boyi, Jean F. O'Barr, and Mary Wyer, 65–78. Chicago: University of Chicago Press.

———. 1988b. "Our Mothers' Grief: Racial-Ethnic Women and the Maintenance of Families." *Journal of Family History* 13: 415–431.

———. 1994. *Across the Boundaries of Race and Class: An Exploration of Work and Family among Black Female Domestic Servants.* New York: Garland.

Dohm, Arlene, and Lynn Shniper. 2007. "Occupational Employment Outlook to 2016." *Monthly Labor Review* (November): 86–125. Bureau of Labor and Statistics. http://www.bls.gov/opub/mlr/2007/11/art5full.pdf.

Drake, St. Clair, and Horace R. Cayton. 1993. *Black Metropolis: A Study of Negro Life in a Northern City.* Chicago: University of Chicago Press.

Du Bois, William E. B. 1899. *The Philadelphia Negro.* Philadelphia: University of Pennsylvania Press.

———. (1903) 1999. *The Souls of Black Folk: Authoritative Text, Contexts, Criticism.* Edited by Henry Louis Gates Jr. and Terri Hume Oliver. New York: W. W. Norton.

Duneier, Mitchell. 2007. "On The Legacy of Elliot Liebow and Carol Stack: Context-driven Fieldwork and the Need for Continuous Ethnography." *Focus* 25 (1): 33–38.

Dyson, Eric Michael. 2005. *Is Bill Cosby Right?: Or Has the Black Middle Class Lost Its Mind?* New York: Basic Civitas Books.

Edin, Kathryn, and Maria Kefalas. 2005. *Promises I Can Keep: Why Poor Women Put Motherhood before Marriage.* Berkeley: University of California Press.

Elder, Glenn H. 1974. "Role Orientation, Marital Age, and Life Patterns in Adulthood." *Merrill-Palmer Quarterly of Behavior and Development* 18 (1): 3–24.

Fagan, Jay, and Rob Palkovitz. 2007. "Unmarried, Nonresident Fathers' Involvement with Their Infants: A Risk and Resilience Perspective." *Journal of Family Psychology* 21 (3): 479–489.

Fass, Sarah. 2009. "Paid Leave in the States: A Critical Support for Low-wage Workers and Their Families." Policy Brief by the National Center for Children in Poverty. Mailman School of Public Health, Columbian University. http://www.nccp.org/publications/pub_864.html, accessed April 18, 2015

Feagin, Joe R., and Melvin P. Sikes. 1994. *Living with Racism: The Black Middle-Class Experience.* Boston: Beacon Press.

Feldstein, Ruth. 2000. *Motherhood in Black and White: Race and Sex in American Liberalism, 1930–1965.* Ithaca, NY: Cornell University Press.

Ferguson, Earline Rae. 2002. "African American Clubwomen and the Indianapolis NAACP, 1912–1914." In *Stepping Forward: Black Women in Africa and the Americas*, edited by Catherine Higgs, Barbara A. Moss, and Earline Rae Ferguson, 73–84. Athens: Ohio University Press.

Ferguson, Karen. 2005. *Black Politics in New Deal Atlanta.* Chapel Hill: University of North Carolina Press.

Fineman, Martha. 2001. "Contract and Care." *Chicago Kent Law Review* 76: 1403–1440.

Foner, Nancy. 2001. *New Immigrants in New York.* New York: Columbia University Press.

Fordham, Signithia. 1993. "'Those Loud Black Girls': (Black) Women, Silence, and Gender 'Passing' in the Academy." *Anthropology and Education Quarterly* 24: 3–32.

———. 1996. *Blacked Out: Dilemmas of Race, Identity, and Success at Capital High.* Chicago: University of Chicago Press.

Foster, Frances Smith. 2010. *'Til Death or Distance Do Us Part: Love and Marriage in African America.* Oxford: Oxford University Press.

Foster, Frances Smith, Beverly Guy-Sheftall, and Stanlie James, eds. 2009. *Still Brave: The Evolution of Black Women's Studies.* New York: Feminist Press.

Fox-Genovese, Elizabeth. 1996. *Feminism Is Not the Story of My Life: How Today's Feminist Elite Has Lost Touch with the Real Concerns of Women.* New York: Anchor.

Frederick, Marla. 2003. *Between Sundays: Black Women and Everyday Struggles of Faith.* Durham, NC: Duke University Press.

Frazier, Edward Franklin. 1939. *The Negro Family in the United States.* Chicago: University of Chicago Press.

———. 1948. *The Negro Family in the United States.* Rev. and abridged ed. New York: Dryden Press.

———. (1957) 1997. *Black Bourgeoisie: The Book That Brought the Shock of Self-Revelation to Middle-Class Blacks in America.* New York: Free Press.

Freeman, Carla. 2000. *High Tech and High Heels in the Global Economy: Women, Work, and Pink Collar Identities in the Caribbean.* Durham, NC: Duke University Press.

———. 2007. "Neo-liberalism and the Romance of Flexibility in Barbados." In *Love and Globalization: Transformation of Intimacy in the Contemporary World*, edited by Mark Padilla, Richard Parker, Jennifer Hirsch, Miguel Munoz-Laboy, and Robert E. Sember, 3–37. Nashville, TN: Vanderbilt University Press.

Freire, Paulo. 1998. *Pedagogy of the Oppressed.* New York: Continuum.

Frey, William. 2004. *"The New Great Migration: Black Americans' Return to the South, 1965–2000."* Brookings Institute Center on Urban and Metropolitan Policy.

Gage, Frances. 1863. "Sojourner Truth." *Independent* New York, April 23.

Gaines, Kevin K. 1996. *Uplifting the Race: Black Leadership, Politics, and Culture in the Twentieth Century.* Chapel Hill: University of North Carolina Press.

Garey, Anita Ilta. 1999. *Weaving Work and Motherhood.* Philadelphia: Temple University Press.

Geertz, Clifford. 1973. "Thick Description: Toward an Interpretive Theory of Culture." In *The Interpretation of Cultures: Selected Essays*, 3–30. New York: Basic Books.

George, Elizabeth. 1998. *Beautiful in God's Eyes.* Eugene, OR: Harvest House.

Gerson, Kathleen. 1986. *Hard Choices: How Women Decide about Work, Career, and Motherhood.* Berkeley: University of California Press.

Giddings, Paula. (1984) 2007. *When and Where I Enter: The Impact of Black Women on Race and Sex in America.* New York: HarperCollins.

——. (1988) 2009. *In Search of Sisterhood: Delta Sigma Theta and the Challenge of the Black Sorority Movement.* New York: Delta Sigma Theta, Inc./HarperCollins

——. 2008. *Ida: A Sword among Lions.* New York: HarperCollins.

Gilkes, Cheryl Townsend. 2000. *If It Wasn't For the Women.* Maryknoll, NY: Orbis Press.

Glenn, Evelyn Nakano. 1985. "Racial Ethnic Women's Labor: The Intersection of Race, Gender, and Class Oppression." *Review of Radical Political Economics* 17 (3): 86–108.

——. 1992. "From Servitude to Service Work: Historical Continuities in the Racial Division of Paid Reproductive Labor." *Signs: Journal of Women in Culture and Society* 18 (1): 1–43.

Goodson, Ivor, and Pik Lin Choi. 2008. "Life History and Collective Memory as Methodological Strategies: Studying Teacher Professionalism." *Teacher Education Quarterly* 35 (2): 5–28.

Gordon, Linda. 1994. *Pitied but not Entitled: Single Mothers and the History of Welfare.* New York: Free Press.

Greenhouse, Carol, ed. 2011. *Ethnographies of Neoliberalism.* Philadelphia: University of Pennsylvania Press.

Gregory, Steven. 1999. *Black Corona: Race and the Politics of Place in an Urban Black Community.* Princeton, NJ: Princeton University Press.

Griffin, Jasmine. 2000. "Black Feminists and Du Bois: Respectability, Protection, and Beyond." *Annals of the American Academy of Political and Social Science* 568: 28–40.

Gutman, Herbert. 1976. *The Black Family in Slavery and Freedom, 1750–1925.* New York: Pantheon.

Guy-Sheftall, Beverly. 1995. *Words of Fire: An Anthology of African American Feminist Thought.* New York: New Press

Gwaltney, John Langston. (1980) 1993. *Drylongso: A Self-Portrait of Black America.* New York: New Press.

Hamer, Jennifer. 2001. *What It Means to Be Daddy: Fatherhood for Black Men Living away from Their Children.* New York: Columbia University Press.

Hammonds, Evelynn M. 1997. "Toward a Genealogy of Black Female Sexuality: The Problematic of Silence." In *Feminist Theory and the Body: A Reader*, edited by Janet Price and Margaret Shildrick, 249–259. New York: Routledge.

Hannerz, Ulf. 1969. *Soulside: Inquiries into Ghetto Culture and Community.* Chicago: University of Chicago Press.

Hansen, Karen V. 2005. *Not-So-Nuclear Families: Class, Gender, and Networks of Care.* New Brunswick, NJ: Rutgers University Press.

Hansen, Karen V., and Anita Ilta Garey, eds. 1998. *Families in the U.S.: Kinship and Domestic Politics.* Philadelphia: Temple University Press.

——. 2011. *At the Heart of Work and Family: Engaging the Ideas of Arlie Hochschild.* New Brunswick, NJ: Rutgers University Press.

Harley, Sharon. 1997. "Speaking Up: The Politics of Black Women's Labor History." In *Women and Work: Exploring Race, Ethnicity and Class*, edited by Elizabeth Higginbotham and Mary Romero, 28–52. Thousand Oaks, CA: Sage Publications.

——. 2002. "'Working for Nothing but for a Living': Black Women in the Underground Economy." In *Sister Circle: Black Women and Work*, edited by Sharon Harley, 48–66. New Brunswick, NJ: Rutgers University Press.

Harley, Sharon, and Rosalyn Terborg-Penn. 1997. *The Afro-American Woman: Images and Struggles.* Baltimore, MD: Black Classic Press.

Harmon, David A. 1996. *Beneath the Image of the Civil Rights Movement and Race Relations: Atlanta, Georgia, 1946–1981.* New York: Garland.

Harris, Alexa, and Adria Y. Goldman. 2014. *Black Women in Popular Culture: An Introduction to the Reader's Journey.* Lanham, MD: Lexington Books.

Harris, Cherise A. 2013. *The Cosby Cohort: Blessings and Burdens of Growing Up Black Middle Class.* Lanham, MD: Rowman and Littlefield.

Harris-Perry, Melissa. 2011. *Sister Citizen: Shame, Stereotypes, and Black Women in the Academy.* New Haven: Yale University Press.

Harrison, Faye. 1995a. "The Persistent Power of 'Race' in the Cultural and Political Economy of Racism." *Annual Review of Anthropology* 24: 47–74.

———. 1995b. "Auto-Ethnographic Reflections on Hierarchies in Anthropology." *Practicing Anthropology* 17 (1–2): 48–50.

———. 1998. "Rehistoricizing Race, Ethnicity, and Class in the U.S. Southeast." In *Cultural Diversity in the South: Anthropological Contributions to a Region in Transition*, edited by Patricia Beaver and Carole Hill, 179–189. Athens: University of Georgia Press.

———. 2008. *Outsider Within: Reworking Anthropology in the Global Age.* Urbana: University of Illinois Press.

Hart, Margaret S., and Michelle L Kelley. 2006. "Mothers' and Fathers' Work and Family Issues as Related to Internalizing and Externalizing Behavior of Children Attending Daycare." *Journal of Family Issues* 27 (2): 252–270.

Hartman, Saidiya. 2007. *Lose Your Mother.* New York: Farrar, Strauss, and Giroux.

Hartmann, Heidi. 1979. "The Unhappy Marriage of Marxism and Feminism: Toward a More Progressive Union." *Capital and Class* 3 (2): 1–33.

———. 1981. "The Family as the Locus of Gender, Class, and Political Struggle: The Example of Housework." *Signs: Journal of Women in Culture and Society* 6 (3): 366–394.

———. 2008. "Impact of the Current Economic Downturn on Women." Testimony Presented to the Joint Economic Committee, at the hearing: "The Employment Situation: May 2008." June 6. Released by Institute for Women's Policy Research.

Hattery, Angela J. 2001. *Women, Work, and Family: Balancing and Weaving.* Thousand Oaks, CA: Sage Publications.

Hayes, Sharon. 1998. *The Cultural Contradictions of Motherhood.* New Haven: Yale University Press.

Hays, Pamela. 1996. "Addressing the Complexities of Culture and Gender in Counseling." *Journal of Counseling & Development* 74 (4): 332–338.

Heiman, Rachel, Carla Freeman, and Mark Leichty, eds. 2012. *The Global Middle Classes: Theorizing Through Ethnography.* Santa Fe, NM: School of Advanced Research.

Hernandez, Graciela. 1995. "Multiple Subjectivities and Strategic Positionality: Zora Neale Hurston's Experimental Ethnographies." In *Women Writing Culture*, edited by Ruth Behar and Deborah A. Gordon, 148–165. Berkeley: University of California Press.

Hertz, Rosanna. 1997. "A Typology of Approaches to Child Care: The Centerpiece of Organizing Family Life for Dual-Earner Couples." *Journal of Family Issues* 18 (4): 355–385.

———. 2006. *Single by Chance, Mothers by Choice.* New York: Oxford University Press.

Hertz, Rosanna, and Faith Ferguson. 1996. "Childcare Choices and Constraints in the United States: Social Class, Race, and the Influence of Family Views." *Journal of Comparative Family Studies* 27 (2): 249–280.

Higginbotham, Elizabeth. 1994. "Black Professional Women: Job Ceilings and Employment Sectors." In *Women of Color in US Society*, edited by Maxine Baca Zinn and Bonnie Thornton Dill, 113–131. Philadelphia: Temple University Press.

———. 2001. *Too Much to Ask: Black Women in the Era of Integration*. Chapel Hill: University of North Carolina Press.

Higginbotham, Elizabeth, and Mary Romero. 1997. *Women and Work: Exploring Race, Ethnicity, and Class*. Thousand Oaks, CA: Sage Publications.

Higginbotham, Evelyn Brooks. 1992. "African-American Women's History and the Metalanguage of Race." *Signs: Journal of Women in Culture and Society* 17 (2): 251–274.

———. (1993) 2006. *Righteous Discontent: The Women's Movement in the Black Baptist Church, 1880–1920*. Cambridge, MA: Harvard University Press.

Hill, Shirley A. 2004. *Black Intimacies: Gender Perspectives on Family and Relationships*. Walnut Creek, CA: AltaMira Press.

Hine, Darlene Clark 1991. "Rape and the Inner Lives of Black Women in the Middle West: Preliminary Thoughts on the Culture of Dissemblance." In *Unequal Sisters*, edited by Ellen Carol DuBois and Vicki L. Ruiz, 292–297. New York: Routledge.

———. (1994) 1997. *Hine Sight: Black Women and the Re-Construction of American History*. Bloomington: Indiana University Press.

Hirsch, Jennifer S., and Holly Wardlow, eds. 2006. "Introduction" and Part I. In *Modern Loves: The Anthropology of Romantic Courtship and Companionate Marriage*, 1–94. Ann Arbor: University of Michigan Press.

Hirsch, Marianne, and Valerie Smith. 2002. "Feminism and Cultural Memory: An Introduction." *Signs: Journal of Women in Culture and Society* 28 (1): 1–19.

Hochschild, Arlie Russell. 1989. *The Second Shift: Working Families and the Revolution at Home*. New York: Viking.

———. 2003. *The Commercialization of Intimate Life: Notes from Home and Work*. Berkeley: University of California Press.

Hoffman, Bruce, and Thomas Vander Ven. 2007. "Mother Blame and Delinquency Claims: Juvenile Delinquency and Maternal Responsibility in Expert Discourses." In *Youth Violence and Delinquency Interventions*, edited by M. McShane and F. Williams. Westport, CT: Greenwood Publishing Group.

hooks, bell. 1981. *Ain't I a Woman: Black Women and Feminism*. Cambridge, MA: South End Press.

———. 1984. *Feminist Theory: From Margin to Center*. Cambridge, MA: South End Press.

———. 1988. *Talking Back: Thinking Feminist, Thinking Black*. Cambridge, MA: South End Press.

———. 1999. "Ain't She Still a Woman?" *Shambhala Sun*. Reposted by Hartford Web Publishing. http://www.hartford-hwp.com/archives/45a/186.html, accessed 12/14/2014.

———. 2000. *Feminism Is for Everybody: Passionate Politics*. Cambridge, MA: South End Press.

———. 2004. *The Will to Change: Men, Masculinity, and Love*. New York: Atria Books.

Hull, Gloria T., Patricia Bell-Scott, and Barbara Smith, eds. 1986. *All the Women Are White, All the Blacks Are Men, but Some of Us Are Brave: Black Women's Studies*. New York: Feminist Press.

Hunter, Tera W. 1997. *To 'Joy My Freedom*. Cambridge, MA: Harvard University Press.

Hurston, Zora Neale. (1935) 1990. *Mules and Men*. New York: Harper & Row.

———. (1937) 1990. *Their Eyes Were Watching God*. New York: Harper & Row.

Hurtado, Aida. 1996. *The Color of Privilege: Three Blasphemies on Race and Feminism*. Ann Arbor: University of Michigan Press.

Hymowitz, Kay. 2005. "The Black Family: 40 Years of Lies." *City Journal of the Manhattan Institute* (Summer 2005).

Jackson, Fleda Mask. 2007. *Race, Stress, and Social Support: Addressing the Crisis in Black Infant Mortality*. Joint Center for Political and Economic Studies Health Policy Institute.

Jackson, Fleda Mask, Mona Phillips, Hogue Taylor, J. R. Carol, and Tracy Curry-Owens. 2001. "Examining the Burdens of Gendered Racism: Implications for the Pregnancy

Outcomes of College-Educated African American Women." *Maternal and Child Health Journal* 5 (2): 95–107.

Jackson, John L. Jr. 2001. *Harlemworld: Doing Race and Class in Contemporary Black America.* Chicago: University of Chicago Press.

———. 2005. *Real Black: Adventures in Racial Sincerity.* Chicago: University of Chicago Press.

Jacobs, Harriett. (1861) 2001. *Incidents in the Life of a Slave Girl.* New York: Dover Publications.

Jacobs, Jerry A., and Kathleen Gerson. 1998. "Who Are the Overworked Americans?" *Review of Social Economy* 56: 442–459.

James, Joy. 1996. *Resisting State Violence: Radicalism, Gender, and Race in U.S. Culture.* Minneapolis: University of Minnesota Press.

———. (1997). 2013. *Transcending the Talented Tenth: Black Leaders and American Intellectuals.* New York: Routledge.

James, Stanlie. 1993. *Theorizing Black Feminisms: The Visionary Pragmatism of Black Women.* New York: Routledge.

Jenkins, Candice M. 2007. *Private Lives, Proper Relations: Regulating Black Intimacy.* Minneapolis: University of Minnesota Press.

Jewell, Joseph Oscar. 2007. *Race, Social Reform, and the Making of a Middle Class: The American Missionary Association and Black Atlanta 1870–1900.* Lanham, MD: Rowman and Littlefield, 2007.

Jewell, K. Sue. 1988. *Survival of the Black Family: The Institutional Impact of U.S. Social Policy.* Westport, CT: Greenwood Press.

———. 1993. *From Mammy to Miss America and Beyond: Cultural Images and the Shaping of U.S. Social Policy.* New York: Routledge.

Jones, Bernie D. 2012. *Women Who Opt Out: The Debate over Work, Mothers, and Work-Family Balance.* New York: New York University Press.

Jones, Delmos J. 1970. "Towards a Native Anthropology." *Human Organization* 29: 251–259.

Jones, Jacqueline. (1985) 2010. *Labor of Love, Labor of Sorrow.* New York: Basic Books.

Joseph, Gloria, and Jill Lewis. 1981. *Conflicts in Black and White Feminist Perspectives.* Boston: South End Press.

Kang, Miliann. 2014. "Are Second-Generation Korean American Women Tiger Mothers? Strategic, Transnational, and Resistant Responses to Racialized Mothering." In *Second Generation Korean Experiences in the United States and Canada*, edited by Pyong Gap Min and Samuel Noh. Lanham, MD: Lexington Books.

Kaplan, E. Ann.1990. "Sex, Work, and Motherhood: The Impossible Triangle." *Journal of Sex Research* 27 (3): 409–425.

Kaplan, Elaine Bell. 1997. *Not Our Kind of Girl: Unraveling the Myths of Black Teenage Motherhood.* Berkeley: University of California Press.

Keating, Larry. 2001. *Atlanta: Race, Class, and the Urban Expansion.* Philadelphia: Temple University Press.

Kessler-Harris, Alice. 1981. *Women Have Always Worked: A Historical Overview.* Old Westbury, NY: Feminist Press; New York: McGraw-Hill.

King, Deborah K. 1988. "Multiple Jeopardy, Multiple Consciousness: The Context of a Black Feminist Ideology." *Signs: Journal of Women in Culture and Society* 14 (1): 42–72.

Kinnon, Joy Bennett. 1997. "Mother Wit: Words of Wisdom from Black Women." *Ebony* (March).

Kuperberg, Arielle, and Pamela Stone. 2008. "The Media Depiction of Women Who Opt-Out." *Gender & Society* 22 (4): 497–517.

Lacey, T. Allen, and Benjamin Wright. 2010. "Occupational Employment Projections to 2018." Bureau of Labor and Statistics.

Lacy, Karyn R. 2007. *Blue-Chip Black: Race, Class, and Status in the New Black Middle Class.* Berkeley: University of California Press.

Ladner, Joyce A. (1971) 1995. *Tomorrow's Tomorrow: The Black Woman.* Lincoln: University of Nebraska Press.

Lamphere, Louise, Patricia Zavella, Felipe Gonzales, and Peter B. Evans. 1993. *Sunbelt Working Mothers: Reconciling Family and Factory.* Ithaca, NY: Cornell University Press.

Lan, Pei-Chai. 2003. "Maid or Madam? Filipina Migrant Workers and the Continuity of Domestic Labor." *Gender & Society* 17 (2): 187–208.

Landry, Bart. 1988. *The New Black Middle Class.* Berkeley: University of California Press.

———. 2000. *Black Working Wives: Pioneers of the American Family Revolution.* Berkeley: University of California Press.

Lareau, Annette. (2003) 2011. *Unequal Childhoods: Class, Race, and Family Life.* Berkeley: University of California Press.

Lefever, Harry G. 2005. *Undaunted by the Fight: Spelman College and the Civil Rights Movement.* Macon, GA: Mercer University Press.

Lehr, Valerie L. 1999. *Queer Family Values: Debunking the Myth of the Nuclear Family.* Philadelphia: Temple University Press.

Lerner, Gerda. 1972. *Black Women in White America: A Documentary History.* New York: Random House.

———. 2005. *The Majority Finds Its Past: Placing Women in History.* Chapel Hill: University of North Carolina Press.

Lewis, Oscar. 1959. *Five Families; Mexican Case Studies in the Culture of Poverty.* New York: Basic Books.

———. 1966. *La Vida: A Puerto Rican Family in the Culture of Poverty—San Juan and New York.* New York: Random House.

Lorde, Audre. 1979. "Open Letter to Mary Daly." In *Sister Outsider*, 66–71. Berkeley: The Crossing Press.

———. 1982. *Zami: A New Spelling of My Name—A Biomythography.* New York: The Crossing Press.

———. 1984. *Sister Outsider: Essays and Speeches.* Trumansburg, NY: Crossing Press.

———. 2007. "Age, Race, Class, and Sex: Women Redefining Difference." In *Race and Gender: An Anthology*, edited by Margaret L. Andersen and Patricia Hill Collins, 52–59. 6th ed. Belmont, CA: Thomson Higher Education.

Low, Setha. 2004. *Behind the Gates: Life, Security, and the Pursuit of Happiness in Fortress America.* New York: Routledge.

Lubiano, Wahneema. 1992. "Black Ladies, Welfare Queens, and State Minstrels: Ideological War by Narrative Mean." In *Race-ing Justice, En-gendering Power: Essays on Anita Hill, Clarence Thomas, and the Construction of Social Reality*, edited by Toni Morrison, 323–361. New York: Pantheon.

Macdonald, Cameron. 1998. "Manufacturing Motherhood: The Shadow Work of Nannies and Au Pairs." *Qualitative Sociology* 21 (1): 25–53.

———. 2009. "What's Culture Got to Do with It? Mothering Ideologies as Barriers to Gender Equity." In *Gender Equality: Transforming Family Divisions of Labor*, edited by Janet C. Gornick and Marcia K. Meyers, 411–434. London: Verso.

———. 2010. *Shadow Mothers: Nannies, Au Pairs, and the Micropolitics of Mothering.* Berkeley: University of California Press.

Mack, V. Kibibi. 1999. *Parlor Ladies and Ebony Drudges: African American Women, Class, and Work in a South Carolina Community.* Knoxville: University of Tennessee Press.

Marcus, George, with Michael M. J. Fischer. 1986. *Anthropology as Cultural Critique.* Chicago: University of Chicago Press.

Marshall, Barbara. 2001. "Working While Black: Contours of an Unequal Playing Field." *Phylon: The Clark Atlanta University Review of Race and Culture* 49 (3–4): 137–150.

Marshall, Martin N. 1996. "Sampling for Qualitative Research." *Family Practice* 13: 522–526. doi:10.1093/fampra/13.6.522.

Massey, Douglas S., and Nancy A. Denton. (1993) 2003. *American Apartheid: Segregation and the Making of the Underclass.* Cambridge, MA: Harvard University Press.

McCabe, Janice. 2009. "Racial and Gender Microaggressions on a Predominantly White Campus: Experiences of Black, Latina/o, and White Undergraduates." *Race, Gender & Class* 16 (1/2): 133–151.

McClain, Leanita, and Clarence Page. 1986. *A Foot in Each World: Essays and Articles.* Evanston, IL: Northwestern University Press.

McClaurin, Irma.1992. "Incongruities: Dissonance and Contradiction in the Life of a Black Middle Class Woman." In *Uncertain Terms: Negotiating Gender in American Culture,* edited by Faye Ginsburg and Anna Lowenhaupt Tsing, 315–334. Boston: Beacon Press.

———. 2001. *Black Feminist Anthropology: Theory, Politics, Praxis, and Poetics.* New Brunswick, NJ: Rutgers University Press.

McCluskey, Audrey Thomas. 1994. "Am I Not a Woman and a Sister? Reflections on the Role of Black Women's Studies in the Academy." *Feminist Teacher* 8 (3): 105–111.

———. 1997. "We Specialize in the Wholly Impossible: Black Women School Founders and Their Mission." *Signs: Journal of Women in Culture and Society* 22: 403–406.

McDonald, Katrina Bell. 1997. "Black Activist Mothering: A Historical Intersection of Race, Class, and Gender." *Gender & Society* 11 (6): 773–795.

———. 2006. *Embracing Sisterhood: Class, Identity, and Contemporary Black Women.* Lanham, MD: Rowman & Littlefield.

McKinley, Catherine E., and Joyce Delaney, eds. 1995. *Afrekete: An Anthology of Black Lesbian Writing.* New York: Anchor Books.

Merton, Robert K. 1968. *Social Theory and Social Structure.* New York: Free Press.

Messerschmidt, Donald. 1981. *Anthropologists at Home in North America: Methods and Issues in the Study of One's Own Society.* Cambridge: Cambridge University Press.

Mikell, Gwendolyn. 1995. "African Feminism: Towards a New Politics of Representation." *Feminist Studies* 21 (2): 405–424.

Milkie, M. A., and R. Peltola. 1999. "Playing All the Roles: Gender and the Work-Family Balancing Act." *Journal of Marriage and the Family* 61: 476–490.

Mink, Gwendolyn. 1995. *The Wages of Motherhood: Inequality in the Welfare State, 1917–1942.* Ithaca, NY: Cornell University Press.

Mixon, Gregory. 2005. *The Atlanta Riot: Race, Class, and Violence in a New South City.* Gainesville: University Press of Florida.

Moen, Phyllis, ed. 2003. *It's About Time: Couples and Careers.* Ithaca, NY: ILR Press.

———. 2005. "Alternative Employment Arrangements: A Gender Perspective." *Sex Roles: A Journal of Research* 52 (5/6): 337–349.

Mohanty, Chandra Talpade. 1988. "Under Western Eyes: Feminist Scholarship and Colonial Discourse." *Feminist Review* 30: 61–88.

Moller, Stephanie, Joya Misra, and Eiko Strader. 2013. "A Cross-National Look at How Welfare States Reduce Inequality." *Sociological Compass* 7 (2): 135–146.

Moore, Mignon. 2011. *Invisible Families: Gay Identities, Relationships, and Motherhood among Black Women.* Berkeley: University of California Press.

Moras, Amanda, Constance Shehan, and Felix M. Berardo. 2007. "African American Families: Historical and Contemporary Forces Shaping Family Life and Studies." In *Handbook of the Sociology of Racial and Ethnic Relations*, edited by Hernán Vera and Joe R. Feagin, 145–160. New York: Springer Science.

Morgan, Jennifer. 2004. *Laboring Women: Reproduction and Gender in New World Slavery*. Philadelphia: University of Pennsylvania Press.

Morgan, Joan. 2000. *When Chickenheads Come Home to Roost: A Hip-Hop Feminist Breaks It Down*. New York: Simon & Schuster.

Morrison, Toni. 1973. *Sula*. New York: Alfred Knopf.

———. 1987. *Beloved*. New York: Alfred Knopf.

———. 2008. *A Mercy*. New York: Vintage.

———, ed. 1992. *Race-ing Justice, En-gendering Power: Essays on Anita Hill, Clarence Thomas, and the Construction of Social Reality*. New York: Pantheon.

Moynihan, Daniel Patrick. (1965) 1981. *The Negro Family: The Case for National Action*. U.S. Dept. of Labor, Office of Policy Planning and Research. Westport, CT: Greenwood Press.

Mullins, Leith, and Alaka Wali. 2001. *Stress and Resilience: The Social Context of Reproduction in Central Harlem*. New York: Kluwer Academic.

Mullings, Leith. 1997. *On Our Own Terms: Race, Class, and Gender in the Lives of African American Women*. New York: Routledge.

———. 2002. "The Sojourner Syndrome: Race, Class, and Gender in Health and Illness." *Voices* 6 (1): 32–36.

———. 2005. "Resistance and Resilience: The Sojourner Truth Syndrome and the Social Context of Reproduction in Central Harlem." *Transforming Anthropology* 13 (2): 79–91.

Murray, Susan B. 1998. "Child Care Work: Intimacy in the Shadows of Family-Life." *Qualitative Sociology* 21 (2): 149–168.

Myrdal, Gunnar. 1944. *An American Dilemma: The Negro Problem and Modern Democracy*. New York and London: Harper & Brothers.

Naples, Nancy A. "Activist Mothering: Cross-Generational Continuity in the Community Work of Women from Low-Income Urban Neighborhoods." *Gender & Society* 6 (3) 441–463.

Narayan, Kirin. 1993. "How Native Is a 'Native' Anthropologist?" *American Anthropologist* 95 (3): 671–686.

Nash, Jennifer C. 2008. "Re-thinking Intersectionality." *Feminist Review* 89 (1): 1–15.

Nelson, Margaret K. 1990. *Negotiated Care: The Experience of Family Day Care Providers*. Philadelphia: Temple University Press.

Ogbu, John.1982. "Cultural Discontinuities and Schooling." *Anthropology & Education Quarterly* 13 (4): 290–307.

Oliver, Melvin. 1980. "The Enduring Significance of Race." *Journal of Ethnic Studies* 7 (4): 79–91.

Oliver, Melvin L., and Thomas Shapiro. 1989. "Race and Wealth." *Review of Black Political Economy* 17 (4): 5–25.

———. 1995. *Black Wealth/White Wealth: A New Perspective on Racial Inequality*. New York: Routledge.

Omolade, Barbara. 1994. *The Rising Song of African American Women*. New York: Routledge.

O'Reilly, Andrea. 2004. *Toni Morrison and Motherhood: A Politics of the Heart*. Albany: State University of New York Press.

Orleck, Annelise. 2005. *Storming Caesar's Place: How Black Mothers Fought Their Own War on Poverty*. Boston: Beacon Press.

Ortner, Sherry B. 2005. *New Jersey Dreaming: Capital, Culture, and the Class of '58*. Durham, NC: Duke University Press.

Osnowitz, Debra. 2005. "Managing Time in Domestic Space: Home-Based Contractors and Household Work." *Gender and Society* 19 (1): 83–103.

Painter, Nell Irvin. 1996. *Sojourner Truth: A Life, a Symbol.* New York: W. W. Norton.

Parker, Kim, and Wendy Wang. 2013. "Modern Parenthood: Roles of Moms and Dads Converge as They Balance Work and Family." *Pew Research Social and Demographic Trends.*

Parker, Lonnae O'Neal. 2005. *I'm Every Woman: Remixed Stories of Marriage, Motherhood, and Work.* New York: Amistad.

Parks, Sheri. 2013. *Fierce Angels: Living with a Legacy from the Sacred Dark Feminine to the Strong Black Woman.* Chicago: Chicago Review Press.

Pattillo-(McCoy), Mary. 1999. *Black Picket Fences: Privilege and Peril among the Black Middle Class.* Chicago: University of Chicago Press.

———. 2007. *Black on the Block: The Politics of Race and Class in the City.* Chicago: University of Chicago Press.

Peirano, Mariza G. S. 1998. "When Anthropology Is at Home: The Different Contexts of a Single Discipline." *Annual Reviews of Anthropology* 27: 105–138.

Perkins, Linda M. 1981. "Black Feminism and 'Race Uplift' 1890–1900." Working Paper, Institute for Independent Study, Radcliffe College, Cambridge, MA.

———. 1983. "The Impact of the 'Cult of True Womanhood' on the Education of Black Women." *Journal of Social Issues* 39 (3): 17–28.

Phillips, Layli. 2006. "Womanism on Its Own." In *The Womanist Reader: the First Quarter Century of Womanist Thought*, edited by Layli Phillips, xix–lv. New York: Routledge.

Pierce, Chester. 1995. "Stress Analogs of Racism and Sexism: Terrorism, Torture, and Disaster." In *Mental Health, Racism and Sexism*, edited by Charles V. Willie, Patricia Perri Rieker, Bernard M. Kramer, and Bertram S. Brown, 277–295. Pittsburgh: University of Pittsburgh Press.

Pittman, Chavella T. 2012. "Racial Microaggressions: The Narratives of African American Faculty at a Predominantly White University." *Journal of Negro Education* 81 (1): 82–92.

Pomerantz, Gary M. 1997. *Where Peachtree Street Meets Sweet Auburn: A Saga of Race and Family.* New York: Penguin Books.

———. 2006. *Wilt, 1962: The Night of 100 Points and the Dawn of a New Era.* New York: Three Rivers Press.

Popenoe, David.1999. *Life Without Father: Compelling New Evidence That Fatherhood and Marriage Are Indispensable for the Good of Children and Society.* Cambridge, MA: Harvard University Press.

Rich, Adrienne Cecile. 1976. *Of Woman Born: Motherhood as Experience and Institution.* New York: W. W. Norton.

Ritchie, Beth. 1995. *Compelled to Crime: The Gender Entrapment of Battered, Black Women.* New York: Routledge.

Roberts, Dorothy. 1997. *Killing the Black Body: Race, Reproduction, and the Meaning of Liberty.* New York: Pantheon.

———. 2005. "Black Club Women and Child Welfare: Lessons for Modern Reform." *Florida State University Law Review* 32 (3): 957–972.

Robertson, Claire C., with Martin A. Klein. 1983. *Women and Slavery in Africa.* Madison: University of Wisconsin Press.

Rodgers-Rose, La Frances. 1980. *The Black Woman.* Beverly Hills, CA: Sage Publications.

Rodriguez, Cheryl. 2001. "A Homegirl Goes Home: Black Feminism and the Lure of Native Anthropology." In *Black Feminist Anthropology: Theory, Praxis, Poetics, and Politics*, edited by Irma McClaurin, 233–257. New Brunswick, NJ: Rutgers University Press.

Romero, Mary. (1992) 2002. *Maid in the USA.* New York: Routledge.

———. 2001. "Unraveling Privilege: Workers' Children and the Hidden Cost of Paid Child-care." *Chicago Kent Law Review* 76: 1651–1672.

Roth, Louise Marie. 2006. *Selling Women Short: Gender and Money on Wall Street*. Princeton, NJ: Princeton University Press.

Sarkissian, Natalia, and Naomi Gerstel. 2012. *Nuclear Family Values, Extended Family Lives: The Importance of Gender, Race, and Class*. New York: Routledge.

Schechter, Patricia A. 2001. *Ida B. Wells-Barnett and American Reform, 1880–1930*. Chapel Hill: University of North Carolina Press.

Schneider, Barbara, and Linda Waite. 2005. *Being Together, Working Apart: Dual-Career Families and the Work-Life Balance*. New York and Cambridge: Cambridge University Press.

Schor, Juliette. 1992. *The Overworked American: The Unexpected Decline of Leisure*. New York: Basic Books.

Scott, David. 2008. "Introduction: On the Archaeologies of Black Memory." *Anthurium: A Caribbean Studies Journal* 6 (1): article 2.

Shapiro, Thomas. 2004. *The Hidden Cost of Being African American: How Wealth Perpetuates Inequality*. New York: Oxford University Press.

Sharkey, Patrick. 2009. "Neighborhoods and the Black-White Mobility Gap." Washington, DC: The Economic Mobility Project: An Initiative of the Pew Charitable Trusts.

Shaw, Stephanie. 1996. *What a Woman Ought to Be and to Do: Black Professional Women Workers during the Jim Crow Era*. Chicago: University of Chicago Press.

Sjoquist, David, ed. 2000. *The Atlanta Paradox*. New York: Russell Sage Foundation.

Small, Mario L. 2009. "'How Many Cases Do I Need?' On Science and the Logic of Case Selection in Field-Based Research." *Ethnography* 10: 5–38. doi:10.1177/1466138108099586.

Smedley, Audrey. 1998. *Race in North America: Origin and Evolution of a Worldview*. Boulder, CO: Westview Press.

Smith, Barbara, ed. (1977) 1982. "Toward a Black Feminist Criticism." In *All the Women Are White, All the Blacks Are Men, But Some of Us Are Brave*, edited by Gloria T. Hull, Patricia Bell-Scott, and Barbara Smith, 157–175. New York: Feminist Press.

———. (1983) 2000. *Home Girls: A Black Feminist Anthology*. New York: Kitchen Table Press/ New Brunswick, NJ: Rutgers University Press.

Smock, Pamela, and Fiona Rose Greenland. 2010. "Diversity in Pathways to Parenthood: Patterns, Implications, and Emerging Research Directions." *Journal of Marriage and Family* 72: 576–593.

Solarzano, Daniel, Miguel Ceja, and Tara Yosso. 2000. "Critical Race Theory, Racial Microaggressions, and Campus Racial Climate: The Experiences of African American College Students." *Journal of Negro Education* 69 (1/2): 60–73.

Sorensen, Anne Scott. 1994. "Women, Family, and Class." *Annual Review of Sociology* 20: 27–47.

Southern Center for Studies in Black Policy. 2004. *Status of Black Atlanta*. Atlanta, GA: Clark Atlanta University Press.

Spelman, Elizabeth. 1988. *Inessential Woman: Problems of Exclusion in Feminist Thought*. London: Women's Press.

Stacey, Judith. 1988. "Can There Be a Feminist Ethnography?" *Women's Studies International Forum* 11 (1): 21–27.

Stack, Carol. (1974) 1997. *All Our Kin: Strategies for Survival in a Black Community*. New York: Harper & Row.

———. 1996. *Call to Home: African American Reclaim the Rural South*. New York: Basic Books.

Stack, Carol, and Linda Burton. 1993. "Kinscripts." *Journal of Comparative Family Studies* 24 (2): 157–170.

Staples, Robert. 1978. *The Black Family: Essays and Studies*. Belmont, CA: Wadsworth Publishing.

Sterling, Dorothy. 1984. *We Are Your Sisters*. New York: W. W. Norton.

St. Jean, Yanick, and Joe R. Feagin. 1998. *Double Burden: Black Women and Everyday Racism*. New York: M. E. Sharpe.

Stocking, George W. 1982. *Race, Culture, and Evolution: Essays in the History of Anthropology, with a New Preface*. Chicago: University of Chicago Press.

Stone, Clarence N. 1989. *Regime Politics: Governing Atlanta 1946–1988*. Lawrence: University Press of Kansas.

Stone, Pamela. 2007. *Opting Out?: Why Women Really Quit Careers and Head Home*. Berkeley: University of California Press.

Sudarkasa, Niara. 1996. *The Strength of Our Mothers: African and African American Women and Families: Essays and Speeches*. Trenton, NJ: Africa World Press.

———. 2007. "Interpreting the African Heritage in African American Family Organization." In *Black Families*, edited by H. P. McAdoo, 29–47. Thousand Oaks, CA: Sage.

Sue, Derald Wing, Kevin L. Nadal, Christina M. Capodilupo, Annie I. Lin, Gina C. Torina, and David P. Rivera. 2008. "Racial Microaggressions against Black Americans: Implications for Counseling." *Journal of Counseling & Development* 86 (summer): 330–336.

Tatum, Beverly Daniel. (1987) 2000. *Assimilation Blues: Black Families in White Communities, Who Succeeds and Why*. New York: Greenwood Press.

———. 1999. *Why Are All the Black Kids Sitting Together at the Table? and Other Conversations about Race*. New York: Basic Books.

Terborg-Penn, Rosalyn. 1998. *African American Women in the Struggle for the Vote, 1850–1920*. Bloomington: Indiana University Press.

Thomas, Jim. 1993. *Doing Critical Ethnography*. Newbury Park, CA: Sage Publications.

Thomas-Hope, Elizabeth. 1998. "Globalization and the Development of a Caribbean Migration Culture." In *Caribbean Migration: Globalized Identities*, edited by Mary Chamberlain. New York: Routledge.

Thompson, Lisa B. 2009. *Beyond the Black Lady: Sexuality and the New African American Middle Class*. Urbana-Champaign: University of Illinois Press.

Trotter, Joe William, ed. 1991. *The Great Migration in Historical Perspective: New Dimensions of Race, Class, and Gender*. Bloomington: Indiana University Press.

Tyson, Karolyn. 2001. *Integration Interrupted: Tracking, Black Students, and Acting White after Brown*. New York: Oxford University Press.

United States Bureau of the Census. 1998. Current Population Reports.

———. 2007. Economic Census.

———. 2008a. "Current Population Survey (CPS)—Definitions and Explanations." http://www.census.gov/population/www/cps/cpsdef.html.

———. 2008b. "Table 5: Determinants of Whether Women Return to Work after Childbirth." http://www.census.gov/population/www/documentation/twps0032/tab05.html, accessed June 16, 2009.

———. 2011. Current Population Survey (CPS). "Annual Social and Economic Supplement." http://www.census.gov/hhes/www/cpstables/032011/perinc/new01_001.htm.

United States Department of Housing and Urban Development. Section 8 Rental Voucher Program Housing Program. http://www.hud.gov/progdesc/voucher.cfm, accessed June 15, 2009.

United States Department of Labor, Bureau of Labor Statistics. 2007. "Table 11. Employed Persons by Detailed Occupation, Sex, Race, and Hispanic or Latino Ethnicity." http://www.bls.gov/cps/cpsaat11.pdf, accessed January 11, 1009.

Urciuoli, Bonnie.1993. "Representing Class, Who Decides?" *Anthropological Quarterly* 66 (4): 203–210.

Uttal, Lynet. 1997. "'Trust Your Instincts': Racial, Ethnic, and Class-Based Preferences in Employed Mothers' Childcare Choices." *Qualitative Sociology* 20 (2): 253–274.

———. 2002. *Making Care Work: Employed Mothers in the New Childcare Market.* New Brunswick, NJ: Rutgers University Press.

Uttal, Lynet, and Mary Tuominen. 1999. "Tenuous Relationships: Exploitation, Emotion, and Racial Ethnic Significance in Paid Child Care Work." *Gender and Society* 13 (6): 758–780.

Valentine, Charles. 1971. "Deficit, Difference, and Bicultural Models of Afro-American Behavior." *Harvard Educational Review* 4 (2): 131–157.

Vander Ven, Thomas 2003. *Working Mothers and Juvenile Delinquency.* New York: LFB Scholarly Publishing LLC.

Vanneman, Reeve, and Lynn Weber Cannon. 1987. *The American Perception of Class.* (Labor and Social Change). Philadelphia: Temple University Press.

Veroff, Joseph, Elizabeth Douvan, and Shirley Hatchett. 1995. *Marital Instability: A Social and Behavioral Study of the Early Years.* Westport, CT: Praeger.

Visweswaran, Kamala. 1997. "Histories of Feminist Ethnography." *Annual Review of Anthropology* 26: 591–621.

Walker, Alice. 1976. *Meridian.* New York: Harcourt Brace Jovanovich.

———. (1982) 2001. "One Child of One's Own: A Meaningful Digression within the Work(s)." In *Mother Reader: Essential Literature on Motherhood,* edited by Moyra Davey, 139–154. New York: Seven Stories Press.

———. 1982. *The Color Purple.* New York: Simon and Schuster.

———. (1983) 2003. *In Search of Our Mother's Gardens: Womanist Prose.* Orlando, FL: Harcourt Books.

———. 1994. *Fictions of Feminist Ethnography.* Minneapolis: University of Minnesota Press.

———, ed. 1979. *I Love Myself When I Am Laughing . . . and Then Again When I Am Looking Mean and Impressive: A Zora Neale Hurston Reader.* Old Westbury, NY: Feminist Press.

Wallace, Michele. 1979. *Black Macho and the Myth of the Superwoman.* New York: Dial Press.

Walsh, Janet. 2011. "Failing Its Families: Lack of Paid Leave and Work-Family Supports in the US." Human Rights Watch. New York. http://www.hrw.org/node/96432, accessed April 18, 2015.

Wardlow, Holly. 2006. "All Is Fair When Love Is War: Romantic Passion and Companionate Marriage among the Huli of Papua New Guinea." In *Modern Loves: The Anthropology of Romantic Courtship and Companionate Marriage,* edited by Jennifer Hirsch and Holly Wardlow, 51–77. Ann Arbor: University of Michigan Press.

Waters, Kristin, and Carol B. Conaway, eds. 2007. *Black Women's Intellectual Traditions: Speaking Their Minds.* Burlington: University of Vermont Press.

Waters, Mary. 1999. *Black Identities: West Indian Immigrant Dreams and American Realities.* Cambridge, MA: Harvard University Press.

Watkins-Hayes, Celeste. 2009. *The New Welfare Bureaucrats: Entanglements of Race, Class, and Policy Reform.* Chicago: University of Chicago Press.

Weise, Andrew. 2004. *Places of Their Own: African American Suburbanization in the Twentieth Century.* Chicago: University of Chicago Press.

Whitaker, Charles. 2002. "Is Atlanta the New Black Mecca? With Its Affordable Housing, Livable Pace, and Reputation for Encouraging Entrepreneurship, Atlanta Is the 'Go To' City for Enterprising African-Americans." *Ebony,* March.

White, Deborah Gray White. (1985) 1999. *Ar'n't I a Woman? Female Slaves in the Plantation South*. New York: W. W. Norton.

——. 1993. "The Cost of Doing Club Work: The Price of Black Feminism." In *Visible Women: New Essays on American Activism*, edited by Nancy A. Hewitt and Suzanne Lebsock, 252–257. Urbana: University of Illinois Press.

——. 1999. *Too Heavy a Load: Black Women in Defense of Themselves, 1894–1994*. New York: W. W. Norton.

White, E. Frances. 2001. *Dark Continent of Our Bodies: Black Feminism and Politics of Respectability*. Philadelphia: Temple University Press.

White, James M., and David M. Klein. 2008. *Family Theories*. Thousand Oaks, CA: Sage Publications.

Williams, Joan. 2000. *Unbending Gender: Why Family and Work Conflict and What to Do About It*. Oxford: Oxford University Press.

——. 2001. "From Difference to Dominance to Domesticity: Care as Work, Gender as Tradition." *Chicago Kent Law Review* 76: 1441–1493.

——. 2010. *Reshaping the Work-Family Debate: Why Men and Class Matter*. Cambridge, MA: Harvard University Press.

Williams, Joan, Jessica Manvell, and Stephanie Bornstein. 2006. "Opt-Out or Pushed Out?: How the Press Covers Work/Family Conflict." The Center for Work Life Law. University of California, Hastings College of Law.

Williams, Rhonda Y. 2004. *The Politics of Public Housing: Black Women's Struggles against Urban Inequality*. Oxford: Oxford University Press.

Willie, Charles Vert. 1981. *A New Look at Black Families*. Bayside, NY: General Hall.

——. 1983. *Race, Ethnicity, and Socioeconomic Status: A Theoretical Analysis of Their Interrelationship*. Bayside, NY: General Hall.

Willie, Charles Vert, and Richard J. Reddick. 2003. *A New Look at Black Families*. Walnut Creek, CA: AltaMira Press.

Willie, Charles Vert, Richard J. Reddick, and Ronald Brown. 2006. *The Black College Mystique*. Lanham, MD: Rowman & Littlefield.

Wilson, William Julius. 1978. *The Truly Disadvantaged: The Inner City, the Underclass, and Public Policy*. Chicago: University of Chicago Press.

——. 1987. *The Declining Significance of Race: Blacks and Changing American Institutions*. Chicago: University of Chicago Press.

——. 2009. *More Than Just Race: Being Black and Poor in the Inner City*. New York: W. W. Norton.

Winkle-Wagner, Rachelle. 2008. "Not Feminist But Strong: Black Women's Reflections of Race and Gender in College." *Negro Educational Review* 59 (3/4): 181–195.

Wolcott, Victoria W. 2001. *Remaking Respectability: African-American Women in Interwar Detroit*. Chapel Hill: University of North Carolina Press.

Wrigley, Julia. 1999. "Hiring a Nanny: The Limits of Private Solutions to Public Problems." *Annals of the American Academy of Political Science* 563: 162–174.

Zavella, Patricia. 1993. "Feminist Insider Dilemmas: Constructing Ethnic Identity with 'Chicana' Informants." *Frontiers: A Journal of Women Studies* 13 (3): 53–76.

Zinn, Maxine Baca, and Bonnie Thornton Dill, 1999. "Theorizing Difference from Multiracial Feminism." In *Race, Identity, and Citizenship: A Reader*, edited by R. D. Torres, L. F. Miron, and J. X. Inda, 103–110. Malden, MA: Blackwell Publishing.

INDEX

ABOUT THE AUTHOR

RICHÉ J. DANIEL BARNES is an assistant professor of sociocultural anthropology in the department of Africana Studies at Smith College.

CPSIA information can be obtained
at www.ICGtesting.com
Printed in the USA
LVHW090556090120
642973LV00001B/3/P

9 780813 561981